child-wise

child-
wise

CATHY RINDNER TEMPELSMAN

HEARST BOOKS

New York

It is the policy of William Morrow and Company, Inc., and its imprints and affiliates, recognizing the importance of preserving what has been written, to print the books we publish on acid-free paper, and we exert our best efforts to that end.

Library of Congress Cataloging-in-Publication Data

Tempelsman, Cathy Rindner.
Child-wise / Cathy Rindner Tempelsman.
p.   cm.
Includes bibliographical references (p.   ) and index.
ISBN 0-688-11740-6
1. Parent and child—United States.   2. Parenting—United States.   3. Child rearing—United States.   4. Child psychology—United States.   I. Title.
HQ755.85.T46   1994
649'.1—dc20   93-41776
CIP

Printed in the United States of America

First Edition

1   2   3   4   5   6   7   8   9   10

BOOK DESIGN BY MARY SARAH QUINN

ILLUSTRATIONS BY STEVEN SALERNO

For
Leon, Audrey, Marina, and Julian
and
for my parents

Foreword

The need for parenting advice has never been greater. While mothers and fathers of the nineties have spent more time on education and career training than any previous generation, they are perhaps the least prepared for parenthood. Unlike previous generations, today's families are less likely to have grandparents and extended family participating in child rearing, which in years past could lessen the strain on parents.

Bookstores are awash with parenting books, each offering solutions to the "problems" that come with raising children. Echoing through the pages of many is the notion that one set of rules applies to all children. But as any seasoned parent or childhood expert will tell you, there is no simple formula for bringing up children.

As a child and adolescent psychiatrist, I emphasize to parents that they strive to understand and appreciate each of their children as individuals—in a sense, to become "child-wise." This requires that they obtain an understanding of normal development, and formulate reasonable expectations of their children. In *Child-Wise,* Tempelsman provides parents with the information and advice necessary to accomplish this important task.

Cathy Tempelsman has synthesized the best of child development theory, while also exploring the real-life experiences of parents and families. In *Child-Wise* she offers insights that help parents distinguish perfectly normal, albeit disturbing, habits or behaviors from those that are truly a cause for concern. Becoming "child-wise" does not mean that your homelife will be entirely stress-free or run smoothly all the time, but it will help you to understand the challenges and demands of childhood.

While there is no set of rules for the first six years (or beyond), there *are* parameters for defining the limits of "normal" behavior, and these are explored throughout the book. Tempelsman carefully balances the "major themes" in a young child's life (attachment, transition, and separation) with discussions of the "minor crises" that often dictate daily life (from the morning rush and messy room to sibling fights and the start of school). In doing so, she offers useful guidelines for defining these limits.

In *Child-Wise,* Tempelsman discusses the ways in which parents and children influence one another, and stresses that it is never too early to forge the bonds of closeness and communication. She takes obvious pleasure in sharing with other parents the insights that have helped her to feel closer to her children. In a skillful, sensitive way, Tempelsman lets other parents know that they are not alone.

All parents are vulnerable to feelings of anger, disappointment, or frustration when their children behave in a difficult or challenging way. To become "child-wise," parents first have to understand themselves and to examine how their own desires and wishes for their children, while well-meaning, may be unrealistic, unnecessary, and provoke family conflict. An understanding of developmental stages is one step toward this goal, but equally important is that parents get to know— and appreciate—each of their children as an individual. These are themes that Tempelsman explores with great empathy and care. *Child-Wise* is a practical and poignant resource for helping parents understand the baffling, upsetting, and extraordinary things children do. Every parent, even those who are childhood specialists, can benefit from the book's insights and expert information.

—HAROLD S. KOPLEWICZ, M.D.
Associate Professor of Psychiatry, Albert Einstein College of Medicine
 Chief, Division of Child and Adolescent Psychiatry, Schneider Children's Hospital

Acknowledgments

I owe an enormous debt of gratitude to those who helped me with this book, and who did so with full and generous support.

The following professionals took time out of busy schedules to discuss the issues of early childhood: Goldie Alfasi, Nora Barron, Virginia Burlingame, Nico Carpenter, Judy Colemen, Lou Cooper, Mark Hochberg, Nina Lief, Andrea Marks, Cathy Nonas, Susan Richenthal, Victoria Ryan, Rebecca Thomas, Stanley Turecki, and Robert Wolf. I appreciate how receptive they were to *Child-Wise* and its themes, and how patiently they answered my questions. I am full of admiration for their devotion to young children and their families.

Two childhood specialists deserve special mention: Dr. Harold Koplewicz, for reading the manuscript early on and clarifying many important facts, and Dr. Francesca Schwartz, for the spirited discussions we had as well as her matchless way of framing and articulating what happens in the early years. Dr. Cyrille Halkin, pediatrician extraordinaire, has now cared for two generations of Tempelsmans. Her wisdom and stamina are beyond compare and have been an inspiration to me.

In the research field, Leon Kuczynski, Grazyna Kochanska, and Jay Belsky were kind enough to share their work, and although I did not speak with Eleanor Maccoby, I benefited greatly from her insights into the circular, reciprocal nature of the parent-child relationship, an idea that is so much at the core of this book.

Many skilled and talented teachers and educators have enriched the lives of my children. In the past two years I felt fortunate to be their student, too. They include Helen Garrison, Margaret Harding, and Mary Adams at The Brearley School and, at the 92nd Street Y, Sue Bayer, Nancy Schulman, Ellen Birnbaum, Ann Obsatz, Nancy Weiss, and Roberta Willenken. Sonja Kim, of Vassar College, was particularly helpful in discussing shy children and how best to help them.

I suffer an embarrassment of riches when it comes to devoted friends and family. Judy Dimon lent her enthusiasm and intelligence to this project from the start, reading an early draft as critically and carefully as I had hoped she would. Likewise, Joan Kaplan contributed her ideas about the nature of childhood and commented on the final manuscript. My only regret is that I could not incorporate all of their excellent suggestions. I also appreciate Diane Thompson's good-natured hand with correspondence, in spite of a heavy workload.

The voices of many friends and acquaintances can be heard throughout *Child-Wise,* albeit anonymously. (All of the children's names have been changed here, with the exception of my own.) If the examples and vignettes in these pages ring true, it is thanks to the honesty and eloquence of other mothers and fathers in sharing their thoughts and concerns.

My parents, Anita and Martin Rindner, set a superb example of how to give a child roots and wings early on, and of marriage at its best. And as always, my wonderful in-laws were there for me, too. I wish to thank Lilly Tempelsman, who provided not just a room of my own but an astute sounding board, frequent meals, and many helpful clippings, and Maurice Tempelsman, whose energy and intellect I so admire.

Wendy Lipkind Black somehow saw the potential for *Child-Wise* before I did, and Megan Newman championed the book through every phase of publication. Each is to be thanked for her friendship and faith.

And finally, I am grateful beyond words to my husband, Leon, who has taught me more about what it means to be a parent, and to love unconditionally, than anything ever written about raising children. This book is as much his as it is mine. And to Audrey, Marina, and Julian, our gems, for everything.

Contents

Child . . . Is Your Baby "Spoiled" or Secure? A
Look at Attachment Behavior . . . The Stress of
Growing Up: Why Older Children Regress . . .
Bottles, Thumbs, and Pacifiers . . . Blankets and
Bears . . . Pacifiers: Pros and Cons: Soothing
the Baby or Shutting Him Out . . . When Is a
Comfort Habit a "Bad Habit"? . . . Red Flag . . .
Childhood Anxiety from an Adult Perspective

What Normally Happens at Night . . . A
Developmental Perspective . . . When Real Problems Begin . . . The Importance of Ritual . . . Working Mothers' Guilt, Single Parents'
Fatigue . . . Understanding Normal Sleep Disturbances . . . Running on Empty: The Anguish of
Sleep Deprivation . . . Red Flag . . . A Final Note
on Bedtime

In the Normal Course of Development . . .
Another Look at the "Terrible Twos": Toilet
Training Through a Toddler's Eyes . . . Saying No:
The Child's "Manifesto of Independence" . . .
From No-Saying to Self-esteem . . . Meeting the
Toddler Halfway . . . Darting Away: Through a
Child's Eyes . . . Separation and Anger . . . Un-
derstanding Your "Stubborn" Child . . . So
Many Ways to Say No . . . A Lesson in Cooper-
ation . . . How Limits Can Help—and When . . .
Teaching Children to Protect Themselves: An-
other Look at Noncompliance . . . Summing It
Up: The Meaning of Unconditional Love

Introduction

If there are so many books about raising children today, it is probably because there are so many parents like me: concerned, caring, well educated, and, yes, ambitious. Being "good" parents isn't enough for us—we want to be the best parents possible.

Like many new mothers, I devoured books about pregnancy and parenting just before and after the birth of our first child, a girl. Along with the arrival of our second daughter came an interest in sibling issues. I enjoyed these books but didn't really believe they applied to us. Our daughter, happy and loved, would welcome the new baby with open arms. And she did—for about two weeks. That's when her "hugs" became lethal and she began hurling shoes into the bassinet when she thought no one was looking.

Our son, by contrast, enjoyed what most third children acquire by birthright: relaxed, experienced parents and two fairly secure sisters who accepted him. (This time the arms were not only open but weaponfree.) Now the "balance of power" in our family had happily shifted, with children squarely outnumbering the grown-ups.

As our children grew, however, I was less and less the "ideal parent" I had set out to become. I found myself falling prey to new habits and new frustrations. Like so many mothers before me, I bemoaned the messy room, the unfed bird, the leftover food. New tensions replaced old ones; the familiar daily battles gave way to unexpected ones, similar only in their intensity. At times in the past I doubted that our eldest child would ever let me sleep later than 5:30 A.M. (still nighttime by most adult standards). Now I had to rouse her for school and coax her out of bed at 7:15 in the morning. Five days a week we struggled to get her dressed, groomed, and fed while I railed, "The carpool will be here any minute!"

I was even beginning to nag.

Once again, I looked for books that might help. Some, with an emphasis on parenting skills, were practical and concise. They gave specific solutions to specific problems. But for the theory that takes us inside a child's mind, I had to go elsewhere, and often the best books were those written forty or fifty years ago, with a professional audience in mind. It was rare to find the two approaches combined in a single volume for parents.

The more I read, though, the more I came to see that many of my children's "bad habits" were hardly bad habits at all.

Much of the behavior that disturbed me, I learned, was not only normal but necessary to their growth. Other reactions arose out of temperament, so that different attitudes toward food and eating, for example, came naturally to each child. Finally, I began to notice a third set of behaviors that could be traced to a single source: me. If my children had developed some difficult, annoying habits, so had I.

Habits are nothing more than *patterns* of behavior, and that is what interests me most as the mother of three very different children. In trying to understand my family better, I have asked what so many parents would like to know: Why do children do the things they do? When are certain reactions normal, and when are they not? And to what extent do we influence our children? In short, what is the connection between a child's puzzling behavior and our own attitudes and expectations?

In the end, I don't believe that any habit or behavior is as telling as the way we respond to it as parents. At the Early Childhood Development Center, in New York City, Dr. Nina Lief told me that we encounter dozens of opportunities every day "either to build the child's self-esteem or to diminish it." Whether we respond with concern or consternation, with faith or with frustration, we send signals every minute.

I'm not sure what surprises me more: the number of issues and annoyances that we fret over as parents, or the predictable, universal nature of these lists. Children forget to flush. They interrupt us when we're on the phone. They squeeze a new baby brother or sister until the infant turns blue. And they swear, through a mouth rimmed with crumbs, not to have pinched another Oreo. Are they social outcasts? Violent or overly aggressive? Pathological liars? No, they are children, and all of these irksome behaviors serve as proof.

In the last fifty years we have learned that children are driven by powerful impulses. Your baby becomes profoundly attached to you in the first few months. One week he is delightedly grabbing at the nose of a new acquaintance. A few months later, the same child buries his face in your shoulder when a stranger comes near. Your toddler darts away from you one minute and clings to you the next. In the first five years, childhood specialists tell us, these stages and many others can be predicted.

What we cannot predict is the degree of distress that each child will feel along the way, or the exact form of his anxiety, for temperament is also at work. I wanted to get a handle on why my children behave as they do, but I also wanted to puzzle out how the same two parents came to raise three remarkably different "souls," and the result is this book.

We are a family of sailors, and it seems as if all three of our children have set out on the same voyage, but that each is destined to chart a slightly different course. In growing up they will travel past many of the same markers. (The milestones of childhood are fairly constant, after all.) But at sea, changing course by a few degrees to the east or to the west makes a difference in how smooth or how turbulent the trip. Similarly, each child is born with tendencies that make his journey unlike anybody else's. As parents, we try to provide enough stability and support to help them through rough seas, even if we cannot always predict when and where the storms will be.

Our children's habits and behavior, I have concluded, are richer in meaning than we may realize. Not just because of what they say about our children, but because of the intense feelings they evoke in us as parents. It may sound mundane, but I honestly believe that our reactions over time to the spilled glass of milk, or the forgotten homework, or even the swipe at little sister, influence not only a child's image of himself but our relationship with that child for many years to come. "Our responses," wrote the late Haim Ginott, "can make a decided difference in the atmosphere of our home."

I began this book after realizing that my children, ages four, six, and nine, generally do what they do for a reason. And as soon as I began looking at what each of them felt and needed *now,* I began to judge their demands and reactions less harshly. This led to my giving them the benefit of the doubt in many difficult situations. I wanted to bring together, in one place, the theory and techniques that helped me to make these connections. And I wanted to write it in a way that speaks to parents today and the special pressures upon us.

What attracts us and teases us about childhood is its spontaneity, its lack of deliberation, the way a small child unself-consciously laughs out loud while playing alone. But even a child's play is layered with meaning. In *A Good-Enough Parent* the late Bruno Bettelheim wrote:

> Through his play, [the child] expresses what he would be hard pressed to put into words. No child plays spontaneously just to while away the time, although he and the adults observing him may think so. Even when he engages in play partly to fill empty moments, what he chooses to play at is motivated by inner processes, desires, problems, anxieties. What is going on in the child's mind determines his play activities; play is his secret language, which we must respect even if we do not understand it.

The child's nonplay behavior tells us a great deal, too. Through it he reveals his thoughts and feelings and fears, so that when any behavior becomes routinely obnoxious or annoying, it behooves parents to find its meaning. The patterns are there, in our children's actions and in our own. And within the patterns are clues: clues to what makes each child special and clues to real problems that may require real help. When we fail to make these connections, we put at risk a child's ability to feel comfortable and happy in the outside world and, just as important, the ability of parent and child to feel comfortable and happy with one another.

Most parents wish there were a way to guarantee each child's happiness. Unfortunately, there is not. But if our goal is to raise children with a capacity to enjoy life, we must begin by creating families where, despite the imperfections, the bad habits, and the inevitable conflicts, we nevertheless value and enjoy one another. And with insight and understanding, I believe we can.

The echoes of my life which I find in my early childhood are too many to be dismissed as vain coincidences. . . . All life is an echo of our first sensations, and we build up our consciousness, our whole mental life, by variations and combinations of these elementary sensations. But it is more complicated than that, for the senses apprehended not only colors and tones and shapes, but also patterns and atmosphere, and our first discovery of these determines the larger patterns and subtler atmospheres of all our subsequent existence.

from *The Innocent Eye* by Herbert Read

child-wise

CHAPTER ONE

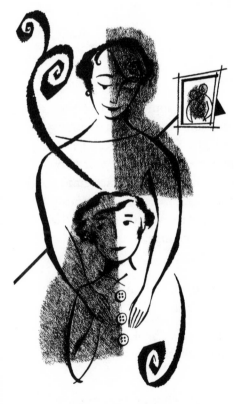

Often, like a child peering over the fence at somebody else's party, she gazes wistfully at other families and wonders what their secret is. They seem so close. Is it that they're more religious? Or stricter, or more lenient? Could it be the fact that they participate in sports? Read books together? Have some common interest or hobby? Recently, she overheard a neighbor woman discussing her plans for Independence Day: her family was having a picnic. Every member—child or grown-up—was cooking his or her specialty. Those who were too little to cook were in charge of the paper plates.

Jenny felt such a wave of longing that her knees went weak.

from *Dinner at the Homesick Restaurant*
by Anne Tyler

1~

Breaking the Patterns
That Keep
Parents and Children
Apart

You probably picked up this book because some aspect of your child's behavior is bothering you. It may be thumb-sucking and whining during the day or refusing to go to bed at night. Sibling fights or school reluctance. Acting shy or acting out. It may be the fact that your baby cries every time you leave for the office. (Or it may be the fact that he doesn't.) It may be an older child's failure to take homework as seriously as you would like, or it may be a messy room. Whatever it is, the *pattern* is one that you would probably like to change.

The message of this book is a positive one:

- ❦ That what we think of as "problem behavior" in our children is often a sign of normal, healthy growth

- ❦ That if you are concerned enough to read a book like this, you are also capable of helping a child whose behavior has you worried

- ❦ That the only coping techniques worth considering are those you feel comfortable with as a parent

- ❦ And, finally, that the relationship between parent and child is one of resilience

A child's unruly behavior does not mean that we have failed, and yet it can fill a conscientious parent with doubts. The simple truth is that there is no "right way" or "wrong way" of raising children. When faced with problems, parents have a choice: we can recoil from the habit and wonder who is to blame, or we can see it as a clue to what is on the child's mind and who that child is. When we choose the latter—when we look for the meaning of problem behavior—parents and children can emerge stronger, closer, and more convinced than ever of one another's love.

"The process of alleviating a disturbing symptom can then become a learning experience from which both parents and children can gather strength," writes the pediatrician T. Berry Brazelton.

From Normal Behavior to Problem Behavior

Before you label a habit a "bad habit," it is important to try to understand why the behavior makes sense from your child's perspective—and why it is disturbing to you as a parent. Some knowledge of child development can help. Many of the conflicts that arise between parents and children occur because of the way parents interpret—and often misinterpret—the things children do.

Even in families where there is genuine intimacy and trust, children will behave in strange, inscrutable ways from time to time. The particular habit may be less important, though, than the patterns that develop as a result.

Daily Battles and the Purpose They Serve

This book is about the many puzzling things that children do. It is about not only accepting the "bad habits" and thorny moments but understanding when, where, and why they generally occur. It is about those aspects of raising children that are frustrating, messy, disturbing, and that simply do not mesh with the idyllic image we may have of a normal, happy family.

I described this book to a kindergarten teacher, and she nodded. "I've thought a lot about how conflict arises in the classroom," she said, "and I finally realized that it isn't a question of *whether* it will arise, it's inevitable. So I began wondering if it serves a purpose, and it does. Children need to test the limits of what's acceptable."

The everyday conflicts between parent and child serve a purpose, too. They have a meaning and a psychology all their own. When we step back and try to understand why our children do what they do, we can distinguish between habits and reactions that are healthy and those that are not. When we see behavior that is not in the child's best interest, we can step in as parents and guide the child toward something better.

Long before children explore conflict at school, they "test the limits" at home. And long before they begin to sound out words, our children are reading us. They see the expression on a mother's face and know, instantly, whether they have delighted or disappointed. We are not half as effective at masking our feelings and concerns as we think. The specific habits and situations that trigger our concern may be trivial, but our handling of them sets the tone for family life.

René Spitz, a French researcher and pediatrician, described these interactions and their meaning nearly fifty years ago. "I cannot emphasize sufficiently how *small* a role traumatic events play in [most children's] development," he wrote. By contrast, he felt that the real fabric of family life was woven in these everyday encounters, in the "endlessly repeated" routines and reactions that come with raising children.

Parents or Interpreters? Three Scenarios

Scene One

A two-year-old toddles over to his mother and asks for a bottle. The mother sighs unhappily and takes the milk out of the refrigerator. This is her first child, and she is beginning to wonder if he will ever drink from a cup. She hands her son the bottle, cautioning him that he is "really getting too big for this" and "ought to" be using a cup instead. The child grabs the bottle and continues to clutch it long after finishing all eight ounces of milk.

The child's playmate, meanwhile, asks his mother for a

bottle, too, and she hands one over without comment. (This is her second child. She recalls that her older daughter used a bottle until age three, when the family dentist suggested a plan for phasing it out.) The child takes the bottle and drinks a few ounces of milk before something colorful catches her eye. Within minutes, she loses interest in the bottle and drops it on the kitchen floor.

Scene Two

A father is standing in line at a pharmacy, waiting for a prescription. Nearby, his robust three-year-old daughter is playing excitedly with some toys on display. *If only she weren't so noisy,* he thinks, aware that her delighted shrieks and giggles are attracting attention. A stiff, self-conscious man, he feels uncomfortable around strangers.

Another child joins his daughter. She is younger, about two, and also begins poking and prodding the display rack. She calls to her mother, who takes obvious pleasure in each noisy, excited sound. The child, a late developer, has just begun talking, and the mother is delighted with the sudden rush of words.

Scene Three

Two anxious four-year-olds arrive at a birthday party. The first insists on being held, and his mother obliges. Ten minutes pass, and the same child asks to be put down. Still, he insists on holding the mother's hand. Another ten minutes go by, and he wanders toward some bright balloons that have caught his eye. He still checks from time to time to see if his mother is there, and each time she smiles and reassures her son that she's nearby.

The other mother, trying to be patient, urges her reticent little girl to "stop acting so shy, there's nothing to be afraid of." When her daughter reaches up for her hand, the mother instead nudges her toward the crowd of guests. But the little girl recoils and clings to her mother for the rest of the party. An hour later, the pair leave feeling dejected and disappointed.

The point of these vignettes is simply that parents read and respond to the same behavior differently, and this is an important starting point for a book about raising children. What is annoying or irksome to one parent arouses empathy or joy in another.

At the same time that we become parents, we also become interpreters. The newborn cries, and we spring to action: Should we feed or soothe? Clean or console? Play with the baby or put her to bed? So begins the process of attunement to a child's needs.

As the child grows, we continue in this role. But spending time with our friends and their children, we also see that other parents react more or less sympathetically to the same behavior. What is acceptable to one mother may be punished or criticized by another. The strong-willed son who makes one parent proud may be a "difficult child" in a different family.

It is impossible to list all of the factors that influence parents' perceptions of their children. It matters whether it is a couple's first child or their second; it matters whether a mother is happy or unhappy about her decision to work or not to work outside the home; it matters whether the child we bring home from the hospital grows into the child we expected to raise; and clearly, our own experiences growing up will make a difference in the demands we make as parents.

But exactly how do these perceptions affect the way we raise our children? What is the connection between our behavior and our child's?

Between Parent and Child

Michael Lewis, a behavioral specialist from New Jersey, offers an example. It is not unusual, he wrote recently, for young infants to refuse food by turning their heads away from a proffered spoon. And yet if you ask three different mothers why their children do this, you will get three different answers. "Some mothers say that the child is being willful," he writes, "others claim that the child is aggressive, and still others believe that the child does not like the particular food or is no longer hungry."

Lewis makes the point that parents read meanings into a child's behavior that might never occur to a more detached observer. These interpretations—fair or unfair, educated or otherwise—then have a profound effect on the way children behave in the future. "So, for example, the mother who believes that the child is being aggressive is likely to react in such a way as to promote aggressive behavior in the child," Lewis writes. "The mother who believes that the child is not hungry is likely to have a child who does not subsequently show aggressive behavior."

So concerned are we about our children and their growth that the same behavior that appears "neutral" to someone else may provoke extreme reactions in us as parents.

We look at what the child is doing *now,* but what we often see is the child *grown tall.* As parents, we hopelessly project the two-year-old's occasional outbursts—"childish behavior" to which he should, after all, be entitled!—onto the adult he will become. Instead of seeing a little boy who fails to put away his toys, we see an unkempt grown man, unable to act responsibly. At other times, a child's behavior recalls the fears and anxieties of our own childhood, or aspects of our personalities that we still long to change. This can also cause parents to overreact or to become overly critical of young children.

In other words, we lose perspective. And each time we do this, we also lose an opportunity to interact with our children in a way that brings us closer.

Nature or Nurture?

Nothing is more difficult to fathom than why children develop as they do. The baby's first birthday arrives and, taking in a group of toddlers, we are struck by the differences we see, even among a small group of children.

One child is tall, another short. One cannot sit still long enough to wait for the birthday cake; another won't leave the table until he has demolished the entire piece. One little boy never leaves his mother's arms; another child shuts out all the excitement by sucking on a bottle and falling asleep.

Oddly enough, though, in trying to explain these differences, we rely on a framework whose roots date back to the eighteenth century: the question of nature versus nurture. In his book *The Disappearance of*

Childhood, Neil Postman traces these two opposing views of childhood to the writers John Locke and Jean-Jacques Rousseau.

It was Locke who drew the image of the *tabula rasa,* the idea that the child's mind at birth is a blank tablet, waiting to be filled. From Locke forward the process of raising children became a more studied, serious pursuit. The child's moral and academic progress became the measure of the parents' success, and parents therefore grew mindful of their role as nurturers.

At about the same time, Postman writes, Rousseau became the champion of the child's natural spirit, spontaneity, and joy, urging parents to nurture and celebrate these qualities, not to civilize young children as Locke instructed parents to do. (Rousseau carried his ideas to the extreme, however. His reliance on nature was more rugged than romantic, and he suggested that children, like animals, should be exposed unprotected to the elements. As for his own offspring, they were abandoned at an early age.)

Those who study young children have wrestled with these two schools ever since, eager to know whether it is "nature" or "nurture" that shapes the child. But for parents, this is not enough. Nature versus nurture is the equivalent of asking who is to blame for disturbing behavior: the parent or the child? Happily, a more helpful model exists.

Mutual Interaction and the "Fit" Between Parent and Child

Many experts today reject the notion that a child's behavior is a function of either nature or nurture. Conceptually, this book is rooted in a theory called *mutual interaction,* which tells us that no single factor prevails in a child's development. Mutual interaction helps to explain why there is no right or wrong way of raising children, and why there never will be. Parents and children clearly influence one another in complicated, profound ways.

Even within the same family, each baby is born into a unique environment. The experiences of a firstborn child bear little resemblance to those of the second or third. One of your children may enjoy being held and cuddled, but another resists the same overtures of affection. One child begs to sit on your lap, devouring one storybook after another, while a different child grows restless after a few minutes. And a colicky infant can leave even the most devoted mother wondering if she really is cut out for this parenting business after all. From the start, then, each child interacts differently with the same set of parents. A parent's relationship, for better or for worse, is essentially different from one child to the next.

Mutual-interaction theory is a useful starting point for parents who want to understand their children better. But to perform any job well, we need specific skills. This book also assumes that a parent's attitude can make a difference and that handling any problem effectively begins with understanding the specific situation and the specific child.

Each section of this book begins with just enough theory to frame a given habit developmentally and then offers parents some practical suggestions for coping. Where other books may offer do's and don'ts, I have simply tried to show that there is always another way of looking at a situation. And when parents are willing to consider a child's point of view in addition to their own, workable solutions will follow.

My hope is that after reading this book parents will begin to think in terms of how well their expectations "fit" with each of their children, and whether the environment they create at home is one that nurtures and celebrates what is special in each child. This may be more difficult for parents of single children, since it is often the birth of a second child that teaches us about temperament. But this effort to accept our children—and to modify what *we* expect of them—is what matters. When we do this, children feel more secure, and we help to relieve the anxiety that is often behind problem behavior.

Usually, in families where there is more than one child, parents will find one son or daughter more difficult to raise than another. One child psychiatrist, speaking of his own three sons, described his youngest child's storms and tantrums. But he did so in a bemused, reconciled way. "Jonathan is the one we will always do push-ups for," he said, smiling. But he quickly added how much harder it would have been if Jonathan, with his mercurial moods, had been their first child!

The challenge for all parents, then, is to find ways of identifying with a difficult child so that they are not constantly at odds. But we must also try to understand the "easy" child, who is difficult only on occasion. This book offers several sympathetic routes, bringing together many ideas and techniques that serve parents and children well, in the first six years and beyond.

Temperament Theory

A good fit between parent and child begins with an appreciation of temperament. Rene Spitz was one of the first to note that temperament and nurturing must go hand in hand.

In the early 1900s Spitz observed infants awaiting adoption in France. At the time, doctors discouraged too much handling or fondling for fear of distorting the child's "true nature." The objective was to place the child with a family that was well suited to its natural disposition. As a result, nurses attended to these babies only for the purposes of routine care and feeding.

What Spitz observed, however, was that these children, left to themselves and emotionally empty, failed to thrive. In fact some died. Spitz urged profound changes in the way orphans and adoptees were treated, changes that became standard practice in foundling hospitals. Today, his views prevail: For healthy development to occur, routine care is not enough. Children need to be nurtured, both physically and emotionally, and this must be done in a way that complements the qualities that they are born with. This *interplay* of nature and nurture will be seen in the growing child's habits, behavior, and general well-being.

Shyness is a good example. Some children are clearly more reserved and cautious than others, but a parent's skillful handling matters: A sensitive mother and father will look for what is age-appropriate caution and what is not. They will respect a quiet child's reserve but at the same time create opportunities for the same little boy or girl to interact with others, so that each small social success leads to another. Nature and experience will influence and modify each other.

For many parents, the birth of the second child proves once and for all the power of biology, the fact that each child is temperamentally unique. If parents are able to relax more, it may be because they know that deep within the swaddling blanket is a person waiting to emerge, not waiting to be formed. Dr. Stanley Turecki, who counsels the parents of difficult children, defines expert parenting as "the particular knowledge of your particular child."

Being a different parent to each child is at odds with the idea many of us have that "good" parents treat siblings the same. Questions of fairness will always arise in families with more than one child. I have yet to see a brother or sister who did not studiously measure two glasses of milk side by side to see which holds more. In families where each child feels respect and appreciation, however, issues of "fairness" may be less divisive.

Good-Enough Parents and "Generous Explanations"

The fit between parent and child can also be improved through empathy. For the late Bruno Bettelheim, whose benevolent view of children imbues this book, empathy is the single most important quality for parents. In *A Good-Enough Parent,* the last book he wrote before his death in 1990, he urges us to give young children the benefit of the doubt. How can we do this? By recalling, as best we can, what it means to be small in a grown-up world.

Bettelheim believed that all children are essentially good. More than anything, he wrote, children want and need their parents' approval, and they will "choose" behavior accordingly. Even when faced with a child's most unruly, unsettling behavior, writes Bettelheim, the good-enough parent assumes that "whatever the child does, he does it because at the moment he is convinced this is the best he can do."

But the good-enough parent then goes a step farther and asks, "What in the world would make me act as my child acts at this moment? And what would make me feel better about it?" Bettelheim reminds us that we cannot find the answers to a child's puzzling behavior without first asking the right questions. This book takes a similar view.

Children often act finicky over food and balk at bedtime. But each child has a different agenda, so to speak. What matters to you is why *your* child is choosing to act in a certain way, and why *you* react as you do to the behavior.

Even parents who have a hard time identifying with a certain child in the family can learn to think empathically. An outgoing, gregarious parent may have a hard time understanding a child's shy demeanor. But perhaps that parent can recall some episode in his childhood in which he felt overwhelmed or anxious. Now, even if their experiences diverge, the emotions they share can bring parent and child closer.

As children grow, their needs grow more complex, more difficult to read. Does the two-year-old really want us to "go away"—or does he want to be held close, as he implores minutes later. By trying to see the world through our child's eyes, we can begin to find Bettelheim's "generous explanations." By finding the true motivations behind a child's actions—no matter how repugnant or rejecting—we cannot help but respond more effectively. For most parents, this leads to the thoughtful response, the feeling that, as parents, we are indeed good enough. When this happens, our warm feelings grow. The child feels reassured that we are on his side after all.

The "Flow of Influence" Between Parents and Children

As parents we cannot "control" a child's behavior, and the more we try to do this the more conflict we can expect. However, we can influence the overall "pattern" of our relationship with a child: positive or negative, supportive or stressful. "What matters most in a child's upbringing," writes Bettelheim, "is often the way the parent handles himself in a given situation, because this is the child's guide to the meaning of what is happening."

In matters of human psychology, the name Sigmund Freud comes to mind. But it was his daughter, Anna Freud, who documented a psychology unique to the growing child. Where her father's ideas were based on the adult patient's memories of childhood (a reconstruction of sorts, dictated by the present), Anna Freud looked at children directly. A keen and sympathetic observer, she is best known for her work with British children who were separated from their families during World War II. While caring for them she observed that each child's reactions to the air raids in London were most influenced by the mother's reactions to wartime trauma.

Air raids, of course, are uncommon events, but childhood anxiety is not. Anxiety is what drives a great many problem behaviors as children cope with the pressures of growing up. In the course of normal development—whether it is learning to go to sleep alone, or to use the toilet, or to negotiate and get along with others—children take their cues from us.

Everyday dramas and conflicts are the inescapable facts of family life. We may be blessed with good health and a strong marriage—but there is no way to avoid a child's tears at separation, or his fear of the dark. What matters is our response. With empathy, we can shrink the shadows on the wall until they cease to exist. Without it, we may imbue those same shadows with inordinate power to frighten the small child.

But when we learn to accept these problems—with understanding, empathy, and humor—more positive patterns can emerge. The daily arguments over putting away the toys or practicing the piano defeat us so easily. We see them coming (they are as predictable as the sun setting in the west) yet they frustrate us time and time again. In many cases, we are mothers and fathers who have managed budgets and unruly bosses and done difficult jobs well through sheer tenacity and dogged preparation. So why are we unable to persuade someone three feet tall to step into six inches of water at bathtime?

In an age of "positive parenting," we still speak of the "terrible twos" as if young children were somehow out to get us. We can hardly resist saying to the small child whose behavior is so baffling, *"Why are you doing this to me!"*

Finding the Answers and Moving Ahead

Character is no more than the combination of qualities that distinguish any individual. And a child's character development is influenced when we introduce morals and standards of behavior in a way that respects what a child is capable of doing and understanding *now*.

Writing about what it means to live life fully, the psychoanalyst and writer D. W. Winnicott reminds us that problem behavior is proof of the child's humanity, not proof that a parent has failed. "The life of a healthy individual," he wrote, "is characterized by fears, conflicted feelings, doubts, frustrations, as much as by the positive features."

Winnicott reminds us of the need to stand by the young child emotionally, even when we would like nothing better than to get up and physically leave the room. This means allowing a child to take charge of confusing feelings and act in a way that makes independence possible. Our goal must be, as one pediatrician eloquently put it, "to give children ownership of their lives."

Summary

Eleanor Maccoby, the noted professor and researcher, writes of a process whereby influence "flows back and forth." To me, the idea was immediately appealing. I was surprised to learn that this focus on the parent-child relationship as a "reciprocal" one is relatively new.

Parents are often advised to "choose their battles carefully." The implication of course is that to raise children is to engage in warfare. And certainly there are families where conflict is the rule, not the exception. When we think about what we want to achieve long-term, however, a more "pacifist" approach is possible. In writing this book I chose a period of time when parents have a singular opportunity to learn to talk to a child, and to learn to listen as well.

From the first year to the first grade we enjoy a unique proximity to our children. We cannot change the process by which children make giant leaps forward, only to be followed by a few steps back, but we can certainly alter the patterns. Many of the "bad habits" children develop have been encouraged—inadvertently, unknowingly—by us. When they act, we react. And ironically, we often reinforce the behavior we would most like to change. But if damaging patterns have been set in motion, we need to ask, "How did this happen, and how can it be changed?" In the end, we can only be heartened by the resilience of the parent-child relationship. For it is never too late to start anew.

CHAPTER TWO

Understanding what children are
up to is the first step in learning to get
along with them.

from *Dr. Spock's Baby and Child Care*

No More "Bad Habits": Ten Questions for Concerned Parents

··

In the first few years parents encounter many habits that they do not fully understand, and comments like these are common:

"She carries that old blanket around with her everywhere. She'll probably still be carrying it at her wedding."

"My son is fifteen months old, and he still cries every time the baby-sitter comes and I go out. He'll never go away to college."

"Our daughter is almost two, and she's impossible. It used to be a pleasure taking her out, but now everything is an ordeal, and she's constantly saying no to us and bossing us around."

A mother may worry that these habits are a sign of abnormal development. In fact they are some of the earliest signs of normal, healthy growth. One therapist told me that the child who consoles herself with a worn blanket does not have a problem—she has solved one! Left alone in her crib at night, or feeling needy during the day, she has learned to find solace. Crying at separation is a sign that the older baby is deeply attached to you—and can anticipate feeling sad when you leave. As for the "bossy" little girl, the pursuit of autonomy (which takes many parents of toddlers by surprise) has begun.

Before you set out to change your child, ask yourself the following:

1. Is your child's behavior age-appropriate?

It's reassuring to learn that in the first six years, many habits develop along normal lines of growth. Louise Bates Ames and Carol Chase Haber, of the Gesell Institute of Human Development in New Haven, Connecticut, are well known for their "ages and stages" approach to understanding children. The three-year-old who lies about taking a cookie isn't really a "liar" after all. He simply can't control his impulses. He then convinces himself of a new truth and, eager for your approval, reports the version that he knows will make you happy.

A two-year-old's willingness to share seems to shift with the wind: he is generous with his possessions one minute and almost miserly the next. A four-year-old may ask countless questions about death, and a six-year-old tends to be messy and forgetful (your daughter wears her sweater to school, but it never seems to come home with her).

It helps to know that most children move through these stages, even though reactions will vary in intensity from one child to the next. When we expect certain issues and habits to arise, though, we are more accepting of what our children do, and we can avoid confrontations with them.

2. Does the behavior tell you something about your child's temperament?

Books about development offer useful guidelines. They tell us approximately when we can expect a child to make certain physical, emotional, and intellectual strides. Specific habits, however, offer clues to your child's *temperament.*

In 1956 two childhood psychiatric researchers named Stella Chess and Alexander Thomas decided that mothers were blamed too often for their children's problem behavior. Chess and Thomas began a landmark study of temperament. Their study revealed that from an early age children display different levels of outgoingness, for example, or sensitivity to noise; activity levels and intensity will also vary. Regardless of a parent's education, skill, or devotion, they asserted, some children will simply be more difficult to raise than others.

Temperament is often behind complaints such as these:

"Food was never an issue with my son, but my daughter won't touch anything but noodles and bread. Sometimes I think she does this just to spite me, but she really seems to have no interest in eating."

"My son insists on wearing the same worn-out sweatpants to school every day. I've tried replacing them with a new pair, but he won't even try them on. He insists that the other ones are more comfortable."

"I always feel embarrassed at birthday parties because my children get so wild. Other kids can at least sit still long enough to watch the puppet show or eat a piece of cake, but mine don't seem able to do this."

Reactions such as these cause many everyday conflicts, especially when parents think children are just being difficult. But a "finicky" eater may simply prefer bland foods. A child who objects to putting on a new pair of pants may be hypersensitive to the stiffness of new clothing; and the children who "go crazy" at a birthday party may, indeed, be easily overstimulated.

Temperamental differences can be seen in other ordinary situations. One child coos contentedly in the car seat, while another cries inconsolably for forty-five minutes before exhausting himself and finally falling asleep. Your daughter enjoys a surprise appearance by you at school one day, but your son—expecting the baby-sitter to pick him up—is upset to see you; like many people, he takes comfort in knowing exactly what to expect.

The good news is that such tendencies do not have to create tension between you and your child. A middle ground exists. The more willing we are to modify our expectations, the more we learn to appreciate the nuances of a child's personality.

3. Are your expectations fair?

Whenever we become overly critical of a child's behavior, we need to step back and ask whether our expectations are realistic, or fair, for a particular child. Often, what we label "problem behavior" is evidence of a "poor fit" between what parents expect and what is either age-appropriate or natural for a given child. Parents who are rigid and rule-oriented, for example, may label a spirited child "difficult."

Harold Koplewicz is chief of the Child and Adolescent Psychiatry Department at Schneider's Children's Hospital and an Associate Professor of Psychiatry at the Albert Einstein College of Medicine, both in New York. He is also an enthusiastic father of three who believes that parenting should be a joyful experience. One problem, he contends, is that parents begin to form expectations for their children even *before* they are born. According to Dr. Koplewicz, pregnant women often make comments such as these:

> *"I know it's silly, but I think he's going to be an athlete because he seems to move around a lot."*

Or:

> *"I imagine he's going to be smart like his father. He's a really brainy guy."*

What if these children turn out to be average athletes or mediocre students? Then their parents' unrealistic expectations are not met, and the children may be harshly judged. Children are quick to sense their parents' disappointment, and their self-esteem suffers in a home where parents rigidly set expectations.

Some parents push reading well before a child is ready either intellectually or emotionally. In another family, parents may criticize a child for his lazy work habits or for never following directions, perhaps ignoring a possible learning disability. The unhappy result is the same whenever parents set goals that their children cannot possibly meet: a pattern of negative interactions between parent and child.

In families with siblings, parents must let go of the notion that being effective, or being fair, means being the same parent to each child. According to child and adolescent psychiatrist Stanley Turecki, expert parenting means recognizing that each child's needs are different. There is nothing wrong with trying to modify problem behavior, but first be sure that your expectations for each child are reasonable.

It also helps to accept the fact that some children are easier to raise than others. If this is the case—if you have to "work harder" to get along with one child in your family—don't despair. Resist the temptation to compare your children with one another *("Rebecca is so much more affectionate than Justin")* and focus instead on what is special in each child *("Justin doesn't enjoy being held the way Rebecca did, but he's developing a wonderful sense of humor.*") If you can learn to value what is different in each of your children, they will all feel special and loved. They will also have an easier time appreciating one another.

4. Is the "bad habit" part of a pattern, or can it be traced to a recent change at home?

A good example is the physical aggression that often follows the birth of a new sibling:

> *"Margaret is almost three, and she's always been so sweet and kind with other children. At first she seemed thrilled with the new baby, but then she started squeezing Emily's head so hard that the baby started to scream. We were appalled! Then Margaret's teachers said she was being rough with the other children in nursery school. It's hard to believe all this is normal."*

Margaret is angry about the new baby and she needs to vent her feelings. Before they can help their daughter, though, her parents must accept that while her physical outbursts are not acceptable, they are indeed normal, and so are the rage and jealousy behind them. The sooner they allow her to express these feelings (without risking their love), the sooner her aggression will cease. The last thing she needs is to feel guilty because she is letting her parents down.

Older children need to verbalize their feelings about any significant change in their lives, whether it is a divorce or a death or a more common event, such as having a new baby-sitter or starting school. Parents may worry that they are "fueling the fires" by bringing up these topics, but the opposite is true. It can be therapeutic to express anxious feelings, and this is often the best way to defuse them.

But now consider a child who has a history of hitting other children:

> *"Our son, Gregory, is three, and his teachers have told us that when he doesn't win a game at school, he gets very angry and hits the other children or storms off. I think he just has a short fuse like my husband and will probably outgrow the behavior if we don't make a big deal about it."*

It's a mistake to assume that children will outgrow problem be-havior, especially when it is aggressive or antisocial in nature. A three-year-old who isn't taught that hitting is wrong will have trouble making friends and getting along with teachers. These negative patterns emerge early, and the longer they are allowed to continue, the more difficult they are to change. Also, while it's true that some children seem to take winning and losing more seriously than others, extreme distress at losing can point to low self-esteem and should not be ignored.

5. Are you reinforcing behavior problems without realizing it?

As parents we both model and reward certain types of behavior. Gregory's parents need to figure out why their child strikes out at other children: Is he imitating what he sees at home, where older siblings may be allowed to hurt one another? Has he found that by yelling or hitting, he usually gets his way? Here is another example of parents who are unaware that they are reinforcing a behavior problem:

> *"It drives me crazy when my daughter whines, especially when she does it in public. The other day, we were waiting in the lobby of my older daughter's school and she started up because she wanted me to carry her. I finally gave in because I couldn't stand to have her make a scene."*

Children are clever, and we cannot blame them for resorting to unpleasant means if it helps them to get their way. Gerald Patterson, of the Oregon Social Learning Center, has studied coercive child be-havior for two decades. He has found that when parents fail to use discipline effectively—when they issue threats but do not follow through on them—children learn to rely on aversive behavior. He calls this a *negative-reinforcement trap*. Frequent temper tantrums, which end with a parent caving in to calm a distraught child, are a good example.

Even with comfort habits, such as bottles and pacifiers, we help to create habits that outlive their usefulness or need. When this happens, we can help children to break these habits by rewarding each small effort to resist falling into old patterns.

6. Can you find similar patterns of behavior in yourself, or in your own childhood?

As children grow, we may be especially unforgiving of qualities we see in them that remind us of ourselves. The parent who performed poorly in school may be overly critical of her six-year-old's homework habits, but her constant rebukes may only discourage her child from trying harder. A mother who recalls her early school years as lonely or unhappy may resonate with anxiety before her own child begins kindergarten, and she may not recognize that what she perceives as her child's fears are really her own.

Our love for a child can be overwhelming in its intensity. But so, too, are some of the negative feelings that our children arouse in us: anger, frustration, impatience, and, perhaps worst of all, a nagging sense that we have "been there" before. When your child behaves in a way that recalls your own shortcomings or faults, you may become overly sensitive to the behavior. Psychologists use the term *projection* to describe this process. (In other words, we often *project* our own feelings onto the motives and experiences of another person.) Since we have such high hopes for our children, it is easy to see why their insecurities and moments of weakness affect us so acutely as parents. Be aware that in looking at your children, you may be seeing yourself. Knowing this may help you to avoid being overly critical of what they do.

It can be maddening to find that, despite our best efforts, we have repeated patterns that we fully intended to avoid. Here is an example of how one shy parent's efforts backfired:

> *"I was very timid growing up, and I swore that my children wouldn't suffer the same way I did. As soon as I could, I started signing up my daughter for playgroups and insisting that she take classes such as gymnastics and ballet, even when she resisted. My plan didn't work, though, and I sometimes think she's even more withdrawn than I was."*

Whenever parents become overly invested in a particular skill or accomplishment, a child's fear of failure multiplies. This is why some children refuse to get into the pool for a swimming lesson, or turn their back on Daddy's favorite sport. In addition, when we stubbornly set these goals for our children, we may disregard their temperament or stage of development. Battling shyness, for example, must be done slowly, with patience and genuine respect for a child's anxiety. Anytime we react to behavior in our children that we dislike in ourselves, we need to proceed with extreme caution. The dynamics of everyday family life also have a way of repeating themselves. One example is sibling strife, as this mother learned.

> *"My two daughters are always fighting, and I tend to feel sorry for my younger daughter. Sometimes I end up sounding exactly like my mother did when she told my older sister to stop picking on me. It only made my sister resent me even more. I can't believe the same thing is happening now in my own family."*

A parent's experiences as a child can inadvertently trigger such conflicts, and it is difficult to address them without resolving the issue first from our own childhood. Whenever parents, like the one above, come too quickly to the side of one child, there is even more jealousy between siblings, and the result is more bullying by the older child in the family. These patterns are surprisingly common. Allowed to continue, they can poison family relationships.

7. How comfortable are you in setting limits for your children?

Childhood experts stress the importance of setting limits. Whether the issue is bedtime habits, bottles and pacifiers, sibling fights, or basic socialization skills, a parent's ability to set limits will strongly influence how a child behaves.

In 1971 Diana Baumrind, a childhood researcher with the University of California, studied 146 preschool children and their families and found three basic patterns of parental authority: *Authoritarian, Permissive,* and *Authoritative.*

The last group, *authoritative parents,* serves as a model throughout this book. According to Baumrind, these parents have high expectations, yet encourage give-and-take and are willing to modify their demands. The authoritative parent "recognizes her own special rights as an adult" but is also "warm, rational and receptive" to the child's point of view. These parents affirm the child's individual interests and special needs, writes Baumrind, while setting the standard for future conduct.

Baumrind found the children of authoritative parents to be "self-reliant, self-controlled, explorative, and content." In other words, they developed many of the qualities that children need to be happy in the world outside the family.

Authoritarian parents, by contrast, are detached, lacking in warmth, and highly controlling. They expect their children to comply to the same fixed standard of behavior regardless of each one's feelings or personality. Baumrind found their children to be "discontent, withdrawn, and distrustful."

And at the other end of the spectrum, *permissive parents* are those who make few if any demands of their children (noncontrolling and nondemanding are two words used to describe them). Yet their children were "the least self-reliant, explorative, and self-controlled."

Baumrind's study helps to explain why some children may be a nightmare at bedtime. On an unconscious level, children sense the parent's role in making the world safe. The mother's "no" protects the child not only from the physical dangers of the external world but from his own aggressive impulses as well. It is widely accepted that when parents fail to set appropriate limits, children may feel more vulnerable at night: the aggressive urges that have not been "tamed" by day may be terrifying to a small child alone in the dark.

Authoritative parents strike a happy balance. They set limits in a way that enhances a child's feelings of security (day or night), and this feeling of safety enables the same child to take initiative and explore the world more actively.

Nancy Samalin, who leads parent workshops in New York and has written two practical books about raising children, believes that parents who have trouble setting limits are often afraid of a child's withdrawing love. "Give your child permission not to like you," she advises parents.

8. Are you reacting to one or two habits or behaviors, or do you feel as if you're criticizing everything?

As children approach kindergarten age, parents may become consumed with criticism, especially of a first child. We simply expect them "to know better." One mother told me:

> *"I feel as if I'm constantly yelling at my kids for one thing or another. 'In this house, we don't do that!' Or: 'In this house, we don't say those things!' Their room is a mess, they're always losing the*

pieces to their toys, and lately they seem to be fighting more. I never thought I'd be this kind of mother."

There's nothing wrong with identifying a problem area—whether it is the morning rush or school stress—and setting out to change it. But at times there is a "snowball effect," as parents harp on all that is wrong with a child but fail to notice those qualities that are worthy of admiration. It is a mistake to try changing everything at once. The director of our children's nursery school once gave me invaluable advice: "Focus on changing one thing at a time with young children," she said, "and try to ignore the things that aren't as important."

Learn to set priorities. Anytime you are about to jump on a child for irksome behavior, stop and ask yourself whether you really must intervene. You can avoid constant, negative encounters by accepting that some behavior is annoying but acceptable. For the sake of perspective, parents must identify and praise the qualities that they genuinely like and admire, especially in a child who is more difficult to live with.

9. Do you attribute your child's "bad habits" or behavior problems to your being a divorced or single parent?

Depending on the specific habit, you may be right: Many experts agree that bedtime, for example, a common enough struggle for young families, is even more difficult in single-parent homes. Most parents are tired by the end of the day. In a two-parent family, when the mother feels tired or tense, the father can take over. But a single parent (or even a parent whose spouse travels frequently) has no such "buffer." And, as discussed in Chapter 4, parents must be able to relax if bedtime is to be smooth.

It is estimated that half of all children born today will live with a single parent at some time in their lives. Even so, a divorced mother may feel isolated and without the support that many intact families enjoy, both emotionally and financially.

The broad principles of child development hold for children in divorced families, too. Research shows that boys are more likely than girls to suffer discipline problems following a divorce. But one reason is that mothers relax their expectations and hesitate to set limits. Ironically, this is interpreted as a lack of caring, and so the child acts out to recapture the parent's attention.

A mother may think that talking about a recent divorce will be too painful for a child or for herself. Chapter 7, about aggression, discusses the importance of allowing children to vent difficult feelings. These principles help to explain the cycles that commonly occur in divorced families, where emotions and living arrangements are more complicated, for adults as well as for children.

10. Do you feel concerned or guilty about how much time you spend with your family?

No book can tell you whether you are, in fact, spending enough time with your children. What is important to understand, though, is how guilt and insecurity may affect your *perceptions* of a child's behavior. According to Jay Belsky, a researcher and professor at the University of Pennsylvania, one component of being a good parent is objectivity. Parents who feel anxious about the amount of time they spend with their children have a harder time saying no to them. These parents also have a tendency to take a child's habits personally.

Where does this guilt and insecurity come from? Certainly it has a great deal to do with our struggle to define the "good mother." During the 1992 presidential election, one news magazine featured a story about Hillary Clinton and Tipper Gore. THE LAWYER AND THE HOUSEWIFE, it stated, as if the two mothers were about to step into the ring. The media perpetuates this notion that women have only two options: a high-powered corporate career or at-home motherhood on a full-time basis. The reality, of course, is that women, struggling to give emotional and financial support to their families, have devised many ways of combining work and family. (Tipper Gore—political advocate and author—is a good example. She is hardly a "typical housewife.")

As long as the mythical "good mother" is the one who stays home full time, women will feel insecure about the decision they make to combine work and family. As a result, we may look to our children to validate our choices. With respect to their habits and behavior, this may put undue pressure on children to behave in a way that makes us look competent.

A mother who works, for example, may blame herself for her child's habits in a harsh, unforgiving way: *If I were staying at home, he wouldn't be so shy.* Or, *She's cranky today because I didn't pick her up at school.*

And the mother who gives up her career to stay at home may have equally unfair expectations of her children (*I gave up my career for my children, and they're still anxious about school. Why did I bother leaving work after all?),* as if the perfect mother raises children who never feel anxious or afraid.

Where there is guilt and insecurity, problem behavior is seen as proof of a parent's failure. This is why guilt can be harmful for both parents and children. Many experts I spoke with attribute bedtime struggles today to this ambivalence and to a basic concern that many parents feel about their relationships with their children and how much time they spend together. Insecurities and difficult behavior are not only normal in the first six years, they also provide important clues to your child and should be viewed as such.

CHAPTER THREE

And once, when the Boy was called away suddenly to go out to tea, the Rabbit was left out on the lawn until after dusk, and Nana had to come and look for him with the candle because the Boy couldn't go to sleep unless he was there . . . and Nana grumbled as she rubbed him off with a corner of her apron.

"You must have your old Bunny!" she said. "Fancy all that fuss for a toy!"

The Boy sat up in bed and stretched out his hands.

"Give me my Bunny!" he said. "You mustn't say that. He isn't a toy. He's REAL!"

When the little Rabbit heard that, he was happy, for he knew what the Skin Horse had said was true at last. The nursery magic had happened to him, and he was a toy no longer. He was Real. The Boy himself had said it.

from *The Velveteen Rabbit* by Margery Williams

3~

Coming to Terms with
Comfort Habits

Scene: Mid-September at a private preschool in New York City. A group of parents is standing behind a one-way mirror, watching their two-year-olds inside the classroom. While the boys and girls play, their parents note with pleasure how easily the children have adjusted—so easily, in fact, that the mothers begin wondering aloud why the teachers are slowly phasing in a full morning of school.

"They seem fine," says one parent.

"Stefanie couldn't wait to come back!" says another.

"Sam is definitely ready for a full morning," adds a third.

But Sam's mother has hardly finished her sentence when she lets out a yawn. She apologizes, explaining that Sam woke her up at four-thirty in the morning—again! He hasn't done that, she adds, since his baby sister was born six months ago.

Stefanie's mother is sympathetic—and slightly puzzled. Her daughter not only woke up several times during the night but she insisted on using a bottle that morning, after giving it up weeks ago.

What's going on? Why have these toddlers, so sturdy and self-assured in their new classroom, resumed "infantile" habits at home? Is there a reason why children resume such behavior at the same time that they start school or learn to use the toilet or become a big brother or sister? The answer is yes. But to see the connection, we need to understand why children first assume these habits in infancy.

Why Comfort Habits Begin

The threadbare blanket. The ever-present pacifier. The ragged stuffed bear with two loose arms and a missing eye. These emblems of early childhood are some of the first "bad habits" that parents bemoan. This chapter also looks at bottles, thumb sucking, and the first strains of stranger anxiety and separation fear. (Bedtime and eating habits, which also concern parents in the first year, are covered in separate chapters.)

Beginning at about six months, writes Dr. Spock, the child feels the "first sense of separateness." Your child is torn between an urge to be independent of you (he pushes your hand away from the bottle or squirms free of your arms) and a desire for the total dependence and comfort of his earliest days when, Spock suggests, "being fed in a parent's arms was all there was to paradise." The *transitional object,* as psychologists call these comforters, is efficient in filling both of these complex needs.

In other words, comfort habits allow the child to take one step back to an earlier feeling, or source, of security. And it is this renewed sense of security that permits a few steps forward, toward independence. Every time a toddler wakes at night or issues new demands for old bottles, he reminds us of the energy and effort he exerts for each step forward.

As parents, we spend so much time wondering about whether we appear to be "in control" of a situation, we forget that our children have the same need. A few hours at school may not seem like a long time. But in that time, your son or daughter is coping with other children's needs, the demands of new adults, and different rules and routines. Imagine how exhausting this must be for a small child!

Each child finds a different way to console himself when he's feeling tired or anxious. Your daughter may twirl her hair or pull on an upper brow; your son may suck his thumb or rock back and forth while stroking a stuffed animal. Early on, it is important to accept and even admire the child's resourcefulness in learning to soothe himself.

Early Signs of Normal Development

First-time parents are relieved to discover that worrisome habits are often proof that a child is developing normally. Some of the changes you see in your baby may surprise you, but you needn't be alarmed. By the end of the first year:

- 🐞 A normally "outgoing" baby may suddenly shrink from strangers and cling to his mother instead

- 🐞 Some children will become deeply attached to a particular blanket or soft toy

- 🐞 Habits such as thumb sucking and pacifiers may be taken up with genuine passion

- 🐞 Saying "bye-bye," which began as a source of delight for your baby, may one day bring on a river of tears and wrenching grief

And, finally, you may find yourself wondering what these reactions say about your child. Behavior that is "normal" can still be troubling to parents, especially when we do not understand it. The pacifier that looked sweet in the mouth of your seven-month-old may begin to bother you now that your child is older, upright, and seemingly "mature." No one will argue that head rocking, which can be just as comforting to a child as an old blanket, is also unnerving. Before you intervene, though, try to understand the purpose these habits serve, as well as the signals you may be sending your child.

Between Parent and Child

It almost seems too obvious to state that children and the adults who provide their constant care develop a special attachment. Learning to cope in a parent's absence, however, is one of the most difficult tasks of childhood.

Parents cannot help feeling concerned when a normally happy baby begins to cry or becomes agitated more easily. But at certain stages of development it is normal for babies to react with increasing distress.

The two most common forms, stranger anxiety and separation anxiety, occur in the first two years. Both have their roots in the profound bond between parent and child, and it is impossible to accept a child's comfort habits without first understanding the anxiety that makes them necessary.

In the First Year: Stranger Anxiety

Stranger anxiety begins sometime after six or seven months. Previously, your baby happily bounced from one set of arms to another. Now the child begins to object to strangers, at times appearing almost terrified by a new face. Why the sudden change in social outlook?

Your child's brain is now developed enough to recognize the difference between your face and a stranger's. If you hold your child and gradually introduce new faces while yours is still in plain view, the child may not be upset. But if a baby looks up expecting to see your face and is met instead by an unfamiliar gaze, there may be tears.

It may help to know that this has nothing to do with whether a child will be "friendly" or "unfriendly." Rather it is an important sign of growth and maturity in the older baby. Like this mother, many parents feel more intensely attached to their child now than ever before:

> *"Zoe was always such an outgoing baby, and we loved letting all our relatives hold her. When she started to protest, I was alarmed at first. But then I had this incredible feeling of closeness. For the first time I felt that she would rather be with me than with anyone else."*

In the Second Year: Fear of Separation

By the sixth month most babies smile and wave "bye-bye," to the delight of their parents. This is especially joyous to the new working mother, who is just beginning to think that maybe she can have it all. One year later, her world turns upside down. The same baby who gurgled good-bye now cries inconsolably when she leaves. Minutes later, the child may be all smiles again. But the mother's stomach churns for the rest of the morning, the sound of her baby's cries echoing inside her head.

Separation anxiety usually occurs between eighteen and thirty-six months. As a parent, you know that you are leaving the house for just a few hours. To your child, though, you might as well be leaving forever, so intense is his feeling of loss once you leave the room. Dr. Spock believes that this fear of separation intensifies at about the same time children learn to walk. In other words, when they first become physically capable of leaving a parent's side, children "soon feel the urge to get back," as if biologically programmed for safety and survival.

What is perhaps most remarkable is how differently each child reacts, as this parent found:

"My sister and I have very similar ways of handling our children (they both turn two next week), but my son has always had a harder time saying good-bye than my niece. Sometimes I think my sister would feel better if her daughter also got upset once in a while!"

While some children hardly fret, others require constant reassurance and a steady, sensitive hand.

Some researchers have claimed that a "securely attached" child will not be upset by brief separations. But Jay Belsky and Margaret Fish, of Penn State University, take a different view. In fact, some of their studies suggest that the baby who protests loudly may be more secure than his less vocal peers. In other words, crying is a legitimate, even healthy way for children to cope with their feelings of loss. (For more on attachment, please see the sidebar on page 34.)

Children usually feel more secure about separation if parents are understanding of their anxiety. Belsky and Fish believe that, as children get older, their reactions to separation are more malleable. In other words, there are things you can do to make separation less traumatic for your child. (Please see Chapter 8 for more about shyness-related anxiety. Chapter 9 offers suggestions for helping a school-age child to say good-bye.)

Try not to be alarmed if your neighbor's son separates more easily than yours. And if you have two or more children, don't be surprised if they handle separation differently. Each child develops at his or her own rate. Brain maturity, personality, and experience will all affect how ready and willing each child is to say good-bye.

Is Your Baby "Spoiled" or Secure?
A Look at Attachment Behavior

Many mothers enjoy soothing a distressed child by holding, cuddling, or singing to him—until an older relative points a finger and accuses them of "spoiling" the baby. Is there a real risk of doing this?

The pioneering work of John Bowlby, a British author and psychoanalyst, suggests that the answer is no. In the 1940s researchers were just beginning to study the impact of losing the mother figure in the first few years of life. Young children who were separated from their mothers not only suffered enormous grief and distress but continued to have adjustment problems later in life. And yet, Bowlby noted, little was known about the nature of the child's earliest ties to the mother: How could we get to the meaning of any *separation,* Bowlby wondered, without first understanding the nature of *attachment?*

In *Attachment and Loss,* Bowlby suggested that the infant's early behavior keeps the mother in proximity to the child, ensuring the care and protection that he needs for survival, and that this eventually leads to a shared sense of intimacy between mother and child.

"The young child's hunger for his mother's love and presence is as great as his hunger for food," Bowlby wrote. When satisfied in his need for the mother, the child feels content and develops happily, exploring the world with vigor. By contrast, when mothers fail to respond—or do so coldly—children tend to demand more attention and grow anxious. Again, Bowlby's analogy is to feeding. The child who eats when he is hungry feels satisfied; the child with an empty stomach grows hungrier and more agitated.

When mothers respond with warmth and affection to a baby's earliest needs, the child is more likely to be *securely attached.* As for the same child's tears and distress when a mother leaves, even temporarily, Bowlby found this to be a natural and healthy expression of loss.

One colleague of Bowlby's also looked at how a child behaved when reunited with the mother. A *securely attached* child welcomed and approached the mother, sought to be picked up, and clung or else remained close by her. In cases of insecure attachment, children either showed no interest in the returning mother or threw tantrums, but "made no attempt to reach her." In other words, the clinging that has you wondering if your child is insecure is a healthy, effective "strategy" for keeping you near.

Despite Bowlby's distinction here between secure and insecure attachment, keep in mind that some ambivalent behavior in a child is always normal when you return from a longer than usual separation. Arriving home from your first grown-ups only vacation, for example, you may be rebuffed by a child who is angry at having been left behind. Or, she may run to your open arms at first, only to "punish" you a short time later by being more difficult than usual. Similar examples can be found in the pages that follow.

Bowlby's findings also have meaning for mothers who work outside the home, and who worry about the strength of the mother-child tie. Attachment, he found, is determined by *social interaction* as opposed to *routine daily care*. Children, he wrote, consistently become "attached" to the person who engages them socially, as if they instinctively respond to the special overtures and presence of a parent.

Interrupting and Darting Away: Separation Anxiety in Disguise?

Separation anxiety is behind many of the baffling things that toddlers and older children do to get our attention.

When young children interrupt, it is usually because they lack the self-control needed to wait their turn. Eager to join in, they must share their impressions *now,* and we are wise to appreciate these early efforts to be social, albeit lacking in politesse. In extreme cases, however, if a child constantly interrupts her mother's phone conversations, separation anxiety may be at work. The mother may be in the same room, but to the child she is "not there."

A toddler may tug at her mother's arm or pick up a toy and throw it at her. But what appears aggressive is the child's best effort to become once again the focus of our attention. (And, as we all know, it works!)

At pickup time in a preschool, it is not unusual to see children dart away from their mothers, forcing the mother to come running after them. This is especially common if the mother has been busy talking with someone else. From the child's perspective, it is a way of bringing the parent back into his sphere.

The Stress of Growing Up: Why Older Children Regress

Early on, comfort habits fill an important need for your child. Try to value this sense of purpose, and you may avoid feeling anxious or embarrassed about your child's particular "vice." There is plenty of evidence that the more anxious you feel about thumb sucking, for example, and the more attention you draw to it, the more you end up reinforcing the very behavior that disturbs you.

Some habits, of course, are more endearing (the worn teddy) and others more repugnant (the blanket, once a lovely shade of blue, now shabby and gray). But they are all a means to an end. In the first few years of life your child must move from being totally dependent on you to being able to cope when you're not there. (It may help to recall your own anxiety the first time you left your baby with someone else for a few hours.) For the young child, comfort habits act as a "bridge" between what is known and what is new.

For the same reason, older children continue to revert to earlier forms of behavior as they take major new steps in development. A child starting kindergarten, for example, may become anxious about saying good-bye or resort to temper tantrums again. Regression is also a hallmark of preadolescence. A nine-year-old may suddenly resume the same behavior that had you worried years before: nervous hair-twirling, nail-biting, anxiety about separation or about making mistakes. To the extent that a child is otherwise able to cope with school and social life, however, these tendencies usually fall into a normal range of behavior.

Do We Expect Too Much, Too Soon?

There is some irony in the fact that our culture expects so much independence at an early age, yet when children develop the coping mechanisms they need, we cry, "Foul!"

Consider the number of accomplishments we expect of a typical two-year-old:

❧ Today, more than half of all mothers with children under the age of six work at least part-time. And over two million children attend day care or nursery school while their mothers work. Early separation from a parent may be a fact of life for these children, but it is an adjustment in any case.

❧ No firm numbers are available, but the majority of preschools and nursery schools either prefer or require that children be toilet trained, roughly by age two and a half—even though childhood experts agree that for many little boys, age three is a better time to begin training.

❧ Millions of American children simply attend the public school in their neighborhood. But in cities across the country many parents apply to private schools. These mothers and fathers probably worry about comfort habits and how "competent" their child appears because the dreaded school interview looms ahead.

I asked the admissions director of a private nursery school what many parents would like to know: What do you look for in a twenty-month-old child? She replied that she isn't terribly interested in whether a toddler still asks for a bottle or carries a worn toy from home. She is, however, watching what happens *between* the parent and child:

> Sometimes a child wants to sit in the parent's lap, but the parent says, "No! You have to sit over there." And that tells us that the parents are not responding to the cues of a child. You can't pick up everything in twenty-five minutes, but you certainly pick up an awful lot. Mothers and fathers who let the child be who he is are the kind of parents a school wants.

Parents, she says, must try to keep things in perspective, whether it is a school interview or a habit such as thumb sucking. Instead, she finds that "starting on a nursery-school level, everything becomes important."

Why Our Reactions Matter

A mother describes her three-year-old's most precious possession:

"Carly has a closet full of toys, but her favorite thing is an old cloth diaper that, for some strange reason, she's been attached to ever since she was a baby. She doesn't take it everywhere, but if she can't find it at night, she gets upset. I'm tempted to take it away, but as my husband points out, it doesn't really seem to be doing any harm."

Like Carly's mother, we're always wondering when a normal habit becomes a bad habit. And often, there is no easy answer. The best we can do with a very young child is to react sympathetically to the need without exaggerating it. And, like Carly's mother and father, we can avoid confrontations over these habits when they appear to help a child more than they hurt.

Whether a blanket remains a bedtime crutch or whether it becomes another "limb" during the day depends a great deal on the signals we send as parents. But what about a four-year-old who continues to use a bottle, or who still screams for his pacifier? One mother told me:

"I didn't mind my son's pacifier when he was a baby. The hospital sent Alex home with one, and he was 'hooked' early. By the time he turned three, I couldn't stand the sight of it, but his pediatrician warned me not to make an issue of it. We compromised by letting him use it at home but not outside. Alex finally gave it up altogether when he turned four."

It may still be what doctors call within normal limits, but parents can begin to distinguish between what an older child *needs to do* and what he or she is simply *used to doing*. At some point, we may decide that it is in the child's best interest to break an old habit.

Bottles, Thumbs, and Pacifiers

Whether babies are fed by breast or by bottle, sucking is a natural reflex for them, and they enjoy it. During what is known as the *oral phase* a child finds physical and emotional well-being through sucking and explores a variety of objects with his or her mouth.

Most experts on early childhood agree that sucking makes a baby feel secure, and this is why many infants first seek out a thumb. Brazelton describes how this "natural and even desirable behavior" begins:

> I found that finger sucking started in the newborn period and was reserved for transitions—when going to sleep, waking up, resting during an exciting play session, or giving up a feeding after being satiated. Later on it was used when a toddler got too excited and needed to calm down. It seemed to be a small child's way of adjusting to the many demands of his world.

What's "Normal"

Although opinions vary, most pediatricians consider bottles, thumb sucking, and pacifiers to be "normal" up to four or five years of age. (At the age of six or seven many children continue to suck a thumb at night, or they return to the habit during the day when feeling tired or overanxious—say, at the start of school.) All of us have different comfort levels when it comes to these habits.

The parents of a cranky baby may be eternally grateful to pacifiers; another mother may find them repugnant. Some parents relish the closeness of holding a toddler while he drinks his bottle at bedtime, and others insist on weaning to a cup before the first birthday. With a firstborn child, parents may be inclined to worry a great deal and try to curb these habits sooner than is necessary. The important thing is to strike a balance between what comes naturally to each child and what feels right, or comfortable, to you as a parent.

When to Worry About Dental Problems

Dental problems nag at many parents, especially those who pain-fully recall what it was like to wear braces in adolescence. By age two many children begin to relinquish a thumb or pacifier. (Ideally, as children get older, these habits give way to other outlets for their anxiety, such as language.) While it is possible for prolonged thumb sucking to cause an overbite, this really depends more on the child's bite and facial structure. In any case, it is best to visit the dentist with your child sometime during the second year.

Pediatric dentists know how to make these visits fun, not fright-ening. Ours offers the children "muscle juice" instead of fluoride, a choice of chocolate or bubblegum-flavored toothpaste, and goody bags on the way out. (I usually avoid issuing ultimatums, so I was surprised one day to hear myself threaten: *"If you don't settle down, we're not going to the dentist!"*)

Battling a "Bite" Problem

If you do have a problem with your child's bite and he has to forgo bottles or pacifiers sooner than he would like, it may help to have the dentist explain this to him. This may prevent a contest of wills between you and your child. Instead, the two of you can work together toward quitting "because the dentist said it will make your teeth healthy." Also, keep in mind that the braces children wear today are a far cry from what we endured thirty years ago. They're lighter, less obtrusive, and may be on and off before your child turns nine.

Baby-Bottle Syndrome

Dental decay can be a bigger issue than bite problems. Pediatric dentists warn that once baby teeth have appeared, children should not regularly be put to bed with a bottle of milk, formula, sugar water, or fruit juice. The acids in these liquids coat the teeth and over time may cause serious decay. (The condition is known as *baby-bottle syndrome*.)

All children occasionally fall asleep while sucking on a bottle of milk, but try not to let bottles become part of the bedtime ritual. (It will only make giving up a bottle more difficult later.) If your child insists on taking a bottle to bed, insist that it be filled with water. Make it part of your older toddler's routine to brush his teeth right after finishing his last bottle before bed.

Helping a Young Thumb Sucker

Thumb sucking is one of the earliest and most natural habits of childhood. In fact, some babies emerge from the womb with their thumbs in their mouths. As for early intervention, less may be more. Pediatric dentists warn that if you come down too hard on three- or four-year-olds, they might replace it with a more aggressive or harmful habit.

Unlike a bottle, which the caregiver must provide, a thumb is something the child can control. It is always there for the child, and this partly explains its appeal. Parents who try to push a pacifier over a thumb may regret it later. The pacifier habit can be just as difficult to break, and many parents dislike seeing one in an older child's mouth.

Many children suck their thumbs when they are anxious about some change at home or a transition. Avoid nagging or overreacting. Your hostility toward the habit will only reinforce it. Instead of looking for quick remedies, try to figure out the source of anxiety. With the young child, separation in general is a big source of fear.

With an older child look for patterns in the thumb habit. If the thumb goes into the mouth every time you approach school, for example, give your child a chance to talk about his class and his teachers and what, specifically, may be worrying him. Maybe he is afraid you won't be there at pickup time, and a little reassurance is all that's needed. Or perhaps your daughter just gave up diapers and needs to know that her teachers will help with going to the toilet. Often, we take it for granted that children know such things when they don't.

But avoid the game of constantly pulling the thumb out of your child's mouth. Children know that you do this because you disapprove of the habit, and this only adds to their anxiety.

How to Help Your Older Child

What about the older child (say, age four or five) who relies heavily on one oral habit or another? Your dentist may be concerned about an overbite, or your pediatrician may believe that normal speech is being delayed by an ever-present pacifier (see pages 45–46). Perhaps your child, eager for a sleepover at her best friend's house, is worried about her "babyish" habits. How can you help curb an oral habit? Like adults, children find it hard to stop "cold turkey." Instead, you can help your child to give it up gradually, providing plenty of small incentives and rewards for her effort to stop.

Try cutting a larger hole in the nipple of the bottle so that sucking on it is less satisfying for the child. Let an older child decide which bottle (morning or night) he wants to give up first. This makes the child feel a part of the process of quitting and also lets him know that you realize it isn't easy.

A mother describes how she gradually replaced bottles for one of her children:

> *"My son, Max, had a hard time giving up his bottle. I let it go for a long time, but after he turned three, the dentist became more insistent. I bought a special cup for him that came with all sorts of attachments: a nipple, a straw, a regular spout for drinking. We agreed that he would use the nipple only at night."*

Some parents object that these thermoses and cups are gimmicky, but others like the fact that they at least eliminate baby bottles symbolically. It helps to have an assortment of appealing children's cups and mugs on hand as well.

Charting Success: Max was an only child, which helped. As this parent explains, having a younger sibling can make it harder for a child to give up bottles:

> *"We tried to help Amanda kick her bottle habit, but she asked for it whenever she saw her baby brother using one, so we started using a chart. Every time Amanda used her cup instead of a bottle, she got a gold star. It sounds hokey, but she loved it. After she earned ten gold stars, we celebrated by taking her to a movie."*

Charts allow children to break bad habits gradually and to track their success. Similarly, if a child goes to school five times without his blanket, he may "earn" something special. Colorful, inexpensive stickers are another way to boost a young child's efforts to break these habits.

Rewards and Incentives: If your son has his eye on a special toy, or your daughter is begging for her first Barbie, there's nothing wrong with using this as an incentive. Acknowledge that these are "big boy" or "big girl" toys and that you're happy to get one if your child can stop using a baby bottle or sucking on a pacifier.

This is more effective than telling a child, *"When you turn four, you can't use a pacifier anymore."* A cutoff date such as a birthday doesn't usually work, and anxiety may simply mount as the date approaches. You can, however, build a child's confidence with words to the effect *"I know you like to have your blanket with you now. But when you're a little older, I'll bet you won't need it as much."*

Above all, keep your child's goals realistic and attainable. Do not punish her for lapses, just reward her for the successes. And remind the child that there's nothing "bad" about what she's doing. You can boost her esteem by listing all the wonderful "big girl" things she does that make you proud, and emphasize that no one is perfect. You might also talk about how difficult it was for you to stop smoking or biting your nails and how good you felt when you did. The more supportive you are, the more secure your child will feel, and of course this also helps to reduce the need for a "crutch."

Blankets and Bears

Any parent who has frantically turned the house upside down at bedtime in search of a lost bear knows how strong these attachments can be. In my experience, the favored bear (each of our three children had one) was a dependable and welcome source of comfort, but it was reserved for nighttime. Except for long car rides or vacations, the bears never left the house. (We claimed that the children would feel sad if their bears were lost, but my husband and I had become equally attached to them. We confessed to each other privately that we would have been devastated to lose such a personal remnant of each child's infancy.)

But if the bear is supposed to relieve a child's distress at bedtime (a kind of separation, as the next chapter explains), why does a child "grieve" when the bear is missing and the parent is not?! Anna Freud explains that the mother's coming and going are unpredictable and create insecurity in the child, who is sensitive to separation. However, the child believes he can control the object of his affection. This illusion is shattered each time the cherished blanket or bear cannot be found, and must bring on the child's distress.

Some families prevent these crises by keeping the bear or blanket in a special place (the top shelf of the closet or inside a drawer) so that it can always be found.

Most children give up these toys on their own in the normal course of development. Your threats to take away the treasured toy will only reinforce your child's dependency. Your daughter may cling to the object even more, perhaps insisting on taking it everywhere out of fear that you'll do something to it when she's out. Try to accept the toy as something the child needs now. Once you do this, you make it easier for your child to "let go" later.

Soothing Rituals and Autoerotic Behavior

There is a fascinating degree of ritual associated with a child's special blanket or bear. Your son or daughter will savor its scent and its feel. Half asleep, a child scratches the same spot until it becomes threadbare and worn.

Some parents worry when their child rubs against a cuddly toy in a masturbatory way. Again, this is normal behavior. Writing about autoerotic behaviors, Anna Freud includes masturbation along with head rocking and thumb sucking. Above all, she explains, they are "spontaneous habits" that help ease the child's transition from wakefulness to sleep, and as long as they do not interfere with the child's active enjoyment of his world (see the section called "Red Flag" at the end of this chapter), these habits are all considered normal.

Pacifiers: Pros and Cons: Soothing the Baby or Shutting Him Out?

Pacifiers have their advocates and their detractors. Child psychiatrist Nina Lief, of New York's Early Childhood Development Center, suggests that while pacifiers often prevent tears, they may not offer real comfort to a child in distress.

Dr. Lief has taught parent workshops for the past two decades. In this time, she has seen a dramatic rise in the use of pacifiers. Sucking is an infant's "primitive comfort mechanism," she notes. But it disturbs her that so many parents today opt to "plug the hole," as she puts it, rather than to understand what the crying is about. She explains:

> To occasionally pacify an infant in this way is all right. But as a child grows, that's not enough. That's not the comforting mechanism [they need]. Some of them need to be held. Some need to be turned over. Some need water. Or a child may be lonesome or scared. You really have to individualize it.

As a new mother I felt hapless when my first child began to wail and someone would ask, "What's the matter? What does she want?" I had no idea. *Why were they asking me?!*

Dr. Lief suggests that many moms turn to pacifiers out of similar feelings of helplessness. "When a child cries, mothers think there's something they must do to stop them, and to shut the child up is the goal." Our culture, she adds, still believes that a quiet child is a good child.

Dr. Lief would rather see a mother respond by holding or caressing or talking to a child in distress. When parents immediately reach for a pacifier, they may stop the baby's crying, but they deprive themselves of the simple and satisfying experience of comforting a child. Parents who can console an infant with their voice, or who find a special, soothing song, will feel a special closeness to the child. This, she says, is true attunement. It takes time, however, a commodity in short supply for many parents. Dr. Lief feels that parents should make the effort whenever they can.

Becky Thomas, Dr. Lief's associate, adds that occasional use of a pacifier is fine, especially during the first few months. But later, if used too often, she warns, it can get in the way of normal speech development:

> When the child makes a sound, however primitive, someone in the child's surrounding area repeats that sound, or makes some kind of notice, or responds facially so that the baby understands that when he makes a sound—not just crying, but when he makes a sound—somebody responds. And when the pacifier is in, it really does inhibit the natural "Aaaah!" a baby makes when he sees a balloon. That sound elicits all kinds of normal and natural and wonderful reactions from the person who's around the baby, and that's normal language development.

Ask Yourself:

Are you offering bottles or pacifiers when real *comfort* is what your child needs?

Well-meaning parents may encourage and exaggerate the need for comfort habits early on. When a child is sad or hurt, for example, we may offer a bottle of juice as consolation instead of simply holding and comforting him until he feels better. This is why bottles and pacifiers become an emotional crutch that, like any addiction, can be difficult to give up.

Are you reinforcing your child's dependency without realizing it?

Parents can help by limiting a child's *reliance* on a specific habit. Nora Barron, who counsels families in Michigan, believes that parents may unconsciously send the message that children need their blanket or bear more than they really do. As an example, she described a mother and a two-year-old getting ready to leave the house. The child asks to take her special bear or pacifier, and the mother, instead of saying no in a firm, reassuring way, replies tentatively. The child senses the parent's uncertainty, feels even more needy, and begins to cry. The parent, wanting to console the child now, finally agrees to take along the bear.

The importance of empathy is discussed throughout this book. When a child looks frightened and upset, it's easy for an understanding parent to mirror his apprehension. There are times when this bolsters the child, proving that he is not alone with this feelings or fears. At other times a child is watching your face for a vote of confidence. Hearing you say "I know you can do it" may be all he needs to leave home without his blanket or bear.

As adults we listen to what someone says, but we also watch the expression on his face. It is no different with young children. They are experts at ambivalence, and if you are trying to offer reassurance, then the look on your face must be as persuasive as what you say.

Do you *create* anxiety by discussing the blanket or bear well before you're ready to leave the house?

Wait until the two of you are on your way out the door. Then casually say, *"Oh, you won't need Teddy today. You can hold my hand. We have each other."* Or: *"It's so easy to lose things in the supermarket. Let's leave Teddy right here by the door."* If you appear confident, the child will feel confident, too. But if you begin to hesitate, you may only end up reinforcing the child's perceived need for the toy.

Do you offer generous praise when your child manages without his thumb or pacifier or bear, even for brief periods?

"I'm so proud of the way you went without your blanket today. What a big girl you are!" It's always more effective to praise a child for behavior that's desirable than to nag and scold him for what he "shouldn't" be doing. Whether the child coped for a few minutes or a few hours, comments like these—along with a hug and a smile—do much to reinforce feelings of self-worth. (In fact, you can engineer a few successes initially by just leaving the house to get the mail or walking

down the block without the pacifier.) Pleasing a parent is a great motivator for young children. In time, the contentment that comes with pleasing you will outweigh that of the offending habit.

Are you giving your child a chance to practice separation?

Parents have long been told that games such as peekaboo, in which the mother "disappears" and "reappears," help introduce older babies to the concept of going away and coming back. But practice with real separation is important, too. Separation anxiety is a normal part of development, but individual reactions are partly explained by experience, that is, by how frequently children have been left in the care of others. A child who has never been separated from her mother may react differently from a child whose mother comes and goes more often.

As children grow, we need to avoid extreme behavior that undermines their sense of security. A mother who is never apart from her young child may be saying to him or her subliminally: *"You are only safe when I'm with you."*

What signals are you sending?

Think about how *you* feel each time you say good-bye, and try to imagine what your child sees on your face. A mother who is unreconciled about working and leaving her child with someone else may be traumatized at the first sign of separation anxiety. Instead of seeing it as a natural stage of development, she may think it means that her decision to work is making her child suffer. The apprehension on her face will only add to her child's anxiety. Now the child has a real reason to worry.

It is important to understand that certain behaviors are inevitable. Like sleep disturbances, some worries at separation can be expected in the second year. If you accept this, then you will avoid reacting to this anxiety as if it's your fault. A mother who feels guilty will appear anxious to the child, as if to affirm the child's anxiety. By contrast, a parent who understands that separation anxiety is normal is more likely to react in a way that soothes and reassures the child.

Does your child have separation anxiety, or does she have difficulty making transitions?

Some children leap toward the unknown from an early age, while others cling to the mother in the face of anything new or unfamiliar. Most children experience separation anxiety in one form or another, but your child may have a difficult time with transitions generally, and one early symptom is the child's extreme grief when you and he must separate. These tendencies are discussed at length in Chapter 8, and I urge parents to read it if their children's separation anxiety is severe and prolonged beyond what is discussed here.

Does your child show signs of *signal anxiety?*

This term refers to distress that begins as soon as a child sees you preparing to leave, also known as *anticipatory anxiety.* In other words, from the time you emerge from the shower to dress for going out in the evening, your child becomes anxious and works himself up. This occurs frequently in children with extreme separation anxiety. If this is the case in your house, try distracting your child, or talk about exactly what is making her so fearful. One mother told me:

> *"My daughter used to cry hysterically when we went out for dinner. Instead of giving her extra reassurance, our baby-sitter took Olivia's reactions personally and became more distant, so Olivia really did end up feeling 'abandoned.' One time, I left a special activity for them to do together, and I gave it to them just before I left the house. It was a great distraction for my daughter, and they had fun together that night. It finally broke this terrible pattern."*

It may also help to ask a child exactly what he is worried about. Parents are sometimes surprised to learn that it is something very specific. The baby-sitter may be neglecting to put on the night-light at bedtime, and your child may be too uncomfortable or embarrassed to ask for it.

Do you have confidence in your child's caregiver?

To let someone else share in the care of your children brings on special pressures. It will be easier for you to handle your child's separation anxiety if you have faith in the day care you've chosen, or the person you've hired to work in your home. If you do not have a good feeling about it, then try to figure out why—and do something about it if necessary.

It's important to realize that no one is going to care for your child exactly as you do. But if you think that something is wrong, trust your instincts. Many parents want to keep their child's environment as stable as possible and will do anything to avoid changing sitters or day-care arrangements. Children are very adaptable, though. The greater your peace of mind, the better you'll feel about saying good-bye, and the less likely it is that you will prolong your child's anxiety.

When Is a Comfort Habit a "Bad Habit"?

Comfort habits do serve a purpose. But you may be wondering, *Can a comfort habit become a "bad habit"?* Here are some guidelines for deciding whether your child's behavior signals a serious problem:

Normal Sequencing: First, does the behavior interfere with what is called normal sequencing in a child's life? For instance, is your two-year-old's pacifier habit interfering with his speech development? Or is your three-year-old's separation anxiety preventing him from enjoying preschool or other activities? If so, the habit may be doing more harm than good, and you should ask your pediatrician for an opinion.

Chronic Withdrawal: Most children turn to comfort habits at night and only occasionally during the day. If your child resorts to a thumb or stuffed toy more than usual, he may not be feeling well. But if you notice that your child prefers a solitary activity such as rhythmic rocking to playing in the park, talk to your pediatrician about it. Your child may be showing signs of withdrawal.

Extreme Reactions: You also want to be on the lookout for extreme reactions that don't fit in with your child's typical behavior. It would be unusual, for example, for the same child who separates easily at preschool to cry inconsolably when you go out for the evening. If this is the case, perhaps it pays to try a new baby-sitter, someone who can make the evening more enjoyable for your child.

If you suspect a sitter of being impatient with your children or unkind, then don't hesitate to listen outside the door for a few minutes after you leave, or to pop in unexpectedly during the day or come home earlier at night than you said. A sensitive child will naturally do better with a sensitive adult. As with any relationship between people, the chemistry between a child and a caregiver has to be right.

Again, some anxiety is normal. But by the age of three or four, chronic anxiety is not considered natural or healthy. If changing baby-sitters does not work, then perhaps you should talk to someone about other possible reasons for your child's distress.

RED FLAG

Separation Anxiety Disorder: As noted earlier, anxiety about separation is normal at certain developmental stages. In addition, children can be expected to have different innate reactions to the stress of saying good-bye. A real anxiety disorder is different, however, in the degree of distress and dysfunction that it causes.

It is not unusual for a two-year-old, for example, to cry loudly when a mother leaves him with a baby-sitter. If the anxiety is within a normal range, the child will become engaged in play a short time later—say, fifteen or twenty minutes. But a child who cannot be consoled—who withdraws and insists on sitting all alone, unable to play happily or become engaged in any activity—is not coping in a healthy way.

Children as old as four or five may still be reluctant to separate but, again, they should be able to play and participate fully within a reasonable time after saying good-bye. If they cannot, then parents should seek professional guidance. As for predicting who is more likely to be affected, the disorder can occur whether a mother works outside the home or not.

Childhood Anxiety from an Adult Perspective

One way to understand how children cope with anxiety is to look at how we cope as adults. Consider, for example, your last promotion at work. A promotion—like the start of school for a young child—is exciting. Even so, adults greet a new job with some ambivalence. You may feel ready for a new challenge—but chances are, you also feel worried. At three in the morning you're consumed by doubts: *What if I'm not up to the challenge? What if I let someone down?*

The security of your old job beckons: familiar office, old friends, approval, and, best of all, a job that you know you can do well. So how do you, as an adult, make the transition? How do you prepare yourself psychologically? You probably start by filling your new office with familiar objects: photographs of your family or mementos from your old job. Maybe you call an old friend for reassurance. You might start biting your nails again or smoking, habits you gave up long ago. But slowly, gradually, you begin to feel comfortable, so that by relying on the old and familiar, you empower yourself to take on something new.

Children feel the same kind of ambivalence and insecurity. They want to please us—but worry that they won't. And your child cannot help wondering why, if you really love her so much, you frown every time she sucks her thumb or takes her blanket in the car.

Like adults, children need confidence to master a new task. And especially during the preschool years they cope with the pressures of growing up by returning to well-worn rituals.

Learning that a particular habit is a normal and even positive sign of development may be enough to change the way you view your child's behavior. But if it isn't—and if you still find the habit to be personally repugnant—there is a danger of constant, negative interactions between the two of you. Again, it is important to remember that many of the habits discussed in this chapter arise out of anxiety, and nothing feeds a small child's anxious feelings more than a parent's disapproval.

Children and parents must separate and come together again throughout their lives. It is important to see the enormity of this task in the first few years, when many comfort habits begin. When we do, we tend to handle an anxious child in a relaxed, reassuring way, and this is why comfort habits tend to subside by the fourth or fifth year. If they do not, we can look for sensitive ways to intervene.

CHAPTER FOUR

That night Lotta was nice to Thomas. He was supposed to sleep in the small guest room by himself, but he was afraid of the dark and cried and wanted the door left open.

"But, Thomas, dear, you're never afraid of the dark when you're at home," Aunt Katie said.

"At home it's his own dark, Aunt Katie. He isn't used to Grandmother's dark," Lotta said.

Thomas was allowed to sleep in our room. Lotta kissed him and tucked him in and said:

"Now I'll sing to you, Thomas, and you won't be afraid any more."

from *The Children on Troublemaker Street*
by Astrid Lindgren

Avoiding Anger and Anxiety at Bedtime

"What hath night to do with sleep?"

John Milton, the English poet, penned those words in the seventeenth century, and it's unlikely that he had young children in mind. But he speaks to many parents today as they struggle with bedtime. At some point most parents have a problem getting a young child to fall asleep, and then, even if the child goes to bed peacefully, staying there all night is another matter.

Rebecca Thomas calls sleep "the issue of the nineties" for parents today. Thomas, who teaches at the Early Childhood Development Center in New York, says that the mothers who come to her workshops are exhausted. And often, so are their children, many of whom are up much of the night. But according to Thomas and her mentor, Dr. Nina Lief, the key to ending the day happily is to begin seeing bedtime the way your child does.

What Normally Happens at Night

Children's bedtime behavior is erratic at best. This mother's experience is shared by many:

"I never understood why my friends had such a hard time with their babies at night. Our son went to sleep in his crib very happily beginning around the third or fourth month. Then one night when he was about eight months old, I tucked him in as usual and headed for the door, but he started sobbing. For several weeks after that it was much harder getting him to sleep."

Many parents find that anxiety about bedtime arises suddenly and inexplicably. Don't be surprised by the following disturbances in the first five years:

- Babies often become fearful of being left alone in the crib at some time between six months and one year.

- These fears may eventually subside only to reappear during the second year, when separation anxiety sets in.

- Your older toddler may be plagued by bad dreams, nightmares, or night terrors, and may wake up screaming and shaken.

- At night your children will act as if they aren't tired and don't need sleep. They are, and they do. (On the bright side, no one can be more charming or delightful than a young child who wants to stay up later.)

And, finally, don't be surprised if you find yourself dreading bedtime battles. For her landmark study of parenting styles, Diana Baumrind selected the bedtime hour for home visits so that young families could be observed "under maximum stress." Rest assured, then, you are not alone.

Bedtime demands a difficult balancing act: the need to give a child structure and the need for sympathetic understanding. The two goals appear to be contradictory. But parents who can appreciate bedtime from a small child's perspective and who also grasp the child's need for sleep can learn to do both. This section looks at bedtime as a *transition* for your child, with suggestions for making the end of the day less stressful.

A Developmental Perspective

At night, when a baby cries in his crib, it is difficult to know what's best. Our grandparents still warn against "spoiling the baby," and at heart we worry about overindulging so that a baby never learns to fall asleep on her own. But this may be because we expect too much too soon. There are still many cultures in which young children typically share a room, if not a bed, with parents or other family members during the first few years. Our basic instinct is to go to a child in distress, and it is probably a good one.

"Parents don't have to rush in at every whimper," says Dr. Cyrille Halkin, a pediatrician for more than thirty years. "But if an adult were talking to you from another room, you wouldn't just ignore what he had to say. It's important to remember that this is your baby's only means of communicating."

Still, she urges parents not to swoop the child from the crib since this may only heighten the child's anxiety, as if to say, "You're right! You aren't safe here without me." Instead, you can come into the room and pat the baby on the back. (Sometimes the baby is uncomfortable because of an air bubble, and this can relieve the discomfort.) Your voice alone can soothe a troubled infant. Above all, remain calm. If you sound or act annoyed, the child grows more fretful and takes even longer to settle down.

Parents are sometimes tempted to take a crying baby out of the crib and play for a few more minutes. But the most common reason for a baby's tears is probably fatigue. Knowing this, you can resist the urge to entertain and focus instead on soothing your tired infant. Many experts believe the best way to teach children to sleep alone is to give extra reassurance early on, even if this means staying in the room with them. The most important thing a parent can do is to help an infant form positive associations with bedtime.

Bedtime as Separation

"The child views going to sleep as a separation," Dr. Lief explains, "and it's a very hard job for a child to separate." For many children, then, real bedtime anxiety begins at the same time that separation anxiety occurs, sometime in the second year (see page 32).

In the two-year-old, Anna Freud found, these disturbances are nearly inevitable:

However carefully and successfully an infant's sleeping habits and arrangements have been handled in the first year of life, difficulties with sleep, or with the ease of falling asleep, intervene almost without exception in the second year.

According to Freud, the older child has become so engaged in the outside world that withdrawing from it is difficult. The child becomes anxious, and this only makes sleep more elusive because he cannot relax enough to let go of the external world. The demands for one more story or for a glass of water are his desperate attempts to stay in touch. But the tired parent grows impatient and angry at these requests, which fuels the child's distress and prevents him from surrendering to sleep. This cycle is at the heart of most bedtime hassles.

Children who have reasonable limits set for them during the day are typically less anxious at night. What's the connection? Even though young children object to them overtly, limits on their behavior—especially dangerous behavior—help to make a child feel safe. For example, a young child may get angry at a mother who insists on taking away a sharp pair of scissors. But on a subconscious level her action makes him feel safe, protected. At night, then, the world will seem less threatening. A child whose parent has trouble saying no in this way may feel more vulnerable at bedtime, as if someone isn't quite protecting him from impulses and actions that could ultimately be harmful, both to himself and to others.

Daytime encounters work in other ways, too. Angry at you that afternoon, your child may have yelled, "I hate you, Mommy! Go away!" Come bedtime, the lights go out and you leave the room—and it occurs to your child what a frightening and horrible thing he said. (*What if Mommy really does go away?*) Perhaps most scary to a small child are the intense emotions and impulses that come from inside him and that he can neither control nor understand.

Easing the Transition

From your child's perspective there are good reasons for resisting sleep. This came home to me one night while I was putting my son to bed and started to doze beside him. He immediately shook me awake. "Don't close your eyes," he warned in earnest, "or you'll see the monsters."

Children hide much of their anxiety behind a sort of daytime bravado. At night these demons are less easily kept at bay. If your child sleeps in his own room, bedtime means being alone. It helps to recall what it is like to be a small child in a dark room at night, the way gently swaying curtains take on a sinister appearance or shadows take on frightening shapes. If you can do this, you will automatically be more attuned to the way your child's mind is working, and you will see that there is a real need for reassurance.

When Real Problems Begin

Children are quick to sense a parent's tension or unhappiness. Once they do, they cannot relax. And if they aren't relaxed, they won't fall asleep. An exhausted child will keep himself awake out of fear of "letting go" of the parent. The parent, sensing that the child will never fall asleep, becomes more irritable and angry, thus filling the child with even more anxiety. Here is one parent's account of this dreadful cycle:

"I swear to myself that I won't get tense, but I've begun to expect a hard time. I literally dread finishing dinner because the struggles begin as soon as I ask the kids to get into pajamas. Bedtime is utter chaos in our house, and it usually ends with me yelling at everyone. I would do anything to make it more pleasant."

Worst of all, bedtime must be confronted seven nights a week. How can this pattern be avoided?

The Importance of Ritual

In general, children do best when they know "what comes next." This is why preschool teachers set up a schedule that hardly varies from day to day: free play, circle time, library, snack, rest time, and so on. It surprises parents to learn that children whose days are structured and fairly predictable are more comfortable taking risks. But during the day, certainty acts like an anchor. It makes a child feel secure, and this enables him to explore the world fully. Similarly, a nighttime routine allows him to let go of the world without fear. Dr. Lief explains:

> *Parents, from the time the child is born, have to set up a* pattern *for the day so that the child is cued in to the fact that after he has his bath, and after he has his supper, then he goes to bed. He has a story read, a record is put on, or a certain toy is put into his crib, and he's turned in a certain position, and Momma says good night and turns out the light and goes out. And she does that* every *night. . . . We also caution parents that they don't "put the child to sleep"; that they have to arrange the bedtime so that it's relaxing and that the child is* overcome *by sleep.*

In families where children go to sleep without major protests, you will usually find a predictable sequence of events, even if the lights go out at different times (eight o'clock one night; eight forty-five the next). But the *order* of events will rarely change: bath, dinner, family time (listening to music, drawing together, playing games), brushing teeth, reading stories, getting tucked in, saying good night.

The good news is that it is never too late to begin such a routine, even with a slightly older child. You just need to stick with it. The most important thing is to find a routine that makes time together enjoyable and is also conducive to falling asleep. If a father arrives home from work late and enjoys "playing rough," that's all right. But he must realize that his children then need time to wind down: reading quietly, listening to music, or just talking together for fifteen minutes.

Experts discourage ending the day in front of the TV. Prime-time programs tend to be violent and aggressive, and this can stimulate a child's imagination in disturbing ways. There are very few programs that are conducive to making a small child feel reassured and safe. Reading together is a far more enjoyable and controlled activity. It can bring parents and children closer, and it has been shown that nothing contributes to curiosity and a happy school life more than an early love of reading. There are many wonderful books that treat bedtime fears with sympathy and humor.

Working Mothers' Guilt, Single Parents' Fatigue

Bedtime can be especially difficult for mothers who work and, even more so, for single parents, as these comments show:

"Ever since my husband moved out, I feel like a shrew at bedtime. But as soon as I get home from work, there's so much to do: dinner, the baths, getting my oldest child to do his homework, getting my daughter to practice the piano—and since there's no other adult around, I have to constantly be 'the heavy.' "

"I'm a little jealous of my husband because he finds it so much easier to say good night to our kids. I work full-time, and I guess I feel guilty about not being with them all day long, so I say good night more tentatively, and our kids (who are very bright) take advantage of it. They get out of bed, or they ask to stay up later. It's hard for me to say no, though."

In my own experience bedtime was a breeze when I stopped working for a time—and stopped counting how many hours I had, or hadn't, spent with my children each day. No longer torn by this guilt, I could finally stand at the door of their room and say to my daughters, then ages one and three, *"It's bedtime now. We had a lot of fun today, but it's Mommy's turn to have some time to herself."* End of discussion.

When I began working again, these lessons stayed with me, with respect not only to bedtime but to other times as well. I learned not to personalize behavior and to realize that a child's reactions aren't always a result of what we do (or don't do) together on a given day. At night our children still ask for the obligatory glass of water and wander back to our room before finally resigning themselves to sleep.

At the end of the day I have simply learned to be more assertive about the need for rest, both theirs and my own.

"Mommy, I'm Hungry . . ."

The lights are turned down low, the bedtime story has tumbled to the floor, and your child is nestled deep inside the covers. (Psychologically you're already sprawled out on the sofa watching the news.) Then you hear those three plaintive words that make it all for naught: *"Mommy, I'm hungry."* Your child looks up at you with wide eyes and, for emphasis, lifts up his pajama shirt to expose an empty belly. Is there a mother or father hardened enough to send a famished child to bed?

Many families establish a "last call" to avoid these last-minute appeals, which effectively stall that final good night. A half hour or so before bedtime, try to get into the habit of announcing, *"Last call. If you're hungry, have something to eat. The kitchen is closing in a few minutes."*

Understanding Normal Sleep Disturbances

There are many reasons why a preschooler who is normally happy at night will either resist going to sleep, resume night wakings, or suddenly begin the day earlier than usual. A disturbance at night can usually be traced to a change in the child's daytime routine. Typical stressors include the start of school or the arrival of a new baby, as this mother found:

> *"When we brought our second child home from the hospital and she awoke for a five A.M. feeding, I found it easy to put her back to bed. But our older daughter, who normally slept until six-thirty or seven, was up for the day."*

One pediatrician told me that an older child's nervous system "goes on alert" when a new baby arrives. Children are sensitized by the change. They feel anxious about sharing their parents and more needy of their attention.

One honest three-year-old confessed to his parents, *"I don't want to go to sleep because then you'll go and play with the baby."* When they showed him that the baby was fast asleep and explained that they were planning to work or read quietly, the little boy felt reassured that he wouldn't miss out on any fun. (For more on siblings, see page 218.)

Have you ever been awakened by your older child calling out the baby's name, in the throes of a nightmare? Many first borns have violent dreams in which they hurt a new baby whom they resent, releasing the feelings that they hide by day. In the morning the same child may smilingly run to greet the baby when she awakens, but don't be fooled by her happiness: She's probably *relieved* to find that the baby is still alive despite her murderous dreams!

Saying Good-bye to the Afternoon Nap

Be prepared to adjust your child's schedule as he or she goes through changes in the amount of sleep needed. Your daughter may still be content to crawl under the covers after lunch—but now she is still going strong at ten o'clock at night. It may be time to eliminate her afternoon nap, or at least begin phasing it out. Try easing the transition by waking her after forty-five minutes or an hour in the afternoon, or opting for one or two rest times (playing quietly or looking at books) during the day. Otherwise, you will have an exhausted, cranky child on your hands in the early evening. It may be a few weeks before both of you settle in to a new routine.

Running on Empty: The Anguish of Sleep Deprivation

Most of us know the sick feeling of having to face a full day at home or at the office on little or no sleep at all, wanting nothing more than to crawl back into bed and have just a little uninterrupted slumber. In the first six years, nearly all children go through periods of night wakings that can wreak havoc on a parent's well-being. Knowing that you aren't alone in your state of exhaustion may help a little (misery does, after all, like company). It is perhaps more reassuring to learn that these periods usually last a few days or a few weeks at most before children settle down again, allowing us the rest we need.

In the meantime, don't expect to be your usual patient self. The day following a night without sleep is long indeed, and your child's small acts of defiance, trying but tolerable after a peaceful night, are bound to wear down even the most understanding mother. What can a sleep-deprived parent do? You might convince a grandparent or a spouse to take over for an afternoon or evening. It is surprising what just a few hours of sleep can do to brighten your outlook.

Ask Yourself:

Are your expectations realistic?

T. Berry Brazelton writes:

> We expect our baby to be active and inquisitive during the day and independent at night. An ideal baby is one who can play all day, mostly alone, but who also can accept nurture when it is offered on the adult's terms. At night he is supposed to give up, subsiding quickly and singlemindedly to sleep.

Expect your child to go through many different phases at bedtime. Some children will easily fall asleep on their own in the first year or so, but they become more anxious as they get older. If this happens, offer reassurance in a way that still allows them to feel safe in the crib.

From time to time an anxious child will ask that you stay in the room until he falls asleep. Opinions vary, but many experts believe that this is an effective way to build up a young child's confidence at night. You can begin by standing near the crib and patting the baby on the back, or try sitting in a chair right near the crib. Eventually, though, you can move the chair farther away from the bed and read quietly until the child is asleep. This is comforting to the child (and a great way to catch up on your reading). In the first three years especially, this is far more desirable than allowing bedtime to become fraught with anxiety. As long as you remain calm, the child will eventually fall asleep.

Many young babies learn to fall asleep in this way, even if it takes a period of weeks or months.

Do you really have a bedtime problem?

Author and parent educator Nancy Samalin urges families to handle bedtime in a way that works for them. Every family is different. If your child habitually falls asleep in your bed and sleeps through the night after being moved into her own room, that's fine—as long as you're happy. But if your three-year-old has you going back and forth to his room for an hour before falling asleep every night, you may begin feeling annoyed, and your anger may be reinforcing his need to see you. Maybe it is time to rethink your bedtime routine or to make some new rules about what is acceptable and what is not.

Most experts agree that it is best not to let a child get into the habit of sleeping in your bed with you. For the child who has trouble falling asleep each night, agree on some quiet activities that he can do in bed by himself, such as reading or listening to music.

Can you decide on a bedtime ritual together?

With an older child, acknowledge that you have a problem and that you would like to make bedtime less tense for everyone. Or try writing a letter explaining that you love your child too much to end the day so unhappily. For this reason, you think it's time to come up with a new plan—together. If bedtime has turned into a contest of wills, your child will be relieved to make a change, too. Once you agree on a new evening routine, put it in writing so that everyone takes it seriously. Again, avoid making TV the last activity of the day. The programming is designed to excite and stimulate, and it can be upsetting to young children.

Do you convey a desire to "get bedtime over with"?

The more you dread bedtime, the more you can be assured of a long, unhappy ordeal. If you come up with an enjoyable routine, then you and your child can anticipate bedtime with pleasure. The end of the day will become more enjoyable and as a result more conducive to falling asleep.

Do you stick to your routine or do you bend the rules too often?

If your routine involves reading together before you tuck your child in, make it clear that he or she can choose three stories, or that you'll read for twenty minutes each night. This way you avoid pleas of *"Just one more book!"* Otherwise, you will end up getting annoyed, your child will be unhappy, and this will defeat the whole purpose of having a routine.

Do you think about how much sleep your child needs?

Sleep is critical to a child's growth. This fact alone should help you say good night with more conviction, especially if you work and you feel guilty putting your child to bed instead of spending time together. By combining this knowledge with a child's view of bedtime, you can offer your child the security he needs early on and also be attuned to normal sleep disturbances.

Do you call it "bedtime" or do you insist that your child must "go to sleep"?

Many children object to being told that they're tired and must go to sleep. It can be less contentious to say, "It's bedtime. You can look at books. You can talk to your sister if she's not too tired. You can play with a toy. But I expect you to stay in bed."

Is there a reason for sudden anxiety at bedtime?

Any difficult change or transition will arouse your child's anxiety and have an effect on how well she sleeps. Examples are moving to a new house, the illness of a sibling, or a divorce. Just hearing you talk about changing schools or baby-sitters can be enough to generate anxiety. One mother was dismayed when her five-year-old developed bedtime anxiety for the first time in her life, but the family had just returned from a vacation where everyone had slept together in one big hotel room. It took weeks for the little girl to feel comfortable going to sleep alone again.

If possible, can someone else take over at bedtime when you've had it?

Single parents often do not have this option, unless they're living with relatives or friends who are willing to help at night. But for other families it pays to let a spouse take over, especially if you become tense at bedtime. Sensitive to your anger, your children will fight falling asleep even more. If you are with the children all day, there is nothing wrong with letting your spouse have some special time with them at the end of the day and giving yourself a little time off as well.

For the younger child who wakes repeatedly during the night, do you try to offer more reassurance during the day?

You're exhausted and overwrought by sleep deprivation, but keep in mind that these periods usually last a few weeks at most before a child sleeps through the night again. Try to pinpoint any other sources of stress (a new baby-sitter to cope with, pressure to give up diapers or bottles), and give the child time during the day to talk about these feelings. Reading stories together can also help. Ask your son why he thinks the child in a picture book is sad or crying, and you may find out, indirectly, what is really troubling him.

For the older child whose night wakings persist, have you tried offering some incentive to staying in bed?

You can call it bribery, or you can call it an incentive. But you want to give your child a reason to hesitate before coming into your room. Once you have some success (waking you up only once in the night instead of four times?!), you can express your appreciation for a good night's sleep: *"I feel great because you didn't wake me up last night! Let's go to the zoo today and celebrate."*

RED FLAG

How can parents tell when nighttime habits call for outside help? The catchwords for any problem behavior are the same: How chronic and how severe is the disturbance? Textbook author Jane Kessler writes:

> The normal child's need for sleep eventually outweighs his anxiety; if there are many successive nights of total wakefulness, or almost nightly nightmares, the problem requires professional attention.

Kessler's other benchmark has to do with how long bedtime anxiety persists. She suggests that by the time your child turns four or five, he or she should be able to fall asleep alone. If not, find out whether the child is troubled by daytime pressures that are too high, or by other emotions, such as anger or fear. These feelings are frightening for a child and need an outlet. Hidden and repressed for too long during the day, they may haunt the child at night and cause serious problems in the long run. In addition, anxiety at night is frequently a symptom of Separation Anxiety Disorder (see page 33), which requires professional help.

A Final Note on Bedtime

As is true for adults, bedtime is always going to be more difficult if a child is in the throes of a stressful event. But some children seem to have a difficult time falling asleep in general, as this mother found:

> *"My daughter is six now but has always had trouble getting to sleep, and the older she gets, the more difficult it is because she's trying to figure out some very big issues. She worries about death, for example, which her older brother never thought about as much. One*

night, she came into my room in tears because she was worrying about whether her pet cat would die."

To be sure, temperament plays a role in many issues of early childhood, and bedtime is no exception. For a child who still lies awake at ten at night, you of course want to rule out whether something is causing undue stress. It is also important to try to discuss troubling issues during the day. At night, though, you may help most by providing a reading light and some books or music cassettes near the bed, or by rubbing a child's back for a few minutes, so that it is easier for her to relax.

You can certainly help to reduce some of the tension and anxiety that plague bedtime in many homes, but do not expect these problems to go away altogether, even as your children get older. There will inevitably be those times when the last words your children hear are shouts of *"Get in your room and go to bed. I've had it!,"* instead of *"I love you."* For better or for worse, though, tomorrow is another night.

CHAPTER FIVE

Eh! poor lad! He's been spoiled till salt won't save him. Mother says as th' two worst things as can happen to a child is never to have his own way— or always to have it. She doesn't know which is th' worst.

from *The Secret Garden* by
Frances H. Burnett

Acting Out and Saying No: The Roots of Self-esteem

A mother of three friendly, outgoing children, I have grudgingly accepted this "Murphy's Law" of being a parent: When we most want our children to be agreeable, they put their most difficult behavior on display. The young child scowls at your boss during a visit to the office, defies you in front of your in-laws, and interrupts constantly when an old friend comes to visit.

Moments like these can be mortifying, and it occurred to me that a book about raising children would hardly be complete without a chapter devoted to these so-called acts of defiance. For many parents this begins with the child's first, furious "No!"

"Can you believe she has an *opinion*?!" my husband used to remark with a laugh when our older daughter, just two and a half, insisted on wearing dresses and party shoes to preschool. But these "opinions" lead to conflict, especially when parents misread the toddler's militance. If we aren't careful, everything becomes an issue, and as this parent notes, these confrontations take a toll:

> "*Getting William ready for school in the morning is hopeless. First he refuses to put on the clothing I've picked out for him, and then he insists on putting on his shoes and socks by himself, which takes a good ten or fifteen minutes. By then we're running late, and I usually start yelling at him. It's a terrible way to start the day.*"

At home we get annoyed and impatient. In public, though, or in someone else's home, it can be embarrassing as well:

> *"I've begun to dread visiting my in-laws. My kids just go crazy. When they start running around the dining room or getting noisy, my mother-in-law says it's okay (she doesn't want to spoil the evening), but I know deep down that she doesn't approve of the way they're behaving. Then I start overreacting to what the kids are doing, which only makes things more tense. By the time we go home, I'm annoyed with them and annoyed at myself for not being able to keep things under control."*

Perhaps this is why so many parents still blame difficult behavior on the "terrible twos," even though these conflicts begin before a child's second birthday and persist well into his third or fourth year. In fact, such behavior marks the beginning of a lifelong process by which parents and children "cling and cleave," as the researcher René Spitz wrote nearly fifty years ago. Labeling it the terrible twos may help us to save face (like teething, it elicits sympathetic nods even from those who don't have children), but it offers little in the way of real understanding.

Conflict is an important theme here, but this chapter is really about the origins of self-esteem. In the second year, to our delight, the child becomes a companion. But just how *companionable* is he? This depends on how well we understand his persistent use of the word no. We can react as negatively as he does, forcing him to dig in his heels even deeper, or we can be gracious about some of his new demands for authority.

In the Normal Course of Development

After months of trying to be just like you, your child suddenly realizes that he also wants to be his own person. In just two years the same baby who was born with the impulse to cling now seems programmed to let go. He asserts his independence with a vengeance! So much so that you may find yourself wondering if he still loves you.

Eager for autonomy, he has opinions about everything, and they don't always make life easy. The same child who happily ate three meals a day may suddenly refuse his favorite meal. And good luck getting out the door if your son's favorite shirt is in the laundry, or the seam on your daughter's tights is crooked.

Some parents describe this stage as a nightmare. But I think it is the child who wakes up one day and feels that he has entered a strange new world.

Before, his home was an accommodating place. When he gathered enough resolve to grab onto a chair leg and stand up, he was hugged—celebrated! His parents blissfully rocked him to sleep, happily fetched bottles, and changed diapers without comment.

Suddenly, we turn a hostile eye on a child's old habits. We frown at the bottle and point to the toilet a lot, and we begin to correct the same baby words that we once mimicked in amusement. Given these pressures to conform and the child's instinctive urge to resist, we can only wonder that we manage to get along at all.

Does life with a toddler have to be one unhappy ordeal after another? Not if we take the time to appreciate how often, and how easily, the small child's efforts are thwarted, and how terribly frustrating it must feel. There is a powerful link between how we handle early negativism and a child's self-esteem, so it is important to understand what is really going on.

Another Look at the "Terrible Twos": Toilet Training Through a Toddler's Eyes

What we call problem behavior in a young child usually corresponds to a new developmental stage, and the terrible twos are no exception. The issue that drives a child's seeming intransigence is in fact his need to assert himself, and the dominant battleground is his body. Your child increasingly thinks of his body as something that he wants to control. The conflicts that normally arise now—over what to wear or to eat—are all manifestations of a need to say, "My body is mine, not yours."

Given the intensity of these feelings, it is easy to see why toilet training can become a battle of wills, leaving a concerned mother to wonder if her home will ever be diaper-free. At the same time that your child is developing an awareness of the body as something that is *his,* parents are exerting new demands about "where to put" something that is very much of the child's body, and with which he may not part so willingly. All of the issues of autonomy, body awareness, and ambivalence about you come into play at once. For the same reason, intense battles over food, discussed in Chapter 9, also commonly arise now.

This isn't to say that it is wrong, or unreasonable, to introduce the toilet at some point before the third year. But if your child is resisting, stop whatever technique you are trying, step back, and look at the broader issue for a moment. Above all, you want to avoid positing this experience as a "Do it my way, or else" situation, which may leave a child with no choice but to prove that what's his is his.

The term *anal retentive* is sometimes used facetiously to describe a compulsive adult, but it has its origins in this developmental phase. Briefly, an anal retentive child is one who literally holds in the feces. It is a more extreme (and disturbing) way of saying what's mine is mine, not my parent's, and may indicate that a parent has been overly controlling.

You and your child share one of the most physically intimate relationships possible. But as your child grows, expect some ambivalence toward you as "the boss" of his body and realize that this results in some of the aggressive behavior aimed at you. This doesn't mean that a child should be allowed to act abusively. Hitting you or yelling at you should not be acceptable—but the anger and ambivalence behind the rage should be: "I see that you're very angry at me now, but you may not hit me or call me names."

In the process of toilet training, as with so many leaps forward in childhood, try to keep things friendly and positive, and do what seems right for your child. There is no need to rush these things, but neither should you feel guilty, as if you are robbing your son or daughter of childhood. At some point in the third year most children, if they haven't been pushed too hard, will come to enjoy and appreciate the special status of no longer needing diapers. Being more like you—or like an older cousin or sibling—is a powerful incentive. And the sense of mastery and control a child gains are rich rewards, indeed.

A new baby or other changes at home may of course slow down the process, but they do not have to. Lead your child toward these milestones, all the while realizing that the process

below the surface is highly complex. To some extent, the decision to reach a new goal must always be your child's.

Saying No: The Child's
"Manifesto of Independence"

Many problems with the newly verbal child begin with how we
interpret the word *no*. Rene Spitz wrote that it is the young child's
"manifesto of independence." Saying no is a milestone, he wrote, "beyond doubt the most spectacular intellectual and semantic achievement
during early childhood." The researcher and psychoanalyst Louise Kaplan insists that the child who rails *"No!"* is much less concerned with
"getting what she wants" than with gaining self-respect.

Spitz observed that very young children may shake their heads
and say no even while they are deferring to a mother's wishes. He
suggests in his book *No and Yes* that the ability to say no is no less than
the key to the "humanization of man," the key to abstract thinking.

What we commonly call negativism is, in fact, a positive and
healthy assertion of the self. The child's no is the very first step toward
learning to think and act independently.

From No-Saying to Self-esteem

One mother describes the frustrations of helping her toddler:

*"Lately it's hard to feel as close to my daughter as I used to. If
I try to help her put on her shoes, she gets angry at me. If I pick her
up, she squirms to be put down. But then when I put her down, she
acts as if I've rejected her. It's as if I can never do the right thing."*

In *Oneness and Separateness*, Kaplan writes of how no-saying begins
when the child realizes that, physically, he and his parent are two
separate beings. He isn't sure he likes this discovery, however. In the
child's view, being separate means being alone, and right now he needs

us to survive. Kaplan describes how this ambivalence can be seen in the eighteen-month-old's constant "moving toward" and "moving away" from the mother, as if he wishes to do both at once:

> The self-aware toddler holds on to his mother and then abruptly lets go of her. Her runs to the door to greet her and then veers away from her open-armed welcome. He clings to her in order to undo their separateness but then angrily pushes her away when she responds to his desperate clinging with a comforting hug.

This struggle explains why saying no assumes such importance in the first few years. "No-saying is the helpless child's way of acting as though he had the power and authority of his parents," Kaplan writes. "The more their 'no's' make him feel vulnerable, the more he has to say 'No' himself."

A good example is a toddler who insistently pats the chair next to him and barks, "Sit here!" The mother may think, "*Gee, he's being bossy!*" and refuse, or she can obligingly sit down, appreciating the child's need to flex some muscle from time to time—to do unto others for a change instead of always being "done to," as Kaplan notes. Tired and angered by the child's defiance, we redouble our no's—and as a result we deflate the child's ego, so that his own defiance goes up a notch as well.

This is the great irony of parent-child conflict, and why it escalates so easily when we fail to see the world through a child's eyes.

It is so easy to feel rejected and demoralized by the child's no-saying and his darting away, until we grasp its meaning. We may still get angry; we may not always share Spitz's enthusiasm for the child's burgeoning independence. When you're late for an important meeting or need to finish dinner and feed the baby, a contrary toddler can be trying. But if we can sympathize with the child's inner struggles *most of the time,* we feel less angry. And in doing this we also permit the child to move, with pride intact, from saying no to saying yes.

Meeting the Toddler Halfway

It surprises some parents to learn that conflict with children is so common, as this mother revealed:

"I had such high hopes for being a parent. I guess I expected family life to resemble one of those Betty Crocker ads on TV, where everyone is smiling and baking cookies and happy to be together. I honestly thought that if I did everything right, I'd never get annoyed at my kids or have to scold them. It took me a long time to see how unrealistic I was being."

In the first three years your child sets the stage for battles that will be repeated in adolescence. In the course of a typical day parents and their toddlers seem to be tugging in opposite directions. And often we are. We want to be building self-esteem, but first we have to persuade a feisty three-year-old that he must wear his jacket after all. Struggling to dress a squirming, defiant two-year-old, what mother hasn't felt incompetent and annoyed⁈ Yet the way we respond—with grumbling impatience or with good-natured despair—will influence a child's earliest impressions of himself, as one mother discovered:

"Matthew used to get so frustrated trying to take off his socks every night, and then he'd get even angrier if I did it for him. One day I rolled down the sock just enough so that he could pull it off by himself. He was so pleased with himself—his face just lit up! I couldn't believe what a difference such a small thing could make."

Meeting the toddler halfway is the most helpful thing we can do. His habit of arguing over food and clothing is his way of asking for some say in his everyday life. Becoming independent does not happen overnight, and it is as if the small child knows that he needs a lifetime of practice. The child who is allowed to exert a little bit of power early on isn't quite so demanding after all.

Our reactions to a child's mastery of each new task set in motion a pattern: Are we supportive of the child's autonomy? Do we share his pride and pleasure? For example, in your rush to leave the house each morning, do you insist on dressing your child? Or do you make a point of letting some of these tasks be his?

Impatient to get the job done or to do it more efficiently, we may inadvertently urge the child to remain dependent. With clarity and grace, Bettelheim writes, "Children need to assert their independence and self-sufficiency at every age, so they can permit and enjoy our taking care of them without any loss of their self-respect."

Darting Away: Through a Child's Eyes

When a child pulls his hand free of ours and runs from our side, it is easy to feel rejected. But a toddler's darting away is further proof of his intense attachment to us. The young child feels the full weight of each separation. And it is ironic, psychologists explain, that the people he loves the most cause him his greatest pain by leaving. This perspective may help to explain why our children sometimes seem so angry or ambivalent toward us when we return.

One working mother described how crushed she sometimes feels after arriving home from the office:

> *"When I walk in the door after work, Katie is always thrilled to see me. Then within ten minutes the trouble starts. She won't listen, or she starts doing little things to annoy me, or she'll refuse to get in the bath. Her baby-sitter says that when I'm not there, Katie is the easiest child in the world, which makes me feel awful. I can't help wondering why Katie is doing this to me."*

Many parents know what it is like to rush home from the office, elated to be with the child they adore. When he doesn't feel like playing, or refuses to sit on your lap, or is just plain cranky, it is difficult not to feel let down.

Separation and Anger

In the second year parents interfere with many of the child's impulses. The result is that all children feel intensely angry and, at one time or another, wish their parents would "go away" or die. Even brief separations may be difficult because a child, feeling guilty, may believe he is being deserted, or punished, for these terrible feelings.

Freud's insights are helpful for working parents who, like Katie's mother, cringe every time the baby-sitter says, "She never does that with me!" On a subconscious level your child experiences separation from you as a "punishment." And if he is to be "rewarded" with your return, he must be very good. "Commands and prohibitions which they formerly opposed at home," writes Freud, "are now religiously observed in the absence of the parents." Eager for you to come back, your finicky son would probably eat liver if your baby-sitter served it, and he wouldn't dream of resisting her at bathtime.

When we reappear, our children are momentarily delighted, but they soon recall their anger with us for having left. Now it is *their* turn to punish *us*.

Your child needs to release these feelings of anger and resentment. If you act wounded, he may repress them—but they won't just go away. They simply grow more frightening, and the hurt that is bottled up will eventually find an outlet in more disturbing habits.

One parent notes:

> *"I used to be so upset when I'd come home and my daughter seemed angry with me. One day I just said, 'You're really upset with Mommy today, aren't you?' She looked at me and said, 'I hate when you go because I miss you so much.' After that she was fine. I realized that I was thinking about my own feelings a whole lot more than hers."*

Understanding Your "Stubborn" Child

Willful. Stubborn. Difficult. Impossible. These are the words we commonly use to describe children when they just won't cooperate. Researchers use the term *noncompliance*. The irony, though, is that our children probably see us the same way!

This became clear to me one night when our two-year-old son insisted on breakfast cereal for dinner, and I insisted that cornflakes were not on the menu. He persisted, however, his voice rising as his anger and irritation with me grew. Fed up, he finally cried, "Mommy, you're making me rude!"

From a young child's perspective we are often the ones who cause problems with our rules and expectations. If *we* would only ease up, give in, relent, *they* would not be forced to dig in their heels quite so often.

There is no question that children fail to comply with many of the requests we make. And much of this "defiance" is reserved for mothers, who still spend more time in the company of their young children than fathers do. But if you find yourself thinking, *My children never listen to me,* then consider for a moment how often we coax, urge, and insist that they do what we say.

In his book *Parent-Child Interaction,* author Hugh Lytton observes:

❦ Mothers issue about one command every two and a half minutes.

❦ Mothers also issue "several directions in succession concerning the same matter more frequently than fathers."

❦ When the father makes a request or issues a command, the mother "backs this up with a reinforcing command of her own more frequently than the other way around." (The result? The father's backing up of the mother's command *increases* the chance that the child will comply, but the same action by the mother typically *decreases* the odds of compliance!)

❦ Two-year-olds went along with "approximately two-thirds of their parents' requests and commands," leading the author of the book to conclude that the so-called terrible twos are "by no means very rebellious."

❦ Finally, children issue "far fewer" commands than do their parents. Parents meanwhile resort to commands and prohibitions far more than they use suggestions or reasoning.

Lytton's book was published in 1980. More recent studies have also found that toddlers defer to their parents as much as 80 percent of the time. So why does it seem as if they never listen?

So Many Ways to Say No

If there are many ways to interpret a child's no, there are also many ways for him to say it. Grazyna Kochanska, a professor at the University of Iowa, also studies parent-child interactions, and she suggests that it is unrealistic of parents to expect children to comply all of the time.

If the issue is safety, compliance must be perfect. "You never want a child to put a fork in the electrical outlet," she says. Beyond this, however, you can expect life with a young child to be complicated. In the second or third year the self emerges, and parents need to recognize this. Compliance is important, but there are some forms of noncompliance that should also be supported.

Kochanska's message is this: Pay attention to *how* your child says no, not just how often.

Normal development can hardly proceed without acts of defiance and the occasional failure to comply. But if a child constantly resorts to physical aggression or whining to get his way, then he is indeed forming habits that will be harmful to him in the long run.

Kochanska's view is a variation of "It's not what you say, it's how you say it." The best we can do is to convey that saying no is acceptable, but that some forms of resistance are not.

What happens in the first few years between parent and child is critical. These are the earliest lessons in socialization. A little girl may find that if she whines and rails long enough, her mother will eventually give in, if only to make her stop. And because this works at home, these are the methods the same child brings with her to the playground and, later, to school.

But another child finds that the opposite is true: He has a much greater chance of getting what he wants by modifying his demands, or using words more persuasively. He knows that his mother will turn a deaf ear to whining, so it doesn't even occur to him to try. Instead, he negotiates. By learning to assert himself in a nonaversive way, he not only gets what he wants more often, but he secures his parents' praises as well. Studies have shown that the children who learn these skills at home are the ones who make friends and adjust more easily to the demands of school.

A Lesson in Cooperation

Eleanor Maccoby, who has studied families for nearly forty years, thinks that parents "get what they give." The ideal parent-child relationship, she has written, is a reciprocal one. Children must have a *desire* to cooperate. And, according to Maccoby, this attitude arises only when children sense that parents are flexible and cooperative, too.

In one study Maccoby tested the idea that children will be more willing to cooperate with parents if parents cooperate with them. To prove her point, Maccoby observed three groups of mothers and children during twenty minutes of free play.

In the first group the mothers followed the children's lead and played *exactly as the children indicated:* the parent did not praise, criticize, or in any way influence the child's actions. She simply went along with whatever the child suggested.

A second group was told to make specific suggestions or commands during the same twenty-minute session, in effect telling the children how to play.

The third group of mothers sat in the room and filled out a questionnaire but did not play or interact at all with their children.

After twenty minutes all of the mothers issued the same set of instructions for cleaning up. The children of the first group of mothers (those who had both interacted with their children and followed their children's lead) cooperated the most. Maccoby found the same results in similar studies, which led her to conclude that family relations are, indeed, a two-way street. And while we know that children will not always comply, her model is a useful and positive one.

How Limits Can Help—and When

So far we have looked at the child's need to share power. But this is not to say that good parents abdicate control. We find it easy to set limits when the issue is safety. Children listen to us when they are about to go near a pot of boiling water because our voices resonate with urgency. But 99 percent of the time there isn't imminent danger; most of life takes place on more ambiguous ground, and children are experts at detecting ambivalence. How can parents know when it pays to say no and when it does not? Is there some helpful advice beyond simply "choosing our battles carefully"?

Setting limits does not mean punishing a child. Like effective discipline, it has its roots in *teaching* a child what is acceptable and what is not. (See page 109 for more about this.) Parents sometimes make the mistake of overreacting to the behavior they want to change when they might be better off ignoring it.

One educator gives the example of a child who tries climbing up the front of the slide instead of using the ladder in back. She recommends simply pointing to the ladder and saying, "This is the way to climb up," without forbidding him to go up the front. When the child walks around to the back and climbs up the proper way, the parent reinforces this: "Good for you! You did a great job climbing up that slide." Since there was little attention gained by climbing up the front, there will be little incentive to try this again the next time. If there is enough of a positive outcome to be gained, then children will naturally choose the behavior that we would choose for them.

What about a child who throws sand in someone's eyes, or keeps grabbing another child's toy, refusing to give it back. Normal child behavior, right? Well, yes. But clearly, if the child isn't taught that throwing sand at people or grabbing others' toys is unacceptable, he will probably continue to do this.

Down the road the child may have trouble making friends at school or interacting with teachers. We will have shortchanged the child socially. There are times when we can change behavior by ignoring it, but at other times we step in so that a child learns how to interact happily with others.

Teaching Children to Protect Themselves: Another Look at Noncompliance

Being allowed to say no contributes to a child's *psychological* health. It is the beginning of autonomy. What we seldom consider, though, is how our views on compliance can influence a child's *physical* safety later.

We are appalled each time we read about child sexual abuse in the newspaper, and we are shocked all over again to learn how frequently these assaults occur. The irony, though, is that in our eagerness to be "good parents" and to raise "good children"—and in our denial of the facts of childhood abuse—we continue to raise children who are easy targets of attack.

According to Flora Colao, who consults nationally on the prevention and treatment of child sexual abuse, children can be taught to protect themselves. But first parents must learn to think differently about what it means to control a child's behavior and, above all, what it means to be "good." In the book *Your Children Should Know*, Colao and coauthor Tamar Hosansky write,

> Good children never lie, are never rude, obey adults, never question authority, keep their voices down, and never hit, bite, or scream. In short, good children are easy to victimize because it would never occur to them to do anything in their own defense, do anything against an adult, or even question an adult.

The more we try to make them "good," the authors conclude, the more vulnerable our children become.

Children with a strong sense of self, who have been taught early on that their opinions matter and that their instincts can be trusted, are in a better position to protect themselves. It is naive to think that we can keep children safe by telling them never to talk to strangers; it is also confusing. We spend a great deal of time coaxing them to greet people they have never seen before. More important, the real risk comes from people they know, such as a troubled teacher or a friend of the family.

Parents can begin to protect children by acknowledging that even a "nice" person whom we love and trust may say or suggest something inappropriate. "Children need to be taught that they have the right to say no to an adult demand or request if their instincts tell them the demand or request is wrong," according to Flora Colao. This is something that cannot be achieved overnight, however. Children will know to trust their instincts in a threatening situation only if they have seen, every day, that their feelings matter, and you can do this in little ways:

❦ Never force a child to hug or kiss a grown-up. Instead, respect a child's right to say no, even if this means hurting Grandma's feelings in the short run. Children should grow up with the understanding that their body is private.

❦ Make it clear that there is always something wrong if a grown-up (or older child) makes threats such as, "Don't tell your Mommy or Daddy, or else . . ." Emphasize that you will not be hurt by that person or angry at your child and that the best thing is always to tell you.

❦ And finally, give your child a vocabulary for understanding different feelings. Young children can be at a loss to describe an incident of intimidation or abuse because they cannot explain how they felt. Something very *wrong* may have occurred, but perhaps the best they can do is to tell you something *funny* happened. Words such as *uncomfortable, afraid, nervous* can be helpful, so help to label these feelings when appropriate (on the first day of camp, for example, or when going to someone's house for the first time). Of course, you also want to praise children for openly expressing their fears. (For more on this, see Chapter 8.)

Ask Yourself:

Do you say no too often?

Nancy Samalin suggests that there are ways of saying no without actually using the word *no*. One example: When a child asks for ice cream just before lunch, try saying, *"Yes, you can have some just as soon as you finish eating your sandwich."* Above all, be aware that the more often a child hears the word no, the greater his need to say no himself.

Do you focus on the quality of your child's no?

Always consider the *skill* with which your children fail to comply with your requests. A parent's job is to give children a broad repertoire for asserting themselves with others. Whining and fighting are methods to be discouraged. These habits serve the child poorly because they perpetuate conflict at home and make it more difficult to form friendships outside the family. The ability to use reason and to compromise are effective, "high-quality" forms of negotiating, and we should encourage these strategies instead.

Do you try to distinguish between "acts of defiance" and self-assertive behavior?

Susan Crockenberg, a professor at the University of Vermont, gives an example of how to do this:

A mother tells her child to pick up toys and put them in a box. If the child says, "No, want to play," he would be asserting himself. If instead he takes more toys out of the box or if he heaves the toys across the room, he would be defying her.

Crockenberg believes that a child's willingness to say no to parents should be taken as a sign of competence, not contentiousness. To the child who says no, there is nothing wrong with allowing a few more minutes and acknowledging that it is difficult to stop doing something enjoyable. But if the child is consistently defiant, then think about whether you also "dig in your heels" more than you need to. And keep in mind that occasional resistance is to be expected with a small child; it's a *pattern* of defiance that you want to avoid.

Try to be reasonable, too. Do you expect your children to come immediately when you call them? If so, think about how many times you ask them to wait a minute because you're tied up on the phone or in the middle of doing something else. One mother confessed to me:

> *"I didn't realize how impatient I was with my children until they started acting that way with one another—and with me! I heard my son yell at his sister one day because she didn't put down her doll as soon as he called her, and it struck me how awful and insistent I must sound to them."*

Do you reward your children for good behavior?

It's easy to fall into the habit of reacting to the things we don't like to see. Toddlers are constantly exploring "cause and effect," though, so that doing these things to get your attention becomes a game, as this mother learned:

> *"Every morning, while I get ready in the bathroom, Isabel unloads the laundry basket. She's been doing this since she could stand, and it drives me crazy. I probably made too big a deal about it. Now as soon as she comes into the bathroom, she dumps it out right away and watches my face for a reaction."*

Your child loves to be applauded, especially by you. Try to give him or her plenty of attention for behavior you like. Many experts urge parents to "catch a child being good." If your child never helps to put the toys away but manages to throw one block back into the closet, cheer him for it. The next time, he may delight you by putting a few more toys away.

Do you try to encourage your child's autonomy?

If you've ever watched a small child chase pigeons in the park, you know that he feels positively drunk with power. When toddlers are given a chance to do small things for themselves at home, they feel both proud and important. Watch your child's face the first time you let him pour his own milk into his cereal bowl. Another source of pride is getting dressed alone, so be sure to buy pajamas and pants that children can put on by themselves. Allow plenty of time as well. If you rush your son or insist on helping, the experience will be more frustrating than fun. As discussed in Chapter 9, many battles at mealtime are also about autonomy, and they can best be avoided if children have a say in not only what they eat but how much. Each decision you allow a small child to make will go a long way toward making life easier.

Do you keep your sense of humor?

Nothing is more important to you than your child's well-being. But do try to have a sense of humor about the everyday trials and idiosyncrasies of the second and third year. Otherwise the atmosphere in your home will be even more charged and tense. If you feel frazzled and have a baby-sitter or other child care available, take time off. Even with insight and a long list of techniques for coping, you should expect your child to push you to the limit from time to time. He is just doing his job. And sometimes this means finding out whether you still love him *no matter what.*

Do you punish or criticize yourself when you lose your temper?

Every mother gets angry—even that seemingly perfect woman who bakes homemade cookies and is always there to pick up her child at school. The parent-child relationship is fraught with emotion. In *Love and Anger* Nancy Samalin describes the dilemma of being a parent:

> *By their nature, children bring to the family environment disorder, aggravation, ambiguity and turmoil. They also bring warmth, humor, boundless energy, and creativity. Loving parents wonder how they can encourage the latter while enduring the former.*

It is important to show our children that we are no more perfect (and no less susceptible to anger) than they are. With a first child especially, expect to feel exasperated at times, if only because contrary, challenging behavior is so unexpected. As determined as you are not to reach the breaking point, there are times when you will. Your child, meanwhile, is more than a little curious about what happens when you do. (*Will she keep on loving me?*) And finally, when your children go through periods of waking several times during the night (or rising before dawn) and you're utterly exhausted, it is impossible to be as patient or as loving as you would like. The more you accept your own limitations—both physical and emotional—the less defeated you will feel by these inevitable low points.

Summing It Up: The Meaning of Unconditional Love

Children need to feel that they can safely reveal an unpleasant side without compromising our love for them. We let a spouse see the anger and frustration that we conceal in public, and we express anxiety at home that we share with no one else. Your child has the same needs, but not the same ability to express them. So try to be tolerant of whatever outlet she does choose, but firm in letting her know that some behavior is simply unacceptable.

My mother used to say that the child who acts unlovable is the child who most needs to be loved. A child who is feeling insecure will test you with impossible behavior. You may be ready to scream and send him away. And at times, leaving the room is a good way to show a child that you've been pushed too far. Other times, though, you can break these patterns by picking up a child and holding him. Instead of feeling snubbed or slighted, be glad that your child feels secure enough to be himself, and give him the reassurance he may be looking for.

It delights us when children mimic our "neutral" behavior, such as talking on the phone or pretending to go to the office. But children also need opportunities to practice being less than perfect. They can afford to be ill tempered with us because it is our love that is most constant. This is the essence of *unconditional love*. For parents, noncompliance quite simply comes with the territory. Our steadfast love provides a safe haven.

CHAPTER SIX

Now you mustn't think Emil was horrid; no indeed. His mother was quite right when she said he was a dear little boy, and he looked like an angel with his curly fair hair and innocent blue eyes. His mother wrote in her exercise book on 27 July: 'Emil was good today. He didn't get into mischief all day long, owing to the fact that he had a high temperature and couldn't get out of bed.'

from *Emil Gets Into Mischief*
by Astrid Lindgren

6~

Parent-Child Conflict:
A "Checklist" for
Everyday Stress

One message of the previous chapter is that willful behavior serves a purpose. The first demons of autonomy are being dealt with, and if we are tolerant of the child's moods and inner struggles, the willfulness is short-lived. Six months or so after the child begins acting "impossible," he usually reverts to his earlier, more endearing habits. This chapter also looks at conflict between parents and children, but from a different perspective. If development tells us why certain *ages* are rife with conflict, why is it that certain *situations* tend to be stressful?

When we stop and think about it, conflict with children is fairly predictable. We know that bedtime, seen through a small child's eyes, is a separation, and this explains why it can be disturbing to them. Is it possible that there are other settings where we fail to make such connections? And if so, what are the patterns of these encounters? Beyond the child's inner struggles, why is it so easy to predict when and where parents and children collide?

Why Some Situations Always
Trigger Conflict

The weekday contest of wills begins with the morning rush, and it often peaks at bathtime. Chapter 9 is devoted to food-related habits, since any activity that occurs at least three times a day seemed to merit special attention. But it is during trips to the store that parent-child strife goes public.

My favorite article about these situations is titled "Avoiding Conflict: Mothers as Tacticians in the Supermarket." Written nearly ten years ago by a professor of psychology, the article confirms what every parent knows: that some settings are inherently more difficult when we have young children in tow. In language worthy of General Norman Schwartzkopf, the author writes:

> The supermarket exemplifies a "triple threat" to a mother: there is food shopping to be done, a child to be managed who is afforded a diverse array of enticing objects, and all the while both mother and child are in the public eye. . . . Trips to the supermarket thus constitute a complex management problem for a mother.

The mothers in this study, however, are heroic in their efforts to cope. They talk with the child to keep him engaged, offer frequent snacks, steer down the center of the aisle where children cannot reach anything, avoid more tempting areas, and, most sensible of all, spend as little time as possible in the store.

Matthew Sanders is an Australian researcher who has studied parent-child interactions since the 1970s. As if to prove that these hassles are universal, he has found several criteria for what he calls high-risk settings. Anytime you have a difficult encounter with your child, there is a good chance that at least one of these factors is bringing out the worst in him or her:

❦ Transitions

❦ Time pressure

❦ Competition for your attention

❦ Conflicting objectives

Each of these aspects is discussed below. Together they offer a window on conflict from a young child's perspective.

Making Transitions Less Taxing

While adults may find it easy to move from one activity to another, many children do not. "Whenever a child is engaged in one predictable activity and is asked to make a transition," Sanders says, you can count on "unpredictable behavior." Here is how one mother describes her son's behavior when she picks him up at nursery school:

> *"Andrew falls apart the second he sees me. The teachers tell me he's fine all morning, but as soon as it's time to leave, he becomes impossible. He screams when I say it's time to go home. Other times he starts hitting me or kicking me when I try to put his coat on him. It's very embarrassing."*

Andrew's mother may notice a pattern, though. Some children—especially those who become highly absorbed in one setting or activity—simply need more time and guidance in making a change. After a busy day at school a tired little boy or girl will find it even harder to do so.

In the course of a typical day children are constantly asked to move from one activity to another. Here are some other transitions that may be difficult for you and your child: getting ready to leave the house in the morning; leaving the playground to come home; getting into the bath when the child is busy playing (and, of course, getting out of the bath a short time later); going back to school after a brief illness. The list goes on.

Leaving a friend's house is difficult for a child who has been playing happily. This poem, written by a sensitive six-year-old, tells us how it feels:

> *when my best friend*
> *comes to my house*
> *or I go to hers a sprinkle of*
> *happiness*
> *melts on*
> *top of me.*
> *when I leave my*
> *best friend*
> *sadness crawls*
> *all over my*
> *heart.*

Any child will resist a pronouncement such as "Stop what you're doing. We have to go now." Many parents find it helps to make the next activity sound appealing, and they distract a child in this way. Instead of asking your daughter to put on her coat to go home after school, ask if she can guess what she's having for lunch. While she's thinking about it, you can start putting her arm through the sleeve of her jacket. Or bring something along with you (a snack or a small toy from home) and say, "As soon as you get your coat on, you can have what's in my pocket."

It also helps to acknowledge how your child feels: "I know you wish we could stay in the park all day, but it's time to go now." "I know you want to watch another video, but after this one is over, the TV is going off."

If a child of five or six still balks at these transitions, then you may have to establish some rules ahead of time. "We'll stay in the park for a half hour, and then we have to leave." If the child still gives you a hard time, don't keep adding five more minutes, or you can expect this to happen again next time. Make it clear that actions have consequences: "If we don't leave now, we won't come back tomorrow." And of course *stick to what you say.* You may all miss the park the next day, but you will have made it clear that you do expect a certain degree of cooperation.

Coping with Time Pressure

The morning rush can be seen as a transition, but what adds to the problem is time pressure. There may be a school bus that won't wait, or parents may worry about being late for the office—or both. It can be exasperating—and futile—to try rushing children, though, since they have a limited concept of time. A three-year-old lives only in the present and can hardly be expected to know what it means to be "fifteen minutes late." By their nature, some children (like some adults) simply move more slowly in the morning. This can be exasperating, especially if you tend to move quickly and expect your child to do the same.

What can parents do to help? The answer is obvious, but it works: *Allow more time.* Getting up a half hour earlier can relieve a lot of pressure in the morning, since you can get yourself ready and then focus on your family's needs.

It may be tempting to lay out your older child's clothing and arrange his things yourself to save time in the morning. But you do this at the expense of teaching him to take some responsibility for himself. One mother solved this problem by having her three daughters select their school clothes (down to the tights and shoes they would wear) the night before. This became a final ritual before bedtime.

Nancy Samalin, who leads parenting groups, encourages parents to sit down with a child at a quiet time and acknowledge that all of you have a problem getting out in the morning. Ask your child, "What can we do about this?" Or, "Is there anything I can do to help?" Any time you can approach an issue as a problem to be solved, says Samalin, your child will probably come up with some good ideas. And since your child thought of them, he has more of a stake in making them work.

One parent describes how a similar approach helped:

> *"In our house, when the morning rush became too heated, we came up with a schedule together and put it in writing. On school mornings everyone had to be dressed before breakfast, and my daughter agreed that it should be her job to pack her book bag the night before and leave it near the door. It was a real relief not to start the day with so much rushing and arguing."*

Weekday mornings may never be as smooth or as relaxed as you would like, and these plans won't work every time, but you can at least avoid the daily fights that get everyone's day off to an unhappy start.

Understanding Jealous Reactions

It is never easy for a young child to share a parent, whether it is with a new baby or with visiting relatives. If children act up when company arrives, it is probably because parents are less attentive to them. But as we all know, children would rather get negative attention from us than none at all.

Speaking of these situations, parents claim, "My son was impossible—I hardly recognized him!" Try thinking about it from your child's perspective. Preparing for guests, you were probably distracted and less patient. Eager to impress his in-laws, your husband may have scolded your son for behavior that is normally acceptable in your home. And all of these changes in us, inexplicable to the child, must throw him off-balance.

In many of the homes he studied, Sanders found that the hour preceding dinner was often tense. The children were as eager as ever for attention, but the mother might be busy preparing dinner. Here is how one mother resolved her three and a half-year-old's demands:

> *"Jeffrey used to give me a hard time when I was trying to make dinner. He'd insist that I carry him or get angry if I couldn't play in his room. I finally learned to give him ten or fifteen minutes of solid time just before I go into the kitchen to make dinner. I let him choose something to do together: read a book, do a puzzle, play with blocks— the important thing is, it's his time. Ten minutes may not sound like a lot, but it's all his and it means a lot to him."*

Young children may be easygoing in the afternoon—until an older brother or sister comes home from school and also begins competing for a mother's attention. Later in the evening parents are busy cleaning up after dinner and talking to each other. Once again, a child may act out as a way of regaining their attention.

Some children find a sibling's birthday party to be highly stressful. The family and friends are gathered, but everyone is fussing over someone else. And who wouldn't be envious of all those presents?

Many parents are sympathetic to the "unbirthday" child. They talk about it ahead of time and acknowledge that the child may feel a little upset or jealous later, but that it's normal to wish it were your party, too. One mother found it helped to talk about her daughter's birthday plans—even though her birthday was months away!

Another mother found that, again, extra time alone before the event went a long way toward defusing jealousy:

> *"We were having my older daughter's birthday party at home in the afternoon. In the morning I took her younger sister out to buy new party shoes and do some last-minute errands. She had a great*

time, and I think having that time alone with me made it easier for her not to be the center of attention later."

Visits with grandparents are often stressful because children may be forced to compete with one another, too, as this mother observed:

"My parents were visiting, and our daughter, Rachel, was acting out a lot. All of a sudden it dawned on me that my mother and father were paying much more attention to my son, who's a few years older. I could see that Rachel was really jealous of her brother and desperate for some attention."

Grandparents may be unaware that they favor one grandchild or another. If this is the case, try to arrange for them to spend time alone with each child. (For more on this, see pages 98–99.)

Compromising as Coping in Difficult Situations

Parents and children have different objectives in any number of situations. As noted earlier, your goal in the food store is to get the shopping done quickly, to buy certain kinds of food, and to spend as little time and money there as possible. The child, however, wants to explore everywhere. And the first thing on *his* list may not even appear on yours.

If you have ever tried taking your child to a museum, you know how different your agendas can be. You want to see the Picasso exhibit because it closes next week, but your four-year-old son only wants to ride the escalator. Perhaps a compromise is possible: Will he agree to three exciting rides up and down in exchange for fifteen quiet minutes looking at paintings?

In the case of a supermarket, try letting your children know ahead of time what is on the list, and let them contribute a few acceptable items.

Letting Someone Else Set the Rules

In his books Haim Ginott also advised parents not to be the "rule-makers" in every situation. In other words, we can avoid conflicts by making it clear that these are someone else's rules and we are expected to obey them. To return to the example of the museum, I recall warning my daughter to stay behind the rope that cordoned off an exhibit. I said this several times, but when a guard came over and scolded her, she instantly complied.

"A child is more likely to obey when restrictions are invoked by outsiders," writes Ginott. This is wonderful advice for young families when they visit in someone else's home: "I'd love to let you vacuum the cat, kids, but Aunt Helen has a rule against that."

"Significant Others":
 Accepting Your Child's Relationships

This chapter looks at conflict between parent and child. Another challenge to us as parents, though, is learning to accept a child's relationships with others. We have images of the perfect grandparent, for example, the gifted teacher, the ideal friend. In truth, though, while these relationships can be great sources of strength and support, they are seldom perfect.

Grandparents

Some women report that after becoming mothers, they begin to feel closer to their parents. But many other adults carry into parenthood the same unresolved issues of their childhoods. If you still feel bitter about the amount of time your father spent traveling while you were young, then you may resent how much or how little time he devotes now to his grandchildren.

Without realizing it, grandparents may favor a firstborn grandchild, or one who is physically more attractive or more compatible with them in temperament. As parents we feel saddened and even angry to see a beloved child go unnoticed or unappreciated. If you are lucky, it may be a matter of sensitizing a parent or in-law to the other child's feelings, or orchestrating some time alone with each child. But this isn't always easy, and in some cases—if you have a poor relationship with your parents or in-laws to begin with, or if they simply aren't receptive—you may have to live with your disappointment.

Teachers

We also suffer in our child's behalf when a sensitive soul is assigned to a tough teacher. Once again, there is the sense that this person will neither see nor bring out the best in your child and that the experience will be a damaging one as a result. But parents have to distinguish between their own reactions to a hard-edged teacher and their child's. This mother found herself in a difficult position at the start of a recent school year:

> "My son was assigned to a very demanding teacher, and I panicked. John was unhappy at first, and we went to speak with the principal. He was very understanding and gave my son a choice of either staying in the class or switching to another one, but John chose to stay. He ended up having a good year, and I could see how much it did for his confidence to learn to get along in what was a very challenging situation."

Some teachers clearly get along better with students than with parents. However, if you see that your child is becoming uncharacteristically fearful or anxious about school, don't hesitate to speak up. You can begin with a conference with the teacher, and if you still aren't satisfied, make an appointment to see the head of the school.

Friends

Finally, when children get to an age where they make friends on their own, you may not always approve of their choices, as this mother found:

> *"Samantha has always been unassertive, and I was frankly appalled when she became good friends with a girl named Annie in kindergarten. I found Annie to be very pushy and aggressive, and it was hard to feel so negatively about my daughter's friend. I kept hoping they would drift apart, but two years later they're still very close."*

Again, it is important to balance your child's needs against your own preferences. Cases like this seem to be common. A quiet child may indeed be attracted to opposite qualities in someone else, and the reverse is also true. But children seem to learn from their exposure to those who are different, so try not to assume that no good will come of it.

Samantha's mother worried that her daughter was being "pushed around" by Annie. In time, though, she found that her daughter learned to be more confident and assertive herself.

All of these situations are unwelcome reminders that there is much we can neither manage nor control in a child's life. As for deciding whether to intervene, parents have to rely on their own good judgment. If you know that your son is self-conscious about being small for his age, then you should certainly ask an insensitive relative to refrain from callous names or comments. But most of the time, it will not be so clear-cut.

Your child's relationships with others will never be perfect, but neither is the world in which children must eventually find their way. Instead of always trying to change a difficult situation, focus on giving your children the resources and confidence needed to deal with a broad range of people and personalities. If you succeed in this, you will have given them a great deal, indeed.

Summary

Despite your frustration, always try to see a difficult moment (or relationship) from your child's perspective. "Seeing the place through your child's eyes might help you to understand his plight," writes Stanley Turecki in *The Difficult Child*. Once you do, you can approach these encounters with greater understanding, and this alone may pave the way for more desirable behavior. Sometimes it helps just to know that all parents find certain situations to be difficult.

CHAPTER SEVEN

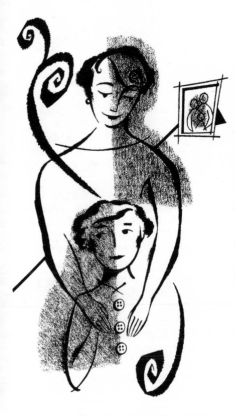

The night Max wore his wolf suit and made mischief of one kind and another his mother called him "WILD THING!" and Max said "I'LL EAT YOU UP!" so he was sent to bed without eating anything. That very night in Max's room a forest grew and grew— and grew until his ceiling hung with vines and the walls became the world all around and an ocean tumbled by with a private boat for Max and he sailed off through night and day and in and out of weeks and almost over a year to where the wild things are.

from *Where the Wild Things Are*
by Maurice Sendak

7~

"Wild Things":
Understanding Anger
and Aggression

For a long time I couldn't understand the appeal of Maurice Sendak's *Where the Wild Things Are*. In one interview Sendak explained that he modeled the book's monsters after his own relatives. These aunts and uncles visited him once a year, pinched his cheeks, consumed enormous amounts of food, and claimed he was so cute, they would eat him up. As a child, Sendak feared they really might.

Then I read Sendak's comments when the book received the esteemed Caldecott Award for Children's Literature in 1984. In his acceptance speech Sendak said,

> [There are] games children must conjure up to combat an awful fact of childhood: the fact of their vulnerability to fear, anger, hate, frustration—all the emotions that are an ordinary part of their lives and that they can perceive only as ungovernable and dangerous forces. To master these forces, children turn to fantasy: that imagined world where disturbing emotional situations are solved to their satisfaction. Through fantasy, Max, the hero of my book, discharges his anger against his mother, and returns to the real world sleepy, hungry, and at peace with himself.

Sendak offers a generous explanation for early aggression. He gives meaning and weight to the disrupting emotions that Max, like all small children, must "tame." Most of all, he reaffirms the child's need for an outlet.

First Signs of "Aggression" Come as a Shock

One day your baby vigorously bangs a toy on the floor, or you watch in horror as your otherwise gentle toddler gives a playmate a premeditated shove off the slide. Tantrums also leave most parents feeling both angry and appalled. Seeing any such behavior for the first time arouses powerful feelings in us as parents, and we seem to feel this most acutely with a firstborn. It is all so unexpected! I can still recall my horror when our oldest child bit my shoulder one day. I know, in retrospect, that it was the innocent act of a hungry six-month-old, but at the time I felt positively betrayed.

Kindness toward others is important to us, and we seek to instill this quality early on in our children. What we forget, though, is that this is *learned behavior.* Grabbing a colorful, coveted toy is what comes naturally to a young, preverbal child; consideration for another's possessions does not. Wanting a mother's exclusive attention is an instinctive reaction; sharing her with a new sibling is not. And until a child finds acceptable outlets for the anger and frustration he feels in these situations and many others, he is forced to rely on impulses that he can neither control nor comprehend.

However, like so many behaviors that are initially offputting or disturbing, early aggression also serves a purpose for the growing child. In fact, it plays a positive role in human development. A true act of aggression is one designed to cause harm. Yet this is seldom the motive when children act out in the first three years. Many milestones of childhood, such as learning to walk, would hardly be possible were it not for the same physical drives that are soon labeled aggressive or negative. Once again, it pays to look at when and why aggression begins, and the role we play as parents in interpreting this kind of behavior. For if it is easy to misread the meaning of a child's outbursts, it is even easier to reinforce them without meaning to.

When Aggression Is Normal

In the First Few Years: Powerful, Positive Urges

Babies use their bodies vigorously as they begin to explore the world around them. This can mean using hands to grasp a toy, or teeth to bite and taste it. Banging the toy on the floor, a baby hears its noise and experiences his power to affect the external world. Within months, your child may *grab* hold of a table leg and, for the first time, stand up. Obviously, then, these are positive impulses that permit the child to grow. In short, biting, scratching, and kicking (the first "aggressive" acts that arouse our concern) hardly begin as violent or hurtful in nature. As children learn to use their bodies, their movements simply become more purposeful.

In the Second Year: The Link Between Frustration and Aggression

The link between frustration and aggression is an important one. By the second year, obstacles seem to multiply. Now your son has both the resolve and the mobility needed to reach a desired object, but he cannot fully understand your protests that the scissors are too sharp or the glass vase too fragile. Another time he may be thoroughly entranced by what a dog has just deposited on the ground. We interfere with these impulses because, most of the time, we must, and yet the child only knows that he cannot satisfy his curiosity. Thwarted in his efforts to explore, he feels angry. And since he cannot yet express himself in words, he lashes out physically instead.

The Older Child

As the child grows, he learns that there is another way. Language not only allows him to express what is upsetting to him but it empowers the child to overcome obstacles in ways that are socially acceptable. In the first few years, try to understand these drives as positive ones.

Gradually help to guide your child toward better outlets, but do expect to see setbacks along the way, especially when a child is overtired or is undergoing a significant change in his life. By the time a child enters school, he should be learning how to cope with anger and frustration in a way that is not hurtful, either to himself or to others.

But how do we get from here to there?

Temperament and Aggression

Given the same frustrating experience, children will react differently to outside limits. One child may obligingly stay away from the electrical outlet the first time he is scolded for going near it. But for another child, each reprimand only increases its appeal, strengthening the child's resolve. It helps to know that, to some extent, many reactions to frustration are temperamentally based, as one father notes:

> "I'll never forget when my younger son asked me for a cookie one day before dinner, and I said no. A few minutes later, I found him standing on a chair, about to climb on the counter and get the cookies down himself. My older son would never have done that! With him, the word no meant no, and he would listen to what I said."

The best we can do is to create an environment in which frustration is generally kept to a minimum. For the child who cannot resist fragile items, this may mean putting them away until she is old enough to know better. We should also realize that children watch us carefully and tend to imitate our own reactions to anger. In other words, no matter what a child's inherited tendencies, he is more likely to engage in aggressive behavior if this is what parents model or condone at home. Studies have shown that children who watch videotapes in which aggressive behavior is seen are more likely to choose the same behavior when they find themselves in a frustrating situation.

What About Gender?

Despite their efforts to be free of bias, many parents with both a son and a daughter sooner or later concede that, yes, little boys behave differently from little girls. There is now a growing consensus that hormone levels account for the gender differences we see in young children's play. Yet too often, we label the boys "aggressive"—as if they were bent on inflicting pain or injury—when we might simply agree that they are more *physically active* (see page 118, about playfighting). Watching our three-year-old son fly through a room wielding a plastic sword or crashing super-heroes into one another, I can see how satisfying it must be for him to act on his frustrations. His Batman cape flying behind him, our son feels less vulnerable to fear. This may also explain why he sometimes leaves a plastic sword beside his pillow at bedtime. (I cannot help wondering how his older sisters, who lacked an arsenal of action figures, vented their own aggressive feelings. I am convinced that they shared the same anxieties and needs.)

The Link Between Fear and Aggression

It is easy to overlook how vulnerable a young child feels. This is how one parent made the connection between aggression and anxiety:

> *"My husband and I went away for the first time, and my parents stayed with our daughter, Jane, who was three. She was fine while we were away, and she was happy to see us when we came back. But within a few hours she started acting funny. When I tried to hug her at bedtime, she got very angry and started hitting me. It was as if she wanted to punish me for leaving her."*

The child's intense attachment to her parents leads to her greatest anxiety: her fear that they will leave her, however temporarily, and her anger at them when they do. Parents who grasp the intensity of this conflict may judge behavior less harshly. They will be less disturbed and probably will not react as if the child has done something unforgivable.

On a psychological level children also do battle with wishes that cannot be fulfilled, and the habits that result can be baffling:

> *"My husband is the most loving father in the world, but lately it's as if our four-year-old son wants nothing to do with him. They used to have so much fun together, but now Jason seems afraid of his*

daddy and is constantly hitting him. I see that my husband feels hurt and a little rejected."

The Oedipus complex explains the psychology behind this kind of aggression and the ambivalence a child sometimes shows toward one parent as a result.

Briefly, a little boy may feel that he must compete with his father for the affections of his mother. (There are similar instances of anxiety when a girl sees the mother as a rival for the father's attention.) These are complicated emotions, occurring on a subconscious level, and the young child cannot make sense of them. He only knows that it is frightening to wish his father would go away or die. When the small child fights an imaginary foe or fears a monster at night, psychologists tell us, the child may be trying to protect himself from the anger his father would feel if he were somehow to discover such feelings.

The irony, of course, is that a parent who fails to make these connections may react angrily. And this, in effect, justifies the child's fears. The father who understands these conflicts will react sympathetically. He may miss their former closeness for now, but he won't react in a way that permanently estranges his son.

Setting Limits on Aggressive Acts

As noted earlier, the word *normal* may be confusing to parents:

> *"I'm not sure how to handle my daughter's outbursts. The books say that temper tantrums are normal, and that children sometimes hit one another. But she's almost four now, and I think she does these things out of habit. I don't want to make her feel guilty, but I do want her to learn how to play with other children. It's hard to find the right balance."*

Like the impulse to crawl and then to walk, aggressive behavior is part of the child's makeup. But if behaving aggressively toward others becomes a habit, it hurts a child for many reasons. Selma Fraiberg urged parents to set limits on aggressive behavior even while understanding its origins. "The right to have a feeling is not the same as a license to inflict it on others," she wrote in her exceptional book *The Magic Years.*

Obviously, we cannot reward aggression. Otherwise, as Fraiberg warns, it will become the child's normal way of doing business. Aggression may begin as an impulse, but we never want to respond in ways that make it acceptable for our children to hurt others.

As noted earlier, the effect of a parent's setting limits is to make the child more secure. "Besides stopping dangerous conduct," writes Haim Ginott, "the limit also conveys a silent message: 'You don't have to be afraid of your impulses. I won't let you go too far. It is safe.' "

About Discipline and Punishment: Do Young Children Need Both?

Many experts agree that a child does not have to be punished per se to learn a lesson. Discipline comes from the word *disciple,* Bettelheim notes, and this is a person who learns from a teacher. As parents *we* are also, in effect, teachers. And if we teach our children well, they will learn to distinguish right from wrong for themselves.

When we approach discipline as learning, this ability to internalize moral behavior will occur in the natural course of growth. Children will make mistakes, but, given half a chance, they will learn from them. Our disappointment and displeasure give them pause—and a strong desire to do better the next time around. However, when parents are too quick to punish (or when they assume that children will not really learn from their mistakes without paying a penalty), these lessons may be lost.

Physical punishment is both unnecessary and undesirable for moral growth. Some experts, among them Penelope Leach, call this "undisciplined discipline." Why? Because instead of gradually teaching children to curb their impulses and behave more humanely, which takes time and effort to do, parents teach aggression instead, acting as impulsively as the child. Thwack! The child is struck, the punishment is invoked—but with no effort at explaining *why* the child behaved wrongly. The slap stings, but it doesn't help a child learn that his actions have consequences. Nor does it encourage him to search for something better. Instead of feeling remorse, he is just plain angry.

If your daughter runs into the street one day, you may spank her without thinking—even though you swore you never would. This is an understandable reaction, and you shouldn't berate yourself for it. It is the parent who uses threats and physical punishment as a matter of course who needs to think this issue through. Parents who lash out physically are modeling the very behavior that they expect children to refrain from themselves, but they are not giving the child alternatives by way of example.

A child who suffers such punishment at home is much more likely to hit someone on the playground or in school. He is only imitating what he knows. Besides, it is behavior he has come to expect of others, so why not be the one to strike out first? But the most dangerous consequences will come years from now. Children who have been punished in this way come to believe that love and physical punishment are one and the same. And it is easy to see what unhappy relationships this can lead to down the road.

Parents who were themselves spanked or beaten as children find it difficult to refrain from this behavior for the same reason. All of us want to believe that our parents acted as they did out of love for us. It takes effort and resolve, but this is a pattern of behavior that is worth breaking. The next generation will be better off without it.

Accepting "Bad Feelings" and Aggressive Play

Why do we get so upset when we witness our child's anger? One reason may be that many adults have never learned to handle or express anger themselves. Growing up, many of us were told that if we didn't have anything nice to say, we shouldn't say anything at all. Or we were told not to say we "hated" someone at school, even though the hatred we felt was real.

Few of us were given effective ways of releasing our angry feelings as children, or told that being angry was okay. As parents, then, it shouldn't surprise us if we have little to offer our children in the way of managing their explosive feelings. What's more, we feel guilty. We see that our child is upset and wonder what we have done wrong—as if by being the "perfect parent," we might somehow prevent a child from ever feeling frustrated or annoyed—in short, from being human! And when children see how uncomfortable their anger makes us feel, they learn to hide it.

Aggressive play is important to a young child's emotional well-being. His demons are many. And as the child grows, he is increasingly aware of his vulnerabililty. You may notice that your four-year-old daughter's imaginative play becomes lurid: "Let's pretend the Mommy dies," she suggests to her friend as they set up their dolls. Many parents wonder whether this type of play signals a preoccupation with death. What appears "morbid" to an adult, however, is a child's effort to explore a mysterious, unfathomable concept. Some children are clearly more troubled than others about dying and may ask about it more often. But most young children worry about "losing" their parents, and they seem to grasp the enormity of death from an early age. They turn to fantasy and imaginative play as a way of satisfying their curiosity and their anxiety.

Language and Aggression

As noted earlier, the little boy who wields a plastic sword feels less vulnerable to fear. Before he can *ask* for a sword, however, the preverbal child is at a loss. In her book *War and Children*, written in 1943, Anna Freud studied the mothers who watched London—and their families—being devastated by air raids: "If they repeated their descriptions often enough their excitement would subside visibly." But the very young child has no such luxury. "This most valuable outlet into speech and conscious thought, which acts as a drainage for anxiety and emotion," Freud wrote, "is denied to young children."

Rage is a valid response to the frustrations of being unable to use language, or to accomplish at all what the adult does so easily:

> *"My daughter is two, and she loves to put on her pajamas all by herself, but she gets frustrated if the pants are inside out or she*

can't get the snaps right. When I try to help her, though, she gets even more upset and starts to yell at me. It's hard to know what to do."

We relish the toddler's smiles when he delightedly buttons his first button. But success is preceded by countless failed attempts, his small head bent over the shirt, his forehead creased until the frustration is too much to bear. In her book *Oneness and Separateness* Louise Kaplan explains that our steady hand only reminds the small child of his helplessness, so he is angry with himself and angry with the parent, who makes him feel powerless.

And how frustrating it must be to have almost completed the tower, or to have linked practically all the yellow Legos, when the grown-up comes from behind, swoops up the child, and straps her into the prison of a high chair because it is time for dinner. Suddenly, the tears and the rage make sense! "Generous explanations" enable us not only to understand the frustrations of being small but to feel sympathetic, too.

It is one of the greatest challenges of parenthood to accept the child's darker feelings along with his gaiety and light. But any behavior, when taken to the extreme, can be dangerous to a child's well-being. The child who constantly feels and acts angry has a problem, and so does a child who appears always to be in control. We know this intuitively. Even so, the first time a child strikes out at a playmate, we may be shaken. We worry, like this mother, that the behavior will become a pattern.

"I was leaving the playground with my son, Jeremy, the other day when he noticed someone else's bike and asked if he could ride it, but the boy who owned it said no. Jeremy was crestfallen and asked again. The child said no again and Jeremy fell apart. He was already tired, and he swung a fist at the little boy, hurting him on the side of his head. Afterward, I could see that Jeremy felt terrible about it."

It was wise of Jeremy's mother to acknowledge her son's sorrow over what happened. He was acting like a tired, frustrated two-year-old, and by talking about what happened later, she was able to convey that what he had done was wrong but that she understood his feelings and loved him nonetheless. The next time, they agreed, Jeremy would have to find some other way of getting over his anger.

Expressing Approval and Disapproval

Children have a strong desire to please their parents, and this in itself is why they are ultimately willing to curb violent or aggressive acts. Nothing means more to our children than to know that they have acted in a way that makes us happy or proud. This is why we are able to teach children what is acceptable and what is not, even while we understand the limits of their restraint. One father describes how this happens:

> "Our son is three, and he started hitting his baby sister a few weeks after she came home from the hospital. We stopped him every time he tried to hurt Jessie, but we realized he was very jealous and tried not to make him feel like a criminal. This went on for weeks, and I was starting to get concerned. Then one day, he was about to hit the baby, but he looked over at us and waited. It was a real breakthrough!"

These are powerful impulses, and the process of taming them is a gradual one.

How can we acknowledge these urges and at the same time temper them? It may be enough simply to hug the child and say, "I know you were angry and wanted to hit your sister, but you didn't, and that made me feel very happy."

At first your child will act sociably because it pleases you. In time, however, the voice inside that helps him to distinguish right from wrong will be his own. (In psychological terms, he will develop his superego.) In the first few years he will learn to decide for himself what is acceptable, or kind, or generous, and what is not. And since the rewards of such behavior are so much greater—those rewards being good friends, a teacher's praise, and, most important, his own sense of pride— your child will gradually learn what it means to act morally and responsibly. It all begins, however, in the early interactions that take place within the family.

Understanding Temper Tantrums

Perhaps no situation leaves parents feeling so powerless and shaken as a temper tantrum. And few experiences are as memorable. The same mother who cannot tell you what she ate for lunch the day before can recall in vivid detail the time, the place, the weather, and a dozen other details of the traumatic scene, including the horrified stares of onlookers.

A small child in the fury of an all-out fit may overwhelm her parents physically, but she has lost control emotionally. Bettelheim writes that it is the child's despair that "throws him into a temper tantrum," stressing the child's inability to control his rage. This is why parents, despite their distress, must do their best to remain calm. Inside, you may feel angry ("*Why is she doing this to me?*"), but your own pique can make a bad situation worse. It's best to convey a sense, however specious, that you are firmly in control.

An occasional tantrum in the first few years is a normal expression of rage. Even so, our goal is to help children find better ways of expressing anger than to lash out physically. Should a child be "punished" for having a tantrum? Most children feel a certain remorse from within. The most important thing is not to cave in to the child's demands just to curtail the scene, or you can count on another one in the future. Experts agree that parents should stand firm, show they understand how powerful and frightening these feelings are to the child, and be willing to talk about what happened when calm returns.

Interestingly, the "time-out" procedure (described on page 115) is *not* recommended for dealing with tantrums. Again, an enraged child feels helpless. Leaving that child alone in his room and closing the door only increases his fear because he knows he cannot control himself. As a parent, then, you want to stand by the child (that is, prevent him from hurting himself or anyone else) instead of shutting him out or giving him a reason to feel abandoned.

Hitting, Kicking, and Biting

Children hit, kick, and bite for many of the same reasons that they throw tantrums. But babies begin doing these things quite by accident. They are using muscles for the first time, discovering what their bodies are capable of doing.

An eighteen-month-old may kick you one day because he wants a cookie and you won't give him one. Once again, he probably does so because he has no verbal recourse for his anger. (His older sister would negotiate for "just half a cookie," or she would *promise* to eat dinner anyway.) We need to let the young child know, in clear, simple language, that this behavior is unacceptable to us: "That hurts me, and hurting people is not allowed."

Parents need to use judgment in deciding whether these outbursts are too frequent. A child who isn't taught to control his temper will have trouble making friends later. The "time-out" procedure can be effective with preschool-age children. If your son is agitated and close to losing control, give him a few minutes alone, or in a quiet place, to cool off before he boils over.

Some children punch or bite when they are provoked by older brothers or sisters. Or they resort to aggression when they feel left out of the big kids' games. If this is the case in your home, your child may need some special grown-up attention, and you may need to make older children mindful of the younger one's feelings. Our reactions to physical aggression are bound to be better if we take into account the frequency and the circumstances of a child's anger.

Most parents notice that children are more prone to hitting, kicking, and biting when they're tired. It is hard work for them to control these impulses. When they are overtired, it becomes nearly impossible. To avoid this problem, see that a two-year-old or three-year-old has a nap if needed, and avoid doing too much on any given day.

Whining, Yelling, and "Verbal Aggression"

Unfortunately, many parents are less vigilant about "verbal aggression," such as whining and yelling.

When young children learn to talk, they still need help in learning to use language effectively. Most of us know the uncomfortable feeling of being in a home (perhaps our own?) where children whine or yell to get their way. For two-year-olds who are chronic whiners, parents must give examples of how to ask for something properly—and give the child what he wants only after he asks for it nicely: "You can't have the paints if you whine or yell at me. Just say, 'Mommy, may I have the paints, please?' and I'll be happy to get them for you." Some children quickly learn to correct themselves if they see that whining doesn't work. With others, you may have to work harder to modify this unpleasant habit.

The Lessons Children Learn at Home

Grazyna Kochanska, who studies family interactions, believes that while aggression may be a basic drive, attitudes toward aggression are shaped early by what a child sees at home. The child's first repertoire of social skills is taught by his parents, and this may or may not include coercive or aggressive habits.

In homes where one parent belittles or ridicules a spouse, children may treat that parent in a similarly demeaning way. If a five-year-old constantly hits a parent or abuses him verbally, it pays to ask whether he has been subtly "taught" to treat this person poorly. And when he alienates other children and adults with similar tactics, we shouldn't be surprised. The behavior a child lives with every day is the behavior that comes naturally.

Common Causes of Childhood Aggression

Generally, the same situations that cause conflict and stress for adults will make children anxious, too. Experts tell parents that aggression typically follows these events:

A New Baby

After the birth of a sibling the older child quickly senses that what she feels about the new baby is the opposite of what her parents *want* her to be feeling, and this leads to a lot of confusion. One mother discovered how much it helps an older child when parents verbalize these mixed emotions:

"I was exhausted from taking care of the new baby and also tending to my three-year-old daughter, who was obviously ambivalent about having a little brother. One day he started crying, and I said, 'Boy, that little guy can be a lot of trouble sometimes.' My daughter looked up at me with an expression of pure relief, as if I had said exactly what was on her mind."

A child has a legitimate feeling of loss now that she must share her mother with a demanding infant. When a child "acts out" by attacking the baby, her parents often act shocked or hurt. Now the child feels guilty too: *"They want me to like this baby, but I hate her!"*

How much easier it is for a child to be told, "It must be hard for you to get used to having a new baby in the family. But maybe you'll enjoy having a little sister more when she gets bigger." Now the child not only feels that her bad feelings are okay but that she is loved no matter what.

Divorce or Remarriage

Parents sometimes make the mistake of thinking that if they do not acknowledge negative emotions, children will not suffer feelings of anger or loss on their own. In truth, though, as Sendak points out, the anxiety is there.

Many children feel angry following a divorce. They may be upset with themselves if they believe their "bad behavior" is what caused one parent to leave. Or they may be angry at a mother who seems to have forced a father out. Whatever the specific situation, children aren't always given a chance to express their feelings. When this happens, sibling fights may erupt, or a child may begin to do poorly at school.

Along the same lines, remarriage also poses special problems for a child, and it may be further complicated by the arrival of stepsisters or stepbrothers. Even in families that manage to resolve these changes happily, the decision to have a new baby may provoke anger and anxiety in older stepchildren, who worry about their mother's or father's "allegiance" to them. The child who talks back angrily or accusingly to an expectant stepmother may be deeply insecure, and the stepmother, no matter how sympathetic or understanding, is bound to feel hurt.

If you find yourself in this situation, suggest that your stepchild speak with someone who can help work through these feelings. Otherwise, the bitterness may have a lasting and damaging effect on your relationship. (Chapter 12 takes a closer look at how divorce affects young children.)

Moving to a New Neighborhood or School

One couple noticed that their two-year-old son, Stephen, slept poorly and resumed "aggressive" play after they moved from California to New York. The first day he attended his new preschool, the children were called to form a circle, but Stephen stayed close to a shelf where he had set up an army of toy figures. Declining to join the group, he told his teacher, "Somebody's got to stay here and protect these." Here was a worried child attempting to gain some control over a world that was now drastically changed.

"Playfighting": Another View of Aggression

Kathleen Connor, a professor at the University of Pennsylvania, thinks that there is a big difference between real aggression and "playful or pretend aggression." What is also overlooked, she thinks, is the parent's role in interpreting aggressive behavior.

"It seems that most children can differentiate between playfighting and aggression," Connor writes, "but adults often find it difficult to make this distinction." She notes:

> Playfighting is characterized by running, jumping, wrestling, and chasing and is accompanied by laughing and smiling. Aggression tends to occur in disputes over objects and is accompanied by frowning, scowling, or crying. The outcome also appears to be different [and] an encounter was playful if the participants remained together at the end of the episode whereas after real aggression they separated.

Connor's work can be reassuring to parents who are not quite sure where playing ends and fighting begins, and when it makes sense to intervene.

Do Men and Women View Aggression Differently?

In many families mothers are more disturbed by aggressive play than fathers. In her study Connor found that after viewing videotapes of children playing, men and women often interpreted the same behavior differently. In one case 75 percent of the males viewed an incident as "playful," while only 38 percent of the female viewers agreed. Connor writes that "people who have engaged in a particular behavior tend to view that behavior less harshly." This may explain why fathers are more tolerant of the kind of rough play they enjoyed while growing up whereas the same behavior is disconcerting to mothers.

Our interpretation of a child's behavior is always important. A mother may feel estranged by her young son's "aggression." But the more she understands it—and the more she understands her reactions—the less likely she is to denounce it. The child whose playfighting is punished or who is never allowed to brandish a sword (either real or imagined) may never be able to avenge his fears through fantasy. The child may seem fine during the day, but at night he may start to feel more anxious or afraid.

Finally, the negative motives we assign to a child's actions are often self-fulfilling. One teacher told me:

> "Parents sometimes say terrible things about their children in front of them, almost as if the children aren't there. And children listen to everything! One mother constantly talked about how 'wild' her son was, and in this case it became a self-fulfilling prophecy."

In short, a child whose mother acts as if she expects him to be aggressive will not disappoint her.

When Aggression Isn't Normal

RED FLAGS

Antisocial and Bullying Behavior

Just as we should not overreact to a child's occasional outburst, there is also a danger in allowing aggression to go unchecked. George Patterson, a child psychologist at the University of Oregon, is most concerned with patterns of aggressive behavior that begin *within* the family. "Clearly," he states, "children do not tend to outgrow these problems."

The term *antisocial* is a subjective one at best. Here it refers to behavior that prevents a child from having happy interactions with others. In other words, whether he or she is dealing with peers or with teachers, an antisocial child typically acts in a way that engenders ill will and animosity, instead of friendship or approval.

In school-age children, Patterson found, such behavior typically leads to academic failure, rejection by peers, and low self-esteem. The five-year-old who cannot coexist happily with teachers and peers at school may be on a self-destructive course. Antisocial behavior is a "powerful marker," according to Patterson, and parents need to stem it, the sooner the better. "Every child has a right to be loved," he writes, "but that right may be denied if parents lack the requisite skills to teach children to be reasonably compliant and noncoercive."

Frequent Temper Tantrums

As seen earlier, an occasional temper tantrum is to be considered normal. Frequent fits of rage, however, are not. If your toddler has these outbursts every day or several times a week, there may be underlying fears or anxieties that need to be addressed. You should also be concerned if your child has difficulty recovering from a tantrum within a reasonable period of time.

As children grow older, their new facility with language should make life less frustrating for them in general. However, a toddler who is slow to develop language skills may continue to rely on preverbal methods. Where his classmates have learned to ask for a toy, he simply grabs it from another child—and is reprimanded as a result. Needless to say, school will be a frustrating experience for the child, and tantrums may intensify as a result. You might want to ask the head of your child's school whether some intervention is called for.

A sudden increase in tantrums may also occur if there is an immediate crisis in the family. If a parent or sibling is hospitalized, for example, an older child will be affected, and her demanding, needy behavior may resemble a tantrum. Be aware that the child may not be able to express feelings about a frightening event such as illness, and this will create anxiety in a small child.

Hyperactivity or Attention Deficit Disorder

Hyperactivity is the most common reason for a child's referral to a psychiatrist. Dr. Harold Koplewicz, a child and adolescent analyst in New York, asserts that many parents make the mistake of waiting until a child is seven or eight before seeking help, even though signs of the disorder are usually present much earlier. The primary symptoms include a short attention span, impulsive behavior, and distractibility.

By the time the school-age child begins treatment for the disorder, doctors have to treat not only the primary symptoms but a host of secondary symptoms. These include poor academic performance, low self-esteem, and inadequate social skills. Often, though, a seriously impaired relationship between the child and his parents sits at the top of the list.

In families with a hyperactive child a chain of negative reactions may occur, as parents and children rob one another of a sense of being loved and competent. At home many of these children never learn the skills they need to get along socially. Sensing their parents' disapproval—and unable to make friends—they feel frustrated and angry, and this fuels their aggressiveness. Many hyperactive children become the "terrors" of the playground, and they do poorly in school. There is medication to treat the primary symptoms effectively. But repairing the child's self-esteem—and his relationship with his parents—takes a much longer time.

Parents should get a professional opinion as soon as they think their child may be hyperactive or overly aggressive. There are cases where these children simply have a more difficult temperament, and parents are able to modify their expectations early on. (In fact, there are childhood specialists who insist that the majority of so-called hyperactive children fall into this category and have been unfairly diagnosed.) But in families where parents wait too long, children may suffer feelings of rejection and anger for their entire lives. Our sensitive handling of early aggression can determine whether acts of antagonism subside as children mature, or whether harmful and lasting patterns are set in motion.

Ask Yourself:

Are you keeping frustrations to a minimum?

As a child becomes more mobile and determined, try to keep prohibitions to a minimum. You will never be able to give in to all of his wishes, but here is an example of how parents needlessly frustrated their toddler:

> "We have a collection of photographs with antique silver frames on a table in our living room, and Allison would be happy to play with them all day long. We don't let her, of course, and she gets very angry at us when we say no. The other day she screamed and kicked my husband, and he yelled back, which really frightened her."

As parents, we should expect to adapt ourselves, and our homes, to the needs of the child *now*. We think of "babyproofing" in terms of creating a physically safe environment for children, but we also need to create a home in which children can explore freely from an early age. And this may mean keeping delicate objects out of reach while a child is still too young to resist such temptations. Like many two-year-olds, one of our children loved tearing at the book covers on the lower bookcases in our apartment. We finally cleared out those shelves and cut down on confrontations with her.

Depending on his age, a child may be incapable of controlling some impulses. A mother asks for problems when she takes a two-year-old into a toy store to pick out a present for his friend, but not for himself.

Altruism is a virtue, but this is not the time or place to teach it. You may only provoke outrage in a tired child who isn't yet old enough to appreciate the joy of giving versus receiving.

Are you overreacting to early aggressive behavior?

In the first three years, many impulses are simply beyond a child's control. In the sandbox your fourteen-month-old wants someone else's bucket, but the other child won't share it. Your child finally throws sand at the other toddler. Rather than acting outraged, remember that what she did is normal and then react in a way that shows it's not acceptable.

Let her know firmly that she is not allowed to do things that hurt other people, and take her home if she does it again. You can say to her, "I know you were angry because you couldn't have that toy, but throwing sand at people is not allowed." You have avoided treating her like a criminal, but you have made it clear that you simply won't allow your child to hurt someone else.

Expect to feel offended the first time your child bites or kicks you, but try not to take these things personally. Otherwise, a sensitive child may feel guilty and ashamed of a normal, powerful impulse. A pattern of overreacting also sends the message that your feelings are fragile, and your children may "protect" you as they grow older. They may not openly express their feelings because they think their anxiety is too painful for *you*.

Are you encouraging aversive behavior, such as tantrums?

It is tempting to give in to a distraught child just to avoid the torment (or embarrassment) of a tantrum. But in doing this you are giving the child no choice but to repeat the scene the next time he cannot have his way. If you want to avoid tantrums in the future, be firm. Simply wait out the storm or, if possible, pick the child up and remove him from the scene of the confrontation. "No child is going to have a temper tantrum for nothing," says family therapist and psychologist Virginia Burlingame. "It's a lot of work."

ɔ you reward your children for the behavior that you like?

When a child with a history of throwing tantrums or hitting and biting other children does try to control her anger, she should of course be rewarded. This can be done by simply letting the child know that you are proud of her—that you know it must have been hard to keep from hitting or biting—and that you're glad she tried. Even if a child does not quite succeed but obviously waits before striking out, you can acknowledge the effort.

Aggression is slowly overcome by "the strength of the positive ties," writes Jane Kessler. Your young child learns to control his or her impulses early on because pleasing you is far more rewarding.

Do you respect and encourage aggressive play?

We can learn from this father's observations:

"My mother came to stay with us for several weeks last summer, and she spent a lot of time with our youngest son, David, who turned three during her visit. After my mother left, David missed her terribly. I was shocked when I overheard him pretending that one of his dolls 'killed Grandma.' It made me realize how much he missed my mother, and how angry he was with her for leaving."

Fortunately, David's father resisted the urge to rush in and say, "David, what a terrible game!" For a child who is too young to express himself, aggressive play is a healthy outlet for anger. David's father saw the behavior as a clue to his son's anger and turmoil, and he helped give voice to feelings that David couldn't express himself. Once he reassured David that his grandmother also felt sad about leaving and would come back to visit again, his games became less aggressive.

Are you helping your child to find acceptable outlets for anger?

The young toddler, writes Fraiberg in *The Magic Years,* is "still a fellow of strong urges and inadequate equipment for controlling his urges." Even before a child can express himself in words or curb his own impulses, we must convey that certain acts are unacceptable. Try "redirecting" your child's anger at another target: "I know you're angry, but you're not allowed to hurt your sister. You can punch this pillow instead, or go yell at your dolls." This approach works for older children, too, especially those who become angry more easily.

Do you talk openly about anger and aggression?

Even after a child acts out in an unacceptable way, it still helps to talk about what happened—and to talk about it in a way that shows you understand the feelings, even if you don't approve of how they were expressed: "You must have been pretty upset today when you hit the boy in the park. Want to talk about it?" We are constantly trying to get children to tell us what they did at school, what they ate at a birthday party, what they did while visiting a friend. But we need to let them know that unpleasant things can be spoken of, too. If your son comes home from school spewing hatred for his teacher, you may be appalled. But if you let him vent his anger verbally, it will probably subside on its own.

When you talk may be just as important as *what you say.* In his book *A Good-Enough Parent* Bruno Bettelheim recommends waiting until after the storm has passed, when a hot temper has cooled and what he calls the "voice of reason" can once again be heard.

With older children keep in mind that they are beginning to understand the rules of making friends, and they want to be liked, so be sure to talk about *why* it's important not to hurt others. Ask your son or daughter, "If you had a choice, would you want to play with someone who kicked and hit, or would you rather play with someone who knew how to use words instead?"

Are you sensitive to what makes each of your children angry, and their different ways of expressing it?

Each child interprets the world differently. It may be tempting to say to your four-year-old, "Why can't you be happy like your older brother about the baby's birthday?" But perhaps your four-year-old has always been more jealous of the baby than your eight-year-old. Is it fair to expect him to react like someone twice his age? In a case like this, it would be better to say, "It's going to be crazy here this afternoon when your cousins come over for Eric's party. If you need some time to yourself or if you get upset, just let me know." Your child will appreciate your understanding, and the fact that you don't think less of him for his "bad feelings" may soften them.

Some children do best on a regular schedule of meals and naps. When a change in routine cannot be avoided, these children may need a lot more preparation to keep from feeling unhinged, or tantrums can be expected.

You may find that winning is very important to one of your children and that she gets angry when she loses. You can't let her win all the time, but perhaps you can remind her at the start of a game that winning is nice, but having fun is more important. Children who are poor sports are often insecure, so you also want to make it clear that you love her no matter how the game ends.

Do you try saying no in a way that acknowledges your child's feelings?

The language we use can go a long way toward defusing a child's anger when he can't have his way. There is often a middle ground: "You had enough chocolate today, but you can pick out some sugarless gum." It also helps take the edge off children's anger by acknowledging their disappointment ("I know you wish you could buy a new toy, but we can't today") and even offering some hope: "Your birthday is coming up soon. Maybe you can put that doll on your list."

Haim Ginott advocates humor and fantasy as a way of deflecting an older child's anger. Your son may be furious because you said no to a new superhero toy, and you may be furious because he already has a dozen of them. Ginott writes, "We set limits on acts; we do not restrict wishes." Instead of getting angry because your child is "greedy," recognize that his wish for a new toy is normal, even if it does not have to be fulfilled. Fantasy can be surprisingly effective: "I'll bet you wish you could have a *hundred* new toys, don't you?" How many of us look longingly at each new catalog that comes in the mail, even though the last thing we need is a new sweater.

Do you try to get to the source of aggressive behavior?

Most adults know what it is like to come home after a bad day at the office, desperate to let off steam. Children have the same need. When our eldest child started kindergarten, her entire mood was affected by what had transpired during the day, with recess carrying extra weight.

Recess, it occurred to me, is the childhood equivalent of the grown-up cocktail party. Success in both cases depends on well-honed social skills. What we dislike most about cocktail parties is that uncomfortable feeling of being adrift, cast off from the small groups that have taken others in. And for a young child, negotiating a place for himself on the playground can be just as emotionally wrenching.

If your son comes home from school and taunts a younger brother or sister or bosses you around, try to get beyond the behavior and find out what is wrong: "You seem very upset. Did anything happen today at school?" There's usually a reason for a sudden onset of aggression, and a child who bosses around a younger sibling may be feeling small himself after an incident at school. A young child can be wounded by a teacher's criticism, or a bully's teasing. It hurts, for example, to discover that a classmate is having a birthday party, but you haven't been invited. You and your children will feel closer if you can avoid reacting to the anger and help them come to terms with an unpleasant episode.

Do you inadvertently allow verbal aggression in your home?

It is important to recognize the patterns of verbal aggression that are common among children. Many parents claim to prevent their children from becoming "whiners" by simply not listening when their children resort to such tactics. "My ears don't work when you use that voice," one father told his children the minute they started whining while they were growing up. Another variation: "That voice hurts my ears so much that I can't even hear what you're saying." If your children whine a lot or yell at you, think about how often you give in to them just to stop this behavior. Giving in only reinforces these unpleasant habits.

CHAPTER EIGHT

Sometimes his mother, who was a cow, would worry about him. She was afraid he would be lonesome all by himself.

"Why don't you run and play with the other little bulls and skip and butt your head?" she would say.

But Ferdinand would shake his head. "I like it better here where I can sit just quietly and smell the flowers."

His mother saw that he was not lonesome, and because she was an understanding mother, even though she was a cow, she let him just sit and be happy.

from *The Story of Ferdinand*
by Munro Leaf

Shyness and Childhood Fear: When Young Children Withdraw

The previous chapter looked at aggressive behavior. Whereas we overreact to the young child's "acting out," the quiet child may suffer a sort of benign neglect. "Shy children don't bother anybody," according to Dr. Judith Hirsch, a physician with the Social Phobia Service at Schneider's Children's Hospital in New York. As a result their problems often go undetected. The overactive five-year-old demands that the world take notice, while the inhibited child seems happy to be left alone. In preschool and grammar school, teachers may even praise the child's quiet habits, in effect reinforcing his withdrawal from the world.

In the Normal Course of Development

As with any childhood tendency, parents need to make distinctions. At one end of this spectrum (also called *internalizing behavior*) is normal, appropriate caution. At the other extreme is shyness so severe that it can cripple a child's self-confidence.

Some children are cautious observers. It's not that they are afraid of joining in, they just warm up slowly. They think before they act. Other children cannot be held back. And even in the same family, from an early age, each child will react differently to the same social settings.

Parents learn early on that temperament plays a hand, as this mother found:

> "It's hard to believe that Maggie and Sarah are sisters, since they couldn't be more different. Maggie is the kind of kid who jumps right in when she goes to a party. She was never afraid of the water or especially worried about the first day of school. She's really quite fearless. Sarah likes to size up a situation. She'll stay on the sidelines as if she's trying to figure out what happens next. And then, as soon as she does, she also joins the group. I used to worry about her, but now I can appreciate that it's just a different way of approaching life."

This chapter looks at why some children seem inhibited and asks:

❦ When is it appropriate for a child to withdraw from someone or something new?

❦ What does it really mean to be "shy" as opposed to "quiet" or "cautious"?

❦ When in the first six years do fears usually arise, and when do they become dangerously inhibiting?

❦ And how can parents tell if they're being overly protective or pushing too hard?

Once again, our handling can make a difference, and parental warmth and acceptance are important. Most children withdraw from time to time, whether they are nervous about the first day of camp or afraid of the dog down the street. When we respect the child's anxiety, fearful behavior is usually short-lived. Our faith in the child boosts his confidence, and this allows him to move forward unafraid.

Stranger Anxiety or Shyness?

For some parents the first signs of stranger anxiety may also trigger concerns about shyness. If you were shy growing up, then you may misread this development and worry needlessly. In the first year stranger anxiety is a normal and healthy development and does not signal chronic timidity or fear. (See page 32 for more about this reaction.)

Penelope Leach, the well-known pediatrician and writer, suggests that the term *stranger anxiety* is misleading. The child is not afraid of strangers per se, she writes, but of the unexpected. The older baby has simply begun to expect certain patterns and routines in his everyday life. Leach writes,

> For example, the baby has learned that when he has been awake for a little while in the morning, either his mother or his father will come to greet him and get him up. If a total stranger were to walk in instead of the familiar parent, his expectations would be shattered and he would cry in fear. Yet that same stranger walking into the house to join the family for tea might well get brilliant smiles.

In other words, in the proper context the reaction makes sense. Jane Kessler writes that a child's reaction to strangers has to do with the ability to distinguish between what is familiar and what is not—a healthy sign of a baby's new powers of discrimination. She poignantly describes what a happy change it is in terms of your child's ability to form close relationships: Her attachment to loved ones leads her "to think about them, remember them, search for them, reject substitutes, and wait for their return."

Understanding Shyness

Shyness is one of the most common of human traits. According to a study by the Stanford Shyness Clinic, 80 percent of adults say that they consider themselves to be shy or were shy at some point in their lives. In fact, the number one fear among adults is of speaking before an audience, an act that universally elicits shy, self-conscious feelings.

Shyness is probably as much a part of the genetic code as the shape of your child's eyes or the color of her hair. Some of us simply find social situations more stressful than others. Researchers have confirmed this genetic component by studying twins and adopted children.

Like many personality traits, timidity is also highly "malleable." Once again, nature and environment work together, and thoughtful parents who have an informed, nurturing attitude can make a great difference in their children's lives.

If you are concerned about your child's shyness, start by accepting the behavior as temperamentally based. Then work with your child to make social situations less threatening, providing extra support where needed. This will help an inhibited child feel more relaxed in new situations. Just as a child with a physical handicap may need a brace, the shy child also needs additional support. A first step, though, is to understand shyness from a young child's perspective.

The "Silent Prison" of Shyness

In their comprehensive book *The Shy Child,* researchers Philip Zimbardo and Shirley Radl do more than define what it means to be shy. They also illuminate the pain and self-loathing behind this pattern of behavior. By referring to the "silent prison," or "psychological prison," of shyness, they show us how their patients, young and old, at the Stanford Shyness Clinic feel about themselves. Saddest of all their findings is the shy person's low self-esteem and the extent to which grown men and women disdain this aspect of their personalities.

For parents, the overriding message is this: Everyone needs practice in social settings. Your shy child's anxiety runs deeper, however, so he needs more time and more practice. One parent sums up the dilemma:

> *"I want to be sympathetic, but I'm afraid of reinforcing my daughter's shyness and making it easier for her to stay that way. It's a very delicate balancing act."*

What can parents do to help? They can be sympathetic to such anxiety but help a child to overcome it a little at a time.

Adult Shyness: Similar Roots, Similar Reactions

It isn't difficult to understand shyness from a child's perspective, since the causes and reactions are nearly identical to those of a bashful adult. At the heart of these feelings is anxiety and fear, as potent as any other phobia. And, as with adults, it is by "practicing" social skills that, little by little, a child begins to feel more comfortable.

The only difference between the adult's shyness and the child's lies in our ability to hide these feelings. In other words, where the shy adult appears aloof or standoffish—or simply doesn't appear at all!—the small child clings to his mother and buries his face in her shoulder. One mother describes her four-year-old daughter's behavior when they entered her new classroom:

> *"If Elizabeth could have disappeared, I think she would have. At the door to the room she took one look and froze. She wouldn't even move until one of the teachers came over to her and asked if she wanted to see the class rabbit."*

Most adults will do anything to avoid going to a party where they don't know anyone. But for some reason we may be impatient with the young child who hesitates on the first day of school, or who recoils from the commotion of a birthday party where there are no familiar faces.

A key to helping shy adults is to let them see that shyness is a highly appropriate reaction to such situations. This is especially important for "chronic shys," who blame themselves for their anxiety and make no distinctions between events that are more stressful than others.

Likewise, says Dr. Judith Hirsch, "There are certain situations where it's normal for children to be shy." At certain stages of development, even a normally outgoing child may become more withdrawn than usual.

Avoiding the Dangers of Labeling

The real value of understanding when and why children act shy is that it helps parents to avoid dangerous labels. A preschool teacher describes how labels hurt more than they help:

> *"Parents sometimes try to make a child feel better by saying, 'Oh, she's just shy,' but it usually reinforces the behavior. If children*

hear it enough, they start to think that they're expected to act that way, and they do."

Many childhood experts agree. With this in mind, parents should avoid excusing a child, as if they fully *expect* a child to withdraw from others. Instead of labeling the child, parents should instead help children understand these feelings. You might try saying, "It's normal to feel nervous about going to a party where you know just a few of the kids. Would you like me to stay a little while, until you've had a chance to meet the other girls?"

We can point out that it is normal to feel uneasy on the first day of camp or when we meet a teacher for the first time and that some people may be more sensitive or anxious than others. One father worried that he would add to his son's fears by talking about them, but the opposite occurred:

> *"I knew that my son, Ben, was very worried about the first day of school, and I didn't want to make him more nervous by talking about it. My mother was visiting one day and she said, 'Oh, your dad was a real worrier before the beginning of school, too.' I started to cringe, but Ben looked incredibly relieved, so I told him what it took me years to learn: that everyone is nervous, but some people hide it better than others. He was still anxious, but talking about it helped him relax a little more."*

Parents who allow their children to express these feelings early on set the stage for a more open relationship later. It begins by acknowledging that these feelings exist, and making it clear that you don't think any less of your child for having them.

When children sense that they have disappointed or "let down" a parent, they feel more estranged than ever. But when parents help a child to see that his feelings are valid, the child feels strengthened instead and is much more likely to overcome his fears.

The Overprotective Trap

As parents, we have a natural desire to help our children avoid feeling upset or anxious. But with a shy child, overprotecting does more harm than good. As parents, we do not flinch from polio vaccinations even though they are painful for our children. In the long run we know that we are protecting them from something more harmful.

Parents of a shy child must take a similar perspective. "Letting a child express distress is okay," says Jay Belsky, a professor at Pennsylvania State University who studies family interactions. The key is to expose children to uncomfortable situations *gradually,* instead of avoiding social settings altogether as this parent did:

> *"The last thing I wanted to do was make my son feel even more uncomfortable around children. When he was very little and we went to a birthday party, I could never get him to play with the other boys and girls, so I just stopped trying. I figured he would come around on his own. Now he's seven, and it's as if he still doesn't know how to make friends."*

This mother meant well, but she went from one extreme to the other. It is easy to imagine her pushing her timid son toward the other children at a party when he needed time to warm up slowly. Discouraged, and afraid of pushing too hard, she did just the opposite, depriving him of experiences that would have made him feel more relaxed with other children. Several years later it shows.

Experts stress above all the child's needs to *practice social skills.* This is the key to treating adult shyness, and it is the key to helping children, too. Every time a child goes to a party or makes a new friend in the park, he has a reason to feel more comfortable, and more confident, the next time around.

Overcoming Shyness, a Little at a Time

For a four-year-old who is too shy to play at a new friend's house, there is nothing wrong with a parent or baby-sitter offering to go along. Nor should you hesitate to invite children to come to your house until your child is ready to venture out. In both cases, the benefits of simply being with other children—making friends and playing games—far outweigh the importance of "being independent" at an early age. If you can leave the room for a few minutes, that's great. Later, you can tell your child that you thought she did a fine job—and isn't she proud of herself, too?

Many parents worry that this attitude is overly indulgent and will perpetuate shyness. But research has shown that inhibited children who are given this nurturing in the first few years are more likely to become uninhibited adolescents and adults. Quiet children need social skills as much as anyone. They simply need more time to develop them. Parents who modify their expectations will avoid making a child feel embarrassed or ashamed.

Remember: Just walking into a strange house and coming face-to-face with someone new is a big step for a timid child. Once you realize this, you can take some pride in your child's accomplishment. And your child will, too. Try to broaden your definition of "social success" according to each child's personality, as this mother did:

"My son was always very independent and outgoing, so I was amazed to see how differently my daughter handled separation. I could drop Timothy off at school or at a friend's house, and he was fine. Caroline was much more anxious and timid in general, and she wanted me to stay with her at birthday parties until she was almost five years old. It didn't happen overnight, but she gradually became more independent. I was glad that I gave her the extra time when she needed it."

Parents act surprised if a child seems less outgoing or less playful upon arriving at someone else's home. But adults also behave differently as guests, or at least take some time to warm up in a social situation. Try to avoid pushing your child or commenting on his behavior. ("I don't know what his problem is—he's never this clingy or quiet at home.") The more accepting you are of this warming-up behavior, the sooner your child will relax and "be himself."

As parents, we have a choice: We can focus on a child's success ("You even played in the room without me for a few minutes!") or we can belabor the "failures" ("Why did you have to run to me every few minutes? Jill didn't come looking for her mother once!") We can guess which child will look forward to the next playdate and which one will ask to stay home.

Ask Yourself:

Is your child really shy, or just slow to warm up?

According to Ellen Birnbaum, a nursery-school teacher, parents and teachers often fail to distinguish between shyness and caution. Children who are labeled shy, she says, "are often highly intelligent, sensitive, observant. They're watching what goes on around them, and this ability to size up a situation serves them well as they grow older." The ability to do this is an asset, not a liability, and as parents we need to respect this thoughtful approach to the world.

When this type of child becomes anxious, it helps to recall earlier successes: "I know you're worried about meeting your new teacher today. Remember how nervous you were about meeting Mrs. Rogers last year? It took some time to get to know each other, but then she turned out to be a real favorite."

Are you labeling your child's behavior?

One expert told me, "If your child had a learning disability, you wouldn't call him 'slow' in front of other people, because this is such a negative label, but parents constantly label their children 'shy.' " Research at the Stanford Shyness Clinic shows that, by age four, children already consider shyness to be a negative trait, and this contributes to their low self-esteem. Just as adults wish they could emulate the person who appears poised and "in control" at a cocktail party, children look up to their socially skilled peers. A child's first impressions of himself come from his parents. Labels are harmful because they become self-fulfilling. As noted earlier, socially inhibited adults are highly critical—even hateful—of this behavior in themselves.

Are your expectations too high?

It's possible that you expect your child to get along in situations that make most adults uneasy. One example is the child who is reluctant to enter a room full of unfamiliar children, even though it makes sense to feel shy in this instance. By realizing this—and by helping your child to understand these feelings—you also help her avoid the pattern of self-blame that makes life so unhappy and unrewarding for shy adults. ("Are you a little excited and a little nervous about starting your pottery class tomorrow?" "You seemed uncomfortable at Christopher's birthday party today. Would it help if we got there earlier next time, before all the other children arrived?") These are examples of how we can boost a shy child's ego by teaching him to respect his feelings.

Perhaps it disturbs you that the other children at school are having sleepovers, but your daughter is still afraid. Does it really matter? If she enjoys playing in other children's homes during the day, maybe that's enough. When she's ready to make this next leap, she will tell you. In the meantime, don't turn sleepovers into a test of real independence.

Are your expectations too low?

Clearly, it can be just as damaging to expect too little. The director of a nursery school told me, "Sometimes parents forget that their job isn't always to make things easy for their children." Parents may allow their shy child to avoid difficult situations, but this deprives the child of what he needs most: practice, along with a vote of confidence.

Have you talked to your child's teachers?

It's important to find out whether shyness is inhibiting your child at school. An older child may do poorly if he is too self-conscious to pay attention to lessons or afraid to speak up in group discussions. Be wary of comments such as "I wish I had a whole class full of nice, quiet children like your daughter." If necessary, sensitize a teacher to your goal of modifying your child's behavior, but without pushing or embarrassing the child in any way. You might make a point of requesting a teacher who is particularly skilled with quiet children. There is no guarantee that the school will comply, but it can never hurt to let your preferences be known.

Do you encourage your child's special talents and interests?

Sonja Kim, who directs the Wimpfheimer Nursery School at Vassar College, says that shy children benefit greatly if they can share special interests with their peers. Encourage your quiet child to play an instrument if she is musically inclined, or suggest starting a special collection that can be shared with others. Whatever the specific skill or subject, it gives inhibited children a way of focusing outside of themselves, and the interest and support shown by other children begins a cycle of positive interactions.

Are you exaggerating the threat of strangers?

Sonja Kim also describes what she calls *acquired shyness*. She sees this in children who have been warned by parents from an early age not to talk to strangers. If they are to explore the world freely, she notes, young children must feel that people can be trusted. This openness to experience is important for a child's psychological well-being and leads to intellectual growth and curiosity. Children who have been taught too early that the world is a dangerous place can be expected to act fearful and inhibited. It is our job as parents to protect our young children and to promote a sense of security.

Do you consider yourself to be shy?

Being the shy parent of a shy child can be difficult, as one mother explains:

> *"I wish I were able to help my children be more outgoing, but I'm still shy myself around other people. It's painful sometimes to see what they're going through, and I wish I were better at teaching them to feel more comfortable."*

Shy parents may be more empathic, but often they don't know how to model the social skills their children need. If you find yourself in this situation, then look for help outside your family. Perhaps an outgoing relative or friend can spend time with your children.

Are you apologizing too much for your child's behavior?

If you've been apologizing for your child's shyness, try becoming an advocate instead. Now, if others fail to elicit a smile and comment, "She's very shy, isn't she?" you can reply, "No, she just takes a little while to warm up to new people." This tells your child that there is nothing wrong with the way she feels and that you respect her reticence. Your faith in her will enhance her faith in herself.

Are you making your child more anxious by overpreparing her?

The mother of a quiet child told me:

> *"I read so many books that talked about preparing shy children for new situations. I finally realized that I was overdoing it for my daughter. She's definitely a worrier, and the more I tried to prepare her, the more frightened and anxious she became. I learned to talk about where we were going a few minutes before we left the house instead of a few days before."*

You know your child best, so find a way of handling social situations that enables you both to relax and enjoy being together.

Have you discussed your child's shyness with your caregiver?

If you work outside the home and your child spends a significant amount of time in day care, or with a baby-sitter or relative, be sure that these people have also been sensitized to your quiet child's needs. Make it clear that your goal is to make your son or daughter feel comfortable with other children. Your caregiver may not be as understanding or as knowledgeable as you are—but at the very least you can make sure that she avoids damaging labels or humiliating comments.

Understanding Childhood Fear

Childhood fears are so common that they are included in nearly every book about raising children. Many parents worry that they will reinforce a fear by being overly sympathetic. It helps to know that when children are permitted to avoid an animal or an object that frightens them, they tend to overcome a fear sooner than if parents push them to confront it. One little boy was startled and shaken by loud noise, so his mother made a point of warning him to cover his ears, or giving him a chance to go in the other room before she turned on the vacuum. His anxiety quickly passed.

Fearlessness and terror live side by side within every child. The same little girl who roars back at the lion in the zoo may cower at the sight of a circus clown. The little boy who dangles upside down at the top of the monkey bars may tremble each time a small dog comes near. But what is perhaps most perplexing to parents is the suddenness with which childhood fears seem to arise.

We try to reassure children that the bear can't come out of his cage and that the shadows on the wall are imaginary. But like the anxiety that drives a child's fears, they are real to a fearful child. The biological "purpose" of fear is survival. In other words, we avoid encounters with things that we think are dangerous. A child who is afraid of dogs is convinced that they will bite him. Therefore, he has a good reason for avoiding them. Brazelton writes:

> It is important for parents to realize at this point that their responsibility is not so much to rid their child of his struggle as to be an anchor for him. The very power of these fears reflects the importance of the mechanisms underlying them.

The occurrence of a specific fear can be seen as a healthy, *adaptive* way of coping for the child—and a highly efficient one at that. Why is this so? The child has unconsciously taken all his anxiety and "localized" it so that he really has to worry about one thing only: the plane ride, the monster in the closet, the pool (see page 143). In some hospitals, chronically ill children learn that injections or other painful procedures will only be done in what is called a "treatment room." Again, the doctors are simply "localizing" fear: the children come to know and dread the treatment room, but they do not have to worry every time a nurse enters their hospital room that something frightening or unpleasant is about to be done to them. Their room, like the healthy child's world at large, can then become a place free of constant anxiety.

The Chronology of Childhood Fear

We can predict certain fears at certain ages. Even so, your son or daughter may have a heightened reaction that is difficult to explain. Some children love pushing the power switch on the vacuum cleaner, but at some point in the second year they suddenly find the noise terrifying.

Such reactions are less random than they appear. Fear of bedtime is best understood as anxiety over separation, and this is most pronounced in the second year. In the first six years many other fears also coincide with the special way a child interprets and internalizes his world.

The toddler is afraid of loud objects, sudden unexpected movements, and new situations and people. Fear is rooted in things that he either sees, hears, or observes for himself. The older child, by contrast, is more afraid of events that he *imagines* or *anticipates* might occur, and this includes the supernatural. (The vacuum's noise gives way to a masked burglar who may crawl through the child's window.) In other words, his mind works overtime now as he worries about the terrible things that *might* happen to him and his family.

What we need to remember as parents is that fear makes all of us feel vulnerable. Many adults dread traveling by airplane; others may shun spiders and snakes to the point of turning away from a photograph of one. When someone is sympathetic to our anxiety, we feel grateful, even relieved. Yet when children openly express their fears—when they admit and expose their vulnerability—they may be met by impatience, pressure, and, worst of all, ridicule.

Often, when we step back and think about what precedes a child's fears, interesting patterns emerge. "Usually in childhood there is a close enough connection between an event and a child's reaction so that we can search our memories and come up with some clues," writes Selma Fraiberg in her classic volume *The Magic Years*. Fraiberg gives common and compelling examples: the little girl whose sudden fear of the rain (and of getting wet) may be traced to toilet training, and her intensive efforts at "staying dry." Or the child who screams in terror at bathtime not long after staring, transfixed, at the water disappearing down the drain one day.

Fraiberg admits that there is surprisingly little we can do to allay a child's anxiety. However, "our knowledge that she is afraid will make a difference in our handling," Fraiberg writes, and often this is enough.

Because it is impossible to cover every single childhood phobia, this section looks at a very common one: fear of the water. Like many of the habits discussed in this book, a child's attitude toward the water will be influenced by many things: his temperament, his particular developmental stage, and the reactions of those around him. The tools available to us as parents are also the same: language, empathy, patience, and faith.

Through a Child's Eyes: Fear of the Water

Shrimps. Kippers. Pikes and Eels. What sounds like a traditional English menu is, in fact, a list of swimming classes for young children at a New York City YMCA. In many U.S. cities, parents may now enroll babies as young as twelve weeks in such programs. As an exercise in fun, these classes are fine. But parents who turn to them in the belief that early exposure will prevent their children from ever being afraid of the water may be missing the point of early phobias.

Taylor Pape has been teaching children to swim for the past fifteen years. She is soft-spoken and friendly in the way that children find honest and appealing. Her teaching style is calm, creative, and always reassuring, like the language she uses with her young charges. Since the late 1970s Pape has taught hundreds of children to swim, both privately and in small groups, and she has seen hundreds of different reactions. "Some children will jump into the water without ever wondering how they're going to get out alive," she notes. "And other children won't get into the water for weeks, until they see that other children have lived through it."

Pape notes that while temperament may contribute to an initial fear of the water, a child's comfort level should be expected to ebb and flow as he grows. "I find that kids will often be very cautious whenever they're working on any kind of major breakthrough: when they're learning to crawl, when they start to walk, when they're working on toilet training, when they start school," says Pape. "My sense of it is that they can't be brave on all fronts at once." (It is probably worth adding that children cannot develop or learn or grow on all fronts at once, either.)

Children internalize the world around them. Expectant mothers are puzzled when a child starts acting "funny" or becomes anxious in the water. They may insist that the child hasn't been told about the new baby. But somehow they do know, says Pape, and it is not unusual for children to reveal their anxiety in a heightened fear of the pool, as if they have to put their fear somewhere.

"The most important thing when dealing with children who are frightened is to respect it—and not to push," Pape says, because it never works—no matter what's behind the anxiety. She acknowledges how tempting it may be to push a child's face into the water to prove that it's not a big deal. "But if they're worried about it," she cautions, "it *is* a big deal." What's more, she says, this type of handling only ends up reinforcing a child's reluctance.

In private lessons Pape may be part teacher, part therapist. One student, a fearful seven-year-old, vented her distress at having had her head pushed under the water at camp the previous summer; she hadn't put her head in the water again since. After twice swimming the length of the pool to check for sharks (another thing that worried her nervous student), Pape listened sympathetically. The child's outpouring lasted almost the entire lesson, with Pape nodding and, from time to time, agreeing that the experience must have been very upsetting. She never urged the child to try again or indicated that this was her goal. Yet at the end of the lesson the little girl asked if she could try getting her ears wet. A few minutes later, proud and elated, she was performing surface dives.

Pape's sensitivity extends to the sometimes daunting language of learning to swim. If a child swears he'll never swim in the deep end, Pape calls it Pennsylvania instead and suggests that they feed the animals there. Children, she says, are more comfortable there as long as it's called anything but *the deep end,* the part of the pool where they know they could drown.

"If I ask them to put their face in the water and they say no, I might say, 'Well, how about just putting your chin in the water, or just putting your lips in the water.'" Pape might also propose an experiment: "What if we cover our face with our hands and put our hands in the water and don't even tell our face about it?" The point, she explains, is to break it down into smaller tasks that children can accomplish, so that one success leads to another. But obviously, her patient acceptance helps to defuse these fears as well.

Still, Pape acknowledges that for some children, the best thing is to back off. She understands that it can be difficult for parents if their child is the only one who refuses to try floating or simply to get into the pool at all. But pushing a child usually backfires. "Sometimes they don't want to fail at something that's so important to their parents," notes Pape, "so they won't try at all."

Having Faith in a Fearful Child

By pushing too hard, parents can transform a child's fear into a contest of wills. This not only strengthens the anxiety but, equally damaging, it gives children a feeling that they have disappointed their parents, undermining their confidence even more. This happens when parents worry that a five-year-old will still be unable to swim ten years later, which is seldom the case. A child who has a new baby sister or who is just starting kindergarten may be reluctant to go in the water one day. If parents can accept this, there's a good chance the child will swim again on the next visit to the pool or to the beach. But if the parents make a point of criticizing or commenting on the behavior to every person they meet, the episode will probably repeat itself.

Ask Yourself:

Are you respectful of your children's fears?

Having empathy for a child is important. If your son is fearful at bedtime, there's nothing wrong with acknowledging that you used to feel nervous at night, too. But avoid being overly dramatic or descriptive: providing too vivid a picture of the beast you feared is neither necessary nor helpful.

Try to use and modify language in a way that acknowledges a child's fear without augmenting it: for example, "Sometimes dogs can be scary, especially when they have a loud bark, but Tara's dog is very gentle and friendly. Would you like me to hold your hand and you can watch the other children pet him?" You can also hold out hope for the future: "I was afraid of that when I was four years old, too. But I don't remember feeling so scared of it when I was a little older."

Have you tried figuring out why your child is afraid?

Therapist Virginia Burlingame tells of a nine-year-old patient who had stopped eating because he was afraid of choking. His family had recently visited a nursing home where, he learned, someone had choked to death. Burlingame uncovered the child's real anxiety, though, by asking *why* he was scared of dying. It turned out that the boy had played some sex games with a friend and then became frightened after his father read a Bible story about hell. In the child's mind, all of these events had been connected: *I'd better stop eating because I might choke,* he thought, *and if I choke and die, I might go to hell.* It didn't help to talk about the remote chance of choking, since the child was really worried about something else. Burlingame's example proves that, however elusive, connections usually exist between a child's recent experiences and his "inexplicable" fears.

Are you trying too hard to convince your child not to be scared?

"There's nothing to be afraid of." Many parents are tempted not only to say this but to prove it, too. To the extent that some fears are "irrational," though, such a statement may be more harmful than helpful. Consider a toddler's fear of the bathtub drain. One mother explains:

> *"Nicholas is two, and he's terrified that his toys will go down the bathtub drain along with the water. The other day, his older sister was determined to show him that his boat was too big to fit, but he panicked even more. I had to explain to her that the best thing for now is just to take the toys out of the bath before pulling out the plug."*

This mother was wise. She saw that her son was too young to understand, and she avoided reacting in a way that intensified or prolonged his reaction. (It is interesting to note that, within a few months, the child's fear had subsided, and he would insist on remaining in the tub so that he could study the last drops of water spiraling down the drain. As is often the case in childhood, his fear was followed by an almost compulsive, close-up interest in what had initially caused his distress.)

Do you talk about the fear openly?

In their book about safety strategies for children, Flora Colao and Tamar Hosansky write that parents may try too hard to eliminate fear instead of accepting it and talking about it openly. Try offering assistance. Ask a child who is scared of going to bed, "What would help you go to sleep?" The answer, writes Colao, may be as simple as leaving an extra light on in the hall or placing a whistle near the bed so that the child can call for help.

You might also look for children's books at the library. Mercer Mayer's *There's a Nightmare in My Closet* is a bedtime classic. Some parents worry that this will only make children more afraid, but the opposite seems to be true. These stories simply legitimize the child's *anxiety*, which is a first step toward coping with fear. (If your child does seem frightened by a particular story, however, don't insist on reading it; the book may be intended for someone older. Ask the librarian to recommend something else.)

Can you break down something frightening into more manageable steps for your child?

Parents can actively help children to overcome a fear by breaking it down into more manageable steps. In Taylor Pape's classes a child who has convinced himself that he can't "swim" will be asked to "kick and scoop" across the pool instead. If your child is afraid of the swings, suggests Penelope Leach, let her sit in your lap the first few times until she feels more secure. Your son, fearful of cats, may find stories about them helpful.

Have you inadvertently turned the fear into a bigger issue than it should be?

Even well-meaning parents can feel frustrated when a child continues to feel afraid, but patience is usually best. There is a good chance that your child is also eager to overcome his apprehension, but if you become too invested in his ability to do this, you may increase his fear of failure. By reassuring your child that everyone is afraid sometimes, you provide more than sympathy: you offer him a way out with his pride intact.

"It's important to try not to back kids into corners where they can't back down," says Pape, and the wisdom of this statement touches not only childhood fears but every aspect of living with children, whether the subject is comfort habits, angry outbursts, or, as Chapter 10 discusses, the early school years.

Do you encourage your children to express their fears?

Textbook author Jane Kessler makes the point that as they grow, children are discouraged from expressing their anxiety:

> Children are praised for courage, which is usually defined as "having no fear." It would be more helpful for children if they were praised for their ability to tolerate anxiety, to proceed to a certain objective despite fear. However, as it is, many children have a fear of showing fear, and anxiety assumes many disguises.

We ought to congratulate children whenever they try to confront something that scares them, even for efforts that don't quite succeed. This not only gives a child the will to try again but brings parents and children closer emotionally. The message that you respect your child— and that you take her struggles seriously—is one that can never be stated enough.

Can you think of changes in your child's life that may be making him or her more fretful?

Many children become more aggressive after the birth of a sibling. Your child may also seem more anxious. What is the connection? "His feelings about the competition from the baby are sure to stir up angry and aggressive wishes," Brazelton explains. "They will surface as fears when the child tries to hold in all of the negative feelings." By giving your child a chance to express feelings that are troubling (or simply letting him know that it is all right to feel this way), you may make him feel more secure—and less frightened—in the future.

RED FLAGS

Extreme Shyness

Childhood experts look at chronicity to distinguish between *fear* and *phobia,* although the two words tend to be used interchangeably in books about early childhood. This chapter gives many examples of inhibitions that are normal in early childhood. How can you tell if your child's cautious behavior and fearful reactions do not fall into a normal range?

"Shyness as a trait seems to run in families," says Dr. Judith Hirsch, but "it can be perpetuated by parents' accepting it." Surprisingly, there are no studies to show that children who are extremely shy are more likely to develop social phobia. But Dr. Hirsch nevertheless urges parents not to become a partner in this pattern of avoidance, regardless of a child's age.

If your son has been in preschool for several weeks, find out whether he has made any friends. If not, you might want to talk to the teacher or the head of the school for an evaluation. You know your child best, though. If you aren't comfortable with their assessment, talk to your pediatrician about where to go for a second opinion.

School Phobia

It is normal for both children and adults to avoid something they fear. However, a child who won't leave the house to go to school may be suffering from *school phobia,* a form of separation anxiety disorder (page 33), and should get professional help. If your child is overly aggressive or puts himself in dangerous situations, this may also result from fear. His anxiety isn't finding an outlet, however, and as a result your child may be developing some harmful habits.

"If you're afraid of elevators, you can avoid elevators," Dr. Hirsch notes. "But you can't avoid people." Social phobia is much more commonly found in adolescents, who actually panic at the thought of certain social situations. Most of Dr. Hirsch's patients don't *want* to avoid people. But many, beginning in childhood, have learned to avoid others because they fear rejection and even ridicule. And this pattern of withdrawal is what keeps many others from getting the help they need as young adults.

CHAPTER NINE

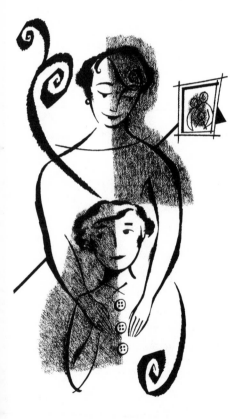

"She won't try *anything* new," said
Mother to Father.
"She just eats bread and jam."
"How do you know what you'll like
if you won't even try anything?" asked
Father.
"Well," said Frances,
"there are many different things to eat,
and they taste many different ways.
But when I have bread and jam
I always know what I am getting, and
I am always pleased."
"You try new things in your school
lunches," said Mother.
"Today I gave you a chicken-salad sand-
wich."
"There now!" said Father to Frances.
"Wasn't it good?"
"Well," said Frances, "I traded it to Al-
bert."
"For what?" said Father.
"Bread and jam," said Frances.

from *Bread and Jam for Frances*
by Russell Hoban

Eating Habits That
Eat at Parents:
When Battles over
Food Begin

This chapter has to do with what children eat, and how to worry about it less. Most parents question at least some aspect of their child's food habits, as these quotes show:

> "My son is three and I think he would happily eat noodles — nothing but noodles—for the rest of his life. The pediatrician says it's normal, but I can't believe he can eat this much starch and still be considered healthy!"

> "Lucy has an incredible sweet tooth, and I worry about it. I was heavy as a child, and I always wish my mother had helped me control my weight more when I was Lucy's age. But I also don't want to make my daughter too self-conscious about the way she looks. You hear so much about teenage girls becoming anorexic these days."

> "I'm very health-conscious, and I try to make sure that my kids eat food that's fresh and nutritious. But it seems as if the more time I spend preparing a dish for them, the less they like it. It makes me crazy."

I can relate to this last comment. Everything our first child ate was not only fresh but prepared by hand, with generous doses of tender loving care. One night when she was about two and a half, I came home late from work and reluctantly ordered some ziti from a local pizzeria. It arrived, cold and congealed from sitting in the tin. But when my daughter tasted it, her eyes lit up as never before. "Mommy!" she crowed, "this is *delicious.*"

Between Parent and Child: Avoiding the Road to Conflict

For most parents, the first few visits to the pediatrician are dominated by questions about feeding a newborn. One mother recalls the intensity of these concerns:

> *"I remember taking Michael home from the hospital and feeling slightly overwhelmed that he was entirely dependent on us for survival. I nursed him, and it was unnerving at first because I didn't know exactly how much milk he was getting. (Maybe I couldn't quite believe that I could provide everything he needed to grow.) Anyway, it was an incredible relief each time we went to the pediatrician and found out that he was gaining weight."*

We tend to view food issues as being of a higher order than many other problems we face as parents. When an older child refuses to go to bed, or fights with his sister, we get angry and annoyed—but we assume that growth will be unhampered. Feeding affects us differently, more emotionally in many ways—but it needn't. There are three important things for every parent to know about feeding young children:

1. Children approach food and eating as individually as they start to talk or learn to swim.

2. Assuming that you make available a balanced diet of nutritious food, a child's natural eating habits are rarely harmful to his growth.

3. Children's attitudes toward food, which are closely related to each age and stage of development, can be expected to change as they grow. Whether a child is mashing his food, refusing to eat it, or craving sweets, these habits have a way of regulating themselves over time.

Like so many habits, a child's food behavior follows along lines of development. In other words, many attitudes and patterns can be predicted. If you can learn to accept some of these habits as annoying but age-appropriate, you will object to them less, and this is the key to keeping food a friendly subject.

Food habits are strikingly individual. (Your best friend's child may live to eat, while your child eats to live—nothing more, nothing less.) Even if we cannot ensure peace at every meal, the good news is that food issues do not have to strain relations between you and your child.

Anna Freud writes of a period, when a child is two or three, when meals become a battleground. Whenever this happens, she warns, the fighting is over something other than food. This chapter is devoted to seeing meals through a child's eyes so that these battles become unnecessary, whether your child is about to celebrate her second birthday or her sixth.

Step One: *Relax*

Goldie Alfasi is a psychologist who has studied feeding difficulties in infants and who also treats adolescents. Her advice to parents of young children can be summed up in one word: relax. She speaks of food issues as both a parent and a professional: "We're so anxious to be good at the things we think are important," she says. "Early on, we equate being a good parent with how we feed our children. You're a 'good mother' if you feed your kid food that is healthy." The result is that we overreact to what children eat (or don't eat) and create problems where none exist.

Don't allow food to become the measure of how successful you are as a parent. It is far more important to establish a pleasant atmosphere at mealtime while a child is young. This means resisting the temptation to correct either their manners or their ideas about what they eat, and when.

Easy Attitude, Easy Feeding

A mother who nurses her baby learns that there is a connection between how she feels and how well her baby eats. If she is nervous or tense, her milk supply will not flow, or "let down," and naturally this gets in the way of a happy eating experience for her baby.

We would be wise to remember this when a baby begins taking meals in a high chair. This mother found that although she got off to a smooth start introducing solids, it was all too brief:

> *"At first I was thrilled to feed Kyle. He was very happy to try new things, and I honestly looked forward to mealtime. Problems began when he was about one and a half. He seemed to be resisting me about everything, including food."*

The breast-feeding baby knew when he was hungry enough to eat, and stopped when he had enough. In an ideal world we would take similar cues from an older child, too. However, the moment we introduce solids, we also impose expectations about how much a child should eat.

Yes, it can be frustrating when a child loses interest after just a few bites. But those few spoonfuls are probably all he needs right now. In general, children will eat when they're hungry. They may be easily distracted, they may not eat a lot, and they may refuse a food that they happily ate the day before. But normal gains in height and weight are proof that your baby is eating well, and this is something you can confirm during visits to your pediatrician. If you have a reason to believe that your son or daughter isn't growing normally, then by all means talk it over.

If you still feel anxious about what your child eats, try to figure out why. Otherwise, you may trigger tension between you and your child. Unresolved issues from your own childhood (such as painful feelings about being underweight or overweight) could be surfacing. You may have to work harder to be balanced about your own child's habits.

Knowing What to Expect

Nearly every nine-month-old gleefully hurls food from his high chair and exults inwardly in his power to land something on the floor. One year later the same child who happily mashed all his food together on his plate may cry inconsolably if his peas touch his potatoes. In general, parents struggle with three types of reactions:

❦ *Food refusal:* children refusing to accept or to try certain foods

❦ *Food fads:* children asking to eat just one food for an extended period of time, almost to the exclusion of other foods

❦ *Matters of etiquette:* that is, how the child behaves at the table, how long he sits, and, of course his "finesse" in getting the food on his plate into his mouth.

In the Normal Course of Development

A child's particular stage will manifest itself in everything he does: his play, his sleep, his reactions to strangers. Understanding this can help you to stay relaxed about his attitudes toward food, even when his behavior becomes difficult or seems to threaten healthy growth.

The First Six Months: The Food-Love Connection

Aside from naming a new baby, one of the first decisions a mother makes is whether or not to nurse her infant. For many women, it comes down to an emotional issue. Breast-feeding is thought to create a certain intimacy between mother and child. And indeed, it is difficult not to feel smitten by the experience of nourishing an infant in such a natural way. This may be why the child's waning interest a few months later comes as such a rude surprise, as the mother of a five-month-old describes:

"I used to be able to nurse Rose anytime, anywhere. As long as she was hungry, she would eat. But now she gets distracted by every

little noise. Sometimes I even turn the lights down very low so that she won't be as tempted to look around and play. I'm thinking of weaning her because she just doesn't seem as interested in nursing anymore."

In some respects Rose's mother is right. It isn't so much that the breast is being rejected but that the world beyond it is being discovered. Seeing her baby's behavior from this vantage point, she will see it as something momentous, rather than as something rejecting.

Parents should not expect a child's need to explore his world to cease just because he is sitting in a high chair. It simply becomes redirected toward the way his food feels and tastes and sticks to the wall, or the way it runs through his fingers when he squeezes it. And since we want our children to explore their world actively, we have to welcome the consequences, even when this means leftover food and a high chair tray happily "painted" with applesauce. For most babies a happy meal is a messy one. You would do well to save the major cleaning up until the meal is over. To wipe your child's face after each spoonful is a guarantee that he will stop looking forward to time in the high chair.

In the first few months parents see many reactions that are temperamentally based—a preference for the taste of one formula over another, for example, or warm milk instead of cold. In general, children react differently to change, and some babies will be stressed by the transition from breast to bottle, no matter how gradually it occurs. There is no way to "disentangle" the effects, but be aware that your own feelings—ambivalence or sadness over weaning, whenever it occurs— will also affect your baby's reactions.

Six Months to Two Years

Another milestone occurs when children begin feeding themselves. It takes great initiative for your child to grab the spoon and try to use it, and an admiring attitude on your part will go a long way. Most mothers find they can still manage feedings as long as the child has a spoon of his own. The more pride you take in your child's independence, the less he has to prove by refusing what you offer. To praise a child's first, clumsy handling of a spoon is also to encourage initiative. To chafe over the food that is "wasted" is to miss the point.

A mother who feels personally rejected by these early attempts at self-feeding is in for a rough time. Her feelings are partially justified, of course. In the child's mind, "food" and "mother" remain one and the same, and this is important to grasp. But it is up to us as parents to have some perspective when children, in rejecting our food, are really making a statement about their need to assert themselves.

Two things can help. First we need to consider a child's autonomy in all areas of his daily life, and whether there are so many obstacles to his authority that food is the only area where he feels he can (and must) make his opinions known. And second, it can help to let others share in the task of feeding, even though you may feel a little resentful:

> *"I found it frustrating that my husband could feed our one-year-old in ten minutes, and it took me almost an hour. With me, Eliza would eat a few bites and then lose interest. She would try to grab the spoon each time it got near her mouth or start playing with her high chair buckle. My husband seemed to get none of these reactions."*

Mothers are usually on the receiving end when a child "acts out." Dr. Nina Lief reminds parents that each human relationship will have "a different rhythm and tempo." Your husband's interactions with the baby will be different from your own. But these differences, which may be especially clear at feeding time, should be valued. Babies are resilient and adaptable, and it's important to appreciate the different ways in which mothers and fathers handle infants.

(In fact, mothers risk alienating their mates if they expect them to hold or care for the baby exactly as they do. Fathers who are constantly criticized or corrected may lose interest in handling the baby, and this is a loss for everyone. The cycle is a dangerous one. Now the same mother feels bitter because she is no longer getting any help at home.)

From Two to Four

Chapter 5 looked at the toddler's ambivalent behavior: his running toward the mother and then abruptly turning away. For the young child, food becomes another vehicle for expressing complex feelings about the adults who control so many aspects of daily life. Anna

Freud gives a fascinating, if extreme, example of a little boy who not only spit out what his mother fed him but scraped his tongue of the last few morsels of food. The child, writes Freud, was so angry at his mother that he literally "would have none of her."

Even behavior that is far less radical, though, can be disturbing to you as a parent. Your daughter refuses lunch one day—but perhaps she ate a bigger snack than usual that morning. A two-year-old who mushes his banana is probably more delighted by its texture than determined to make you angry. As Dr. Nina Lief puts it, young children are on a voyage of discovery, and sitting in a high chair is just part of it. They don't simply eat food, they explore its many properties. From your son's perspective there is no reason why a plate of mashed potatoes should not be subject to the same manipulation as what he finds in the sandbox or in a container of Play-Doh.

In this age group a child's "offenses" often arise from a disregard for convention. A catsup-lover will douse everything on his plate with the heavenly red stuff. And since there's nothing inherently wrong with this, there is no reason to object. Try not to be offended by the toddler's culinary trial and error. It is best to let him enjoy it.

In the end, "motives" hardly matter. Whether the toddler spits out food to assert himself or because he didn't like the color of it to begin with, the best we can do is to avoid overreacting. Tolerating these behaviors, or simply ignoring them, is perhaps the best guarantee that this, too, shall pass.

From Four to Six

By this point we may be victims of patterns that we have inadvertently set in motion. The child who has been labeled finicky from the moment he first picked up his fork may have no choice but to behave this way. Unless we have been willing to meet children halfway in terms of modifying our expectations of what they eat, then conflicts may reach a new pitch as they become more vocal in their food likes and dislikes.

School-age children are becoming aware of their physical appearance, and they are vulnerable to how we, as parents, feel about their bodies, too. One mother describes her reactions to her daughter's body:

"I kept waiting and waiting for Andrea's 'baby fat' to disappear. When she was about five, I realized that it was here to stay. I know that kids can be very mean to each other, and I worry about how she'll feel if she's overweight. I don't want to make her self-conscious, but I do want her to feel good about her body so I try to help her watch what she eats."

No matter how subtle you are, a five-year-old catches on if you are trying to control her weight. A young baby develops his first image of himself from the love and affection that are reflected in a parent's face. This process, known as *mirroring*, continues with older children as well.

Your six-year-old cannot distinguish between your feelings about her body and your feelings about her. Food habits may take a turn for the worse if your child thinks that your love is conditional on how she eats or how she looks. Nevertheless, we can teach children to watch what they eat for the right reason (to be healthy) instead of for the wrong reason (to be thin or attractive).

Sweets are also a big concern, as this mother explains:

"I feel as if I'm being tested at every turn. If I tell Jake that he can have some cookies, he wants to know how many. If I say two, he wants three. Meanwhile, I wish he would eat more fruit, but he seems to have no interest in anything that's healthy."

It is ironic but true that we reward children from an early age with the food we least want them to eat. On a subconscious level some children feel "punished" if they aren't given a sweet dessert. Others, sensing that a mother or father "disapproves" of their weight, may feel compelled to test a parent's love by constantly demanding ice cream or cake.

Finally, as children get older, our concerns over etiquette are another source of stress. It isn't enough now to see that food is being eaten, we would also like to see it consumed with some civility. We just have to keep these expectations age-appropriate and avoid changing them all at once.

Know Your Child:
What Body Type and
Temperament Tell You

Eating habits are highly individual. If you are feeding an only child, this may not be obvious. But if you have two children or more, you notice that their food preferences are as distinctive as their personalities. One mother describes her dilemma:

> *"My kids are like day and night when it comes to eating. My son has always been a finicky eater. He has three or four foods that are acceptable, and that's it. But his younger sister will eat anything. I'm trying to get one to eat more and the other one to eat less. Needless to say, it doesn't make mealtime easy."*

One child will try anything, and the other one acts insulted if you reheat the noodles instead of preparing them fresh. In short, children come to the table with distinct attitudes. The sooner you become attuned to these differences, the less you will find yourself arguing over food.

Studies in Contrast: Ectomorphs, Endomorphs, and Mesomorphs

A fascinating area of study, called *constitutional psychology,* looks at a person's body type for clues to behavior and personality. It is especially helpful for understanding a child's eating habits.

Dr. William H. Sheldon was the first to look systematically at physical build, or *morphology,* in his book *Varieties of Temperament,* which he wrote in 1942. After observing hundreds of men and women, Sheldon came up with three basic types:

The *endomorph* has a rounded, soft body and enjoys food. This is the person who "lives to eat." A hedonist of sorts, the endomorph takes comfort in, well, comfort. A glutton for food, he may also be a glutton for affection, seeking others for consolation when upset or disgruntled.

An endomorphic child is one who will eat without urging, who probably tries new food willingly, tends to be on the high end of a normal weight range (if not slightly over), and climbs into your lap for emotional nourishment or consolation after the two of you have had a fight.

The *ectomorph,* in contrast to the type described above, has a long, angular body and appears more fragile. With a small appetite and a high metabolism, ectomorophs rapidly burn up what little calories they take in. A child with the classic ectomorphic profile can be a challenge. Emotions are not easily or openly expressed. Instead of openly resolving a conflict, this type of child may brood in solitude, behind a closed door.

The *mesomorph* has a hard, square body and is more motivated by physical activity than by food. The mesomorphic child is more inclined to lose himself in some physical activity than to sit and confide in a friend when something is bothering him, and his attitude toward food falls somewhere in the middle of the two types discussed above.

Sheldon makes the point that, temperamentally, most of us are combinations of the above. But if you are alarmed by your children's eating habits, they may lean more heavily toward one type than the other.

You can avoid conflicts over food by attuning yourself to each of your children. But understanding temperament is also helpful for what happens beyond the dinner table. Any "bad habit" will be less daunting if you know your child well. You may still set out to change behavior that is undesirable. But if you see a habit as part of an overall personality, or body type, you will probably find it less offensive and will deal with it more effectively.

A quiet parent with a "mesomorphic" daughter may cringe at the level of noise every time she enters the room. ("She never sits still.") Meanwhile, the parent who learns to appreciate a child's robust, active nature is bound to have an easier time developing a close, loving relationship than the parent who attempts to change behavior that comes naturally to a child.

Again, instead of asking, "Why is this child doing this to me?" parents can accept that each child is simply different, and that many food habits are innate. Some children prefer lunch, for example, and eat a big meal in the middle of the day. If this is the case, then why not allow that child to eat a smaller dinner? Many parents worry about sending a child to school without a big breakfast. But as we all know, some children have no interest in eating as soon as they wake up. If this is the case, pack some crackers for your child to eat en route. Most children are happy to eat when they feel hungry.

Shifting the Focus: Toward Healthy, Nutritious Options

Some experts claim that children, if left on their own, can maintain a healthy, balanced diet. The original research in this area is cited in many guides to early childhood. However, it is usually distorted and can be terribly misleading to parents.

In the early 1900s doctors believed that infants could not digest fruits, vegetables, or meat, and parents were told to wait at least two years before introducing these foods. A pediatrician named Clara Davis set out to prove otherwise. Over a period of at least six months she fed three infants, between six and nine months of age, a steady diet of these solids. At the end of her study Davis wrote that her "adult" diet was a success: "young children could choose their diets and thrive without adult direction as to just what and how much of these foods they should eat."

She also noted, however, that individual meals were "a dietician's nightmare." She observed what any seasoned parent knows: that children's eating patterns are erratic at best. The babies in the study binged on starches at one sitting, only to lean heavily on fruits or vegetables at another. But the food they consumed *over time* was adequately balanced for healthy growth.

Quality Versus Quantity

Davis's work is frequently cited to support a "hands-off" view of feeding children. What we rarely hear about is Davis's own note of warning. She cautioned that her exclusive use of nutritious foods in the infant study constituted a "trick." "Self-selection," she warned, "can have no, or but doubtful, value if the diet must be selected from inferior foods."

Simply put, Davis believed it was the parent's job to provide a balanced and steady diet of nutritious foods. She noted that although the body seems to regulate how much healthy, natural food it takes in, the same mechanism does not appear to exist for what we call junk food today.

When laboratory rats are given free access to a "supermarket diet" (cookies, cheese, sweets, salami, etc.), the animals tend to overeat and some become obese. Although it has never been tested, the same tendency is thought to be true for children and adults. Our role, then, is twofold: to provide nutritious foods in abundance, letting children choose from them freely, and to rely less heavily on foods that are lower in nutritional value.

"Sorry, Kids, We Just Have Fruit"

Cathy Nonas, a nutritionist living in New York, suggests that parents are responsible for many attitudes that children form about food. Often, she says, when a child asks, "What's for dessert?" the answer is an apologetic "Sorry, nothing but fruit." By doing this, we simply increase the power and appeal of sweets.

Nonas urges a balanced approach. For every plate of cookies that you put on the table, be sure there is a bowl of fresh fruit, too. Children will help themselves to both. In her home Nonas has sugary cereals alongside more nutritious brands. The sweet ones are allowed for snacks. But if one of her children eats cereal for dinner, it must be one with some nutritional value.

Research has shown that, in general, the heavier you are (even if this means being at the high end of a normal range), the more susceptible you are to disease. And this, says Nonas, is the best argument for teaching children to choose food sensibly. While buying a granola bar, you and your older child can look at the labels together to see which is lower in fat, and buy frozen yogurt together instead of ice cream.

Keeping Diet Concerns in Perspective

The message we send about body image is disturbing, since it is so confined to looking a certain way. Many mothers make their daughters anxious about eating and dieting, as this parent found:

> *"I guess I didn't realize how much I talk about my weight. Just the other day I heard my seven-year-old daughter complaining that her thighs are too heavy. She told her friend that she was going to go on a diet! I was so taken aback. I realized that that must be what I sound like to her."*

It is distressing to learn that as early as the second grade many girls are unhappy about their appearance. But we all know that children imitate the adults in their lives. It shouldn't surprise us if our children set the same high standards for their appearance that we do.

RED FLAGS

The following are some warning signs with respect to a child's eating habits:

❧ *Sudden changes in growth.* Babies normally go through growth spurts, but your pediatrician will be concerned about a child who shows a sudden drop in growth rate.

❧ *Frequent illness.* According to Dr. Alfasi, some children with allergies may look as if they have colds. If your child is frequently congested (especially if there is a history of allergic reactions in the family), he could be sensitive to a particular food. Allergies to shellfish, berries, lactose, peanuts, and soy are common in young children.

❧ *Extreme food fads.* Nearly all children go through a stage of insisting on peanut butter sandwiches, for example, or noodles. Over the course of a few weeks, however, your child should be eating at least some small quantities of other foods as well. Visit the pediatrician if your child tires easily or seems weak, since there could be a vitamin deficiency or anemia.

❦ *Constant battles over food.* Finally, if you have reached the point where you dread meals, try talking to someone who can help you to relax. A sympathetic friend may be able to put things into perspective, and your pediatrician can reassure you that your child is growing normally. A child will eat if he is hungry, and he will stop when he is full. This is when to stop the meal instead of coaxing a child to keep eating.

A Note on Eating Disorders

When parents talk about eating problems, they often express concerns about *anorexia nervosa* in the same breath. Anorexia is a psychiatric disorder that is characterized by extreme efforts to become thin, bordering on starvation. It mainly affects girls between the age of twelve and twenty, although doctors report that the number of anorexic boys is on the rise.

Hilde Bruch, a professor of psychiatry at the Baylor College of Medicine, wrote *The Golden Cage* based on her experiences counseling seventy anorexic patients. She explains in her book that there is no way to predict who will develop the condition. There are surprisingly few links between early eating habits per se and anorexia. In reconstructing her patients' pasts, however, Dr. Bruch did find disturbing trends with respect to issues of autonomy and control. Many of her patients were described by their parents as "never giving any trouble."

"To please and not give offense had been a basic rule of life," she writes, and this tendency was reinforced by well-meaning parents, who treated any attempts at self-assertion as "disturbances." It is another compelling example that self-assertive behavior is vital for a child's healthy development.

Allow a child who is worried about her body to tell you why she feels unhappy about it. What you say in response may be less important than simply listening and letting the child know that this is a subject that can be discussed.

Avoiding Fights over Food

If You Think Your Child Weighs Too Much . . .

A first step is to distinguish between a real overweight problem and plumpness, and your pediatrician can help you to do this.

With children, it's important to focus on good health, not appearance. Avoid suggesting that your child will "look better" if he loses weight. A child quickly assumes this means that there is something "wrong" with the way he looks now, and your disapproval can be just as devastating as being teased by peers.

Overweight should be presented not just as a question of cosmetics but in terms of what a child's body is able to do. You can explain to your son that he won't be able to run as fast, or that he'll have less energy if he eats food that adds fat to the body.

Focus on forming better eating habits, not "going on a diet." Make it a family project for everyone to begin eating healthier foods, and keep a selection of appetizing, low-fat foods in the house. Cathy Nonas says that the overweight child still needs autonomy. Give one or two cookies if he asks for them, she says, but offer to cut up some fruit or slice some cheese if the child is still hungry and wants to eat more. And enlist the child's help in keeping less fatty foods at home. Sit down together and come up with some low-fat foods that you can buy at the store. (Many food companies today are promoting fat-free versions of popular cookies and snacks.)

By switching to low-fat milk and margarine, and offering frozen yogurt instead of ice cream, you can trim unneeded calories, cholesterol, or fat from a child's diet. Pretzels, for example, contain less fat than potato chips. "Fat is something that all children have to be cautioned about," says Cathy Nonas. She explains that "fat storage" in the body has been found to correlate with certain kinds of disease, so that all of us stand to gain by keeping intake to a minimum.

Small portions are a good idea, too, since people who are overweight may feel more compelled to clean their plate. Finally, avoid using food as a reward in general. You can celebrate good news by going ice-skating together or taking a walk. Besides, a child who grows up active won't put on extra weight. Children need to be taught that exercise is important for good health.

If You Think Your Child Eats Too Little . . .

Other parents worry about a child who is thin:

"My in-laws are always trying to get my son to eat. I've tried explaining to them that he's fine, and that he just has a very small appetite, but they look at me as if I never feed him! What makes it even harder is that they try to coax him into eating by telling him that he can't have dessert until he finishes his dinner—and then they give him these enormous portions of food that he couldn't finish in a whole week."

Children need surprisingly small quantities of food for healthy growth. Parents of a small eater should know that normal gains in weight and height are proof of an adequately balanced diet. Again, your pediatrician can confirm that your child's diet is healthy simply by looking at his rate of growth.

For a small eater large portions are unappetizing and defeating. By contrast, if you give a few pieces of meat, the child may triumphantly ask for more. In general, a small quantity of food usually contains all the nutrients and minimum requirements for a young child.

Small eaters also do better with frequent snacks instead of three big meals. Our pediatrician advised us to let one of our children get up from the table and come back for more a few minutes later. If your child loves pasta for dinner, don't fight it. You can offer some cold cuts and carrot sticks as a mid-afternoon snack.

In general, the less you say, the better. Bribes won't work, but humor might. We used to threaten our younger daughter with mock consternation: "Whatever you do, *don't* eat that meat on your plate!" She could hardly contain her glee at "defying" us each time we turned around and found another bite missing.

And finally, don't give up on trying to offer new foods or assume that something will be unappealing. When green peppers appeared on our table one day, the pickiest eater in our family surprised us all by devouring three slices. (Another unexpected favorite of hers is Japanese seaweed, known as *nori!*)

Ask Yourself:

Do you give as much freedom and autonomy as you possibly can?

We exert tremendous control over what and when a young child eats. As much as possible, though, try to make eating your child's decision. Each time you "announce" a meal, you may diminish its appeal. By contrast, many a toddler will happily join you at the table if he sees you eating, as if children know instinctively that meals should be social. (There is nothing more appealing to a hungry child than the food on *your* plate. I have happily sacrificed many a bagel to a child who turned down one of his own a few minutes before.) Clearly, the decision to eat has to be theirs. Choice can be conferred in many ways, as this father found:

> *"We used to put all the food on my daughter's plate for her, and she never seemed very interested in it. Now that she's a little older and sits at the table with us, we let her serve herself from the big bowls. The first time she did this, she was thrilled. She obviously felt very grown up."*

Children should be given their own cutlery as soon as they grab for the spoon, and, whenever possible, they should be given a few different foods to choose from. You are the one who does the shopping and determines what is available. Beyond this, however, try giving the impression that it is your child who decides what he or she eats.

Do you "editorialize" every time you offer your child food?

It's difficult to serve dinner to a child without some morsel of advice:

> *"Be sure to eat some of the meat."*

> *"Don't just eat the noodles. There's spinach on your plate, too."*

> *"I'm not giving you any dessert tonight until you finish your dinner."*

The result is that young children feel backed into a corner. No one likes being told what to do. If a waitress brought you a plate of food and insisted that you try the potatoes first, you'd be indignant!

Nor should you impose your values about which foods go together and which do not. To a young child this is one big adventure. From his perspective there is no reason why the carrots shouldn't be dipped in the catsup, too.

If you are still skeptical about how parents influence a particular food's appeal, then think about how often young children beg for pizza and ice cream. Have you ever heard of a mother imploring her child to eat one more slice or to finish the scoop in the bowl?

Do you give your children small portions?

Children hate being coaxed into eating, but they happily thrust an empty plate toward you and ask for more. Some grown-ups admit that they find large portions of food unappealing. For children who naturally have small appetites, large quantities of food can be demoralizing, as this parent discovered:

> *"My son was never much of an eater, and I was constantly urging him to eat more. I finally realized that he did better if I gave him just a few pieces of meat and let him ask for seconds. It made him feel good to be able to finish dinner and not think that I was annoyed at him for leaving food on his plate."*

Small children may feel overwhelmed by a plate heaped with food. They know from the start that there is no hope of emptying it, so they don't even try. If a parent is constantly upset about what's left on the plate, a child has no choice but to feel poorly about himself. A child's minimum daily requirements, both in calories and in nutrients, are small. Smaller portions may also prevent an overeater from consuming more than he needs.

Are you willing to find substitutes for foods your child needs but doesn't like?

A child who hates milk may like chocolate milk. Cheese, spinach, and yogurt are other sources of calcium, and so are some of the fruit juices that come in individual boxes. Always assume that there are alternatives to the basic requirements. Your pediatrician can help you find ways to supplement, or substitute, for important nutrients.

Are you respectful of each child's attitudes toward food?

Two mothers recount two different food habits that they found a way to resolve:

> *"My son is a small eater, and he tends to wait too long between meals. He just forgets to eat, and then he acts grouchy. I had to teach him to pay more attention to his body and to take a snack between meals."*

> *"My daugher loves sweets, and she wasn't eating much fresh fruit. I thought about not keeping any cookies in the house, but I also didn't want her to start craving sweets. Instead I explained to her that it's okay to eat cookies once in a while, but that her body also needs things like fruit to be healthy. She was very receptive."*

Instead of fighting with a child and trying to withhold a favorite food, just be sure that there are other appealing, nutritious foods available, too. Don't give up if a child refuses to sample a new food the first or second time you serve it. Research shows that frequent exposure to a wide variety of foods is the best guarantee that a child will eventually try them. Our daughter watched us eat pancakes every weekend for five years before finally asking to taste one.

Do you serve the most nutritious foods at the start of a meal?

Let's face it: given a choice, many children will automatically start with the serving bowl of spaghetti. As we've seen, children do a fair amount of self-regulating of unprocessed foods. But there's nothing wrong with setting out the most nutritious foods first and putting out the pasta a few minutes later. Needless to say, children are hungrier at the start of the meal, and therefore more open to trying new foods.

Are you helping to form many food biases?

If your child's craving for sweets drives you crazy, it shouldn't. Researchers have found that the foods we use to reward young children, such as ice cream and candy, become more "valued" by them. (In one study, the same food was introduced to children either neutrally, appearing in a lunch bag one day, or with some fanfare as a "special treat." The group that was "rewarded" with the food gave it higher marks.)

Ask yourself, Dr. Alfasi says: When was the last time you said to your child, "I'm so proud of you. Let's go out for broccoli!" Many of us imbue sweets with a certain power. In a symbolic way they make a child feel loved and rewarded. And for the rest of our lives many of us turn to sweet foods as a form of consolation, a way of making ourselves feel better.

By the time we become parents, we have also adapted cultural norms about what is appropriately eaten at various meals. Needless to say, these ideas don't make sense to young children, and so we find ourselves arguing about Oreos at seven o'clock in the morning.

The sugar contained in cookies, however, may be less harmful than many of the other "food legacies" we pass on to our children. These include using too much butter and salt, habits that are known contributors to heart disease.

Do you personalize your child's behavior at the table?

In the first chapter I borrowed Michael Lewis's example of how different mothers will interpret a child's refusal of food. One mother described the child as acting willful. A second claimed her child was being aggressive. And a third felt that the child was no longer hungry. Be aware that the way you interpret a child's behavior plays a role in whether or not it continues.

Perhaps you were brought up to empty your plate at every meal. If this is the case, you may expect your children to do the same. But some children have a small appetite and little interest in trying new foods. Getting upset at every meal will turn food into a constant source of stress between you and your child, and these arguments will no doubt spill into other areas.

Do you focus on a balanced *diet* instead of balanced *meals*?

As long as you are making nutritious foods available, you can rely on your children to balance their intake—not at every meal, but over a period of days or weeks.

Leann Birch, a researcher in Urbana, Illinois, has found that while children eat erratically, "daily intake is relatively constant, because children adjust their energy intake at successive meals." In other words, your daughter who eats a small breakfast every day probably compensates with a larger lunch. Your son may wolf down a bowl of pasta at lunch and dinner today, but at another time his body will naturally crave more vegetables and meats. As Clara Davis found, the body is efficient at regulating consumption. The key is to provide nutritious foods for your child to choose from.

Can you stop coaxing your child to eat "one more bite"?

"This bite is for Grandma . . . this one is for Grandpa . . ." The game seems benign enough. But research into early feeding patterns shows that this urging of the child, while it may result in a clean plate, can take a long-term toll on a child's budding autonomy, not to mention his innate sense of how much food his body needs. Children should be taught to eat until they feel full and then to stop. They should not think of eating as a way to secure love and approval.

Are you flexible about what your child eats—and when?

Many children enjoy eating breakfast foods, such as cereal, bagels, and eggs, any time of the day. Instead of fighting this tendency, use it to your advantage. For a child who needs calcium, a bowl of cereal or a bagel spread with cream cheese may be appealing and nutritious, day or night.

One mother describes how she "sneaks" nutritious foods into her children:

> *"I've discovered that I can get a lot of healthy foods into my children when they're busy watching a favorite TV show or video. They're not big on meat and vegetables, so I put together a plate with*

cut-up fruit and cheese. Then if they just want pasta at dinner, I don't worry about it."

A word of caution, though: Don't overdo the food-TV connection. This is a common pattern of behavior in adults who are seriously overweight. "You will never see an obese person who doesn't eat while doing something else," warns Dr. Alfasi.

Do you try to make mealtime enjoyable?

Focus on making meals social and free of stress. In our family we often take turns telling one another the best thing and the worst thing that happened to each of us that day. Some families swear by a schedule of dinner "themes" to keep meals enjoyable:

> *"In our house, Monday is picnic night. We spread a blanket on the floor and have cold salads and finger foods. Tuesday night is 'barbecue' night, a fancy name for hamburgers and hot dogs that get cooked on the stove anyway. We celebrate the end of the week with Friday night at the movies. It's the only time the kids are allowed to eat in front of the TV, so it's a real treat."*

The mother quoted above mentioned that these "themes" also eliminate a lot of the meal planning that can be tedious for busy parents.

Do you get through dinner with no problems, only to argue over dessert? One family solved this problem by introducing an "ice cream night." Knowing that they could count on sundaes every Wednesday, the children stopped begging for sweet desserts the rest of the week.

Have you given your children some say in planning what's for dinner?

Obviously, you can not always do this. But if you are choosing between chicken and hamburgers anyway, why not let your children decide? When the choice is theirs, children are much more inclined to eat what's on their plate. When I asked our pediatrician about my daughter's waning appetite one day, she said, "Sometimes we feel like eating steak and sometimes we just want a salad." Her comment made me realize that children shouldn't always be expected to eat the same foods with the same gusto.

When possible, do you let your child help in preparing meals?

Bob Sloane, a caterer and the author of *Dad's Own Cookbook,* says that children are more enthusiastic about sampling food that they have helped to prepare. If nothing else, they're more curious about the final product, and this makes them more open-minded. You can use this to your advantage—and get some needed help in the kitchen at the same time.

Have you made others sensitive to your child's food habits?

Tell your baby-sitter not to force or urge your children to eat, and insist on small portions of food. Grandparents should also be aware of your feelings and those of your children. A grandmother may ooh and aah about how much of her homemade meat loaf your older child ate, without realizing that your younger child, who can't stomach the stuff, feels like a disappointment.

Do you expect your children to sit at the table for long periods?

Young children are fidgety, and they cannot sit still for long. You may have to be satisfied with five minutes of good behavior at the table until they're older. In the meantime, don't create problems by asking them to do the impossible.

As for table manners, you can begin by asking them to monitor your own. "Will you help me remember to keep my elbows off the table? Sometimes I forget." This is a nice, neutral way to introduce the idea of etiquette. (Just make it clear that other adults are not to be corrected! It can be awkward when your five-year-old tells your boss not to chew with his mouth open.)

Have you lost your sense of humor?

Goldie Alfasi laughs when she recalls a game called Sharks that her family played at dinner when her children were small. Her sons would sit under the table, where she and her husband passed food along to them. In general, a relaxed attitude is the key to keeping food free of conflict.

When etiquette reached a new low in our home, I drew inspiration from a Walt Disney movie and made a "Beauty and the Beast" chart. Our children laughed at the thought of "earning" a star in the Beast column—but at least they got the message and made an effort to improve their table manners.

When Less Is More

This applies not only to the portions we serve but to the amount of time we spend preparing. Children can be fed simply and healthfully. One secret is this: The less we fuss over what we prepare for them, the less we tend to fight over it. Carrots are a case in point: most children find a raw one appealing. A cooked carrot, however, is something that you can't give away in many homes. Children like crunchy foods, and this applies to vegetables, too. And ironically, the more we cook vegetables, the less nutrients remain. I usually put a few raw carrot sticks on my children's plates. I have yet to find an acceptable way of cooking them.

Arguing over broccoli and peas, we forget that eating is something children like to do. As parents we need to focus more on which foods we make available so that children naturally grow accustomed to a healthy, low-fat, balanced bill of fare. Only then can we give them both the freedom to eat as they choose, and the opportunity to form food habits that will serve them well.

CHAPTER TEN

Miss Jennifer Honey was a mild and quiet person who never raised her voice and was seldom seen to smile, but there is no doubt she possessed that rare gift for being adored by every small child under her care. She seemed to understand totally the bewilderment and fear that so often overwhelms young children who for the first time in their lives are herded into a classroom and told to obey orders. Some curious warmth that was almost tangible shone out of Miss Honey's face when she spoke to a confused and homesick newcomer to the class.

Miss Trunchbull, the Headmistress, was something else altogether. She was a gigantic holy terror, a fierce tyrannical monster who frightened the life out of the pupils and teachers alike. There was an aura of menace about her, even at a distance.

from *Matilda* by Roald Dahl

School-Related Problems and Stress

While driving the carpool one morning, I asked whether any of the girls had been to a square dance at their school the previous weekend. One of them, a kindergartener, told me she had gone, but that she hadn't enjoyed it. "The dances were too hard, and I couldn't do them," she explained thoughtfully, "so I had to get my stomach ached and go home."

I could find no better example that for every school-related incident we fret over as parents—for every tear at separation and for every sudden, suspicious stomachache—a child's ego and self-respect are on the line.

Education is so important to us, it is easy to panic at the first sign of a problem at school:

"My daugher is three and she started nursery school a few weeks ago, but she still cries when I try to say good-bye. I'm the only mother who has to stay in the room, and I'm a little embarrassed about it. I can't help thinking that Ilana's not as secure as the other boys and girls."

"Meredith is in kindergarten, and she gets a lot of stomachaches, especially on Monday mornings. I think it's a very academic program for five-year-olds, and she's concerned about doing well because she likes the teacher so much. As a parent, though, I'm torn. I'm glad

that she wants to do well, but it kills me to see a five-year-old under so much pressure already."

"Joseph is six, and he constantly forgets either his lunch or his homework. I want to be sympathetic, but I'm tired of making the extra trip to school each time he forgets something. I'm beginning to think he's completely irresponsible. The worse thing is I find myself getting annoyed with him over little things now, too."

These are the incidents that make us wonder, *If she can't remember her homework now, how will she ever cope with college!* We worry that if we are too accepting of these early travails—if we "let him off easy" now—then we will make the child even more irresponsible later.

But many issues that arise in school are reminders that children are, at heart, insecure, vulnerable, and terribly concerned about pleasing us. And it is in this spirit of understanding that we can handle school-related stress sensibly and well.

Don't Be Surprised If . . .

Parents may fret over a long list of problems with their school-age children. This chapter covers the following:

- ❦ Crying at separation
- ❦ Reluctance to go to school
- ❦ The transition to kindergarten
- ❦ Nervous habits and hypochondria
- ❦ Reading readiness
- ❦ Perfectionism
- ❦ "Sloppy" homework habits
- ❦ Aggressive behavior

It would be foolish simply to dismiss these problems as "normal" and therefore of little consequence. They are important issues and they can soon affect a parent's relationship with a child. No one enjoys feeling taunted by a child who insists "I'm *not* going to school today!" But if we try to understand where these reactions come from—and why they are, in fact, so common—we can handle them in a way that strengthens a child instead of estranging him from us or from school.

Learning, like eating, can be fun for a young child, or it can be forced, becoming a constant source of friction between parents and children. This chapter is about having expectations that make it possible for children to enjoy going to school and to get the most out of it.

In the Normal Course of Development

Two to Four Years

To be capable of having a happy school experience, a child must be able to tolerate being away from the mother. Many educators believe that a child should be at least two and a half years old before starting school, but this does not guarantee that he is ready. No matter how bright or precocious your child, it is important to look at his emotional maturity (what is referred to below as "behavior age") as opposed to birthday age.

Experts explain that, before starting school, children must have reached the stage known as *object constancy.* In other words, they must understand that even when people and objects are out of view, they do not cease to exist. Otherwise a child may fear that the absent mother has vanished forever, so his distress on separating from her is legitimate. Anna Freud observed that if this is the case, there is nothing that even the most skilled, sensitive parent or teacher can do to console the child.

Even if a child is ready or "mature," however, separation must be done gradually. The mother and child should be apart for small periods of time at first (with the mother close at hand), and the child should be allowed to see the mother if he wishes. The experience of separation is then neither hurried nor forced. And for the child it is neither taxing nor traumatic.

Even among children who are "ready" to separate, reactions will vary. Like the mother quoted at the beginning of this chapter, many parents worry that a child who separates slowly is insecure. But this may not be the case. Teachers point out that some children quickly see that being at school means *not* being with Mommy, and this can make separation more stressful. It may take days or weeks for another child to arrive at the same conclusion, and he may suffer a delayed distress as a result.

Between the ages of two and four, children are just learning to get along with others and to see their peers as playmates, but they are still highly narcissistic. Preschoolers are especially susceptible to fatigue, and the more tired they feel, the more difficult it is for them to resist grabbing a toy from someone else, for instance, or hitting a classmate during a squabble.

Aggressive behavior in the classroom is often related to events at home. A common stressor for young children is the birth of a new sibling; others include marital conflict, divorce, moving, or talk of a new school.

Four to Six Years

From four to six, children make two important transitions: from preschool to kindergarten, and from kindergarten to first grade. Anytime a child attends a new school, parents should expect some anxious behavior or acting out. Some children will revert to egocentric or "babyish" behavior, such as clinging, at the start of school each year.

In first grade many six-year-olds begin doing homework. It helps to see this as another transition in your child's life. After years of urging our children to *play well with others,* now we expect them to *work alone.* Some children will handle the solitude required to do homework more easily than others, but there are ways (discussed at the end of this chapter) to keep homework from becoming a source of friction.

You may also be concerned about stomachaches and "nervous habits." Some may be as benign as twirling hair while doing homework or biting on the end of a pencil. But what about nail biting or twitches? It is almost a knee-jerk reaction for parents to assume that school pressures are too high. What I have tried to show in this chapter, however, is that parents play a role in *interpreting* school for the child. In other words, what a child expects of himself at school has a great deal to do with the values and expectations that we convey to our children at home. Unresolved issues and significant events at home will also find an outlet in behavior at school.

Going Public: Emotional Issues for Parents

"We talk about a *child* going to school," says Francesca Schwartz, a child and adolescent analyst in New York, "but really the *family* goes to school." She notes that the start of school "reorganizes" the family in a new way, with parents relinquishing some of their control over the child.

Some parents resent the influence of teachers and administrators. No one else had to know whether a child still sucked his thumb at night or wet the bed. But school problems take us public, so to speak, and some parents feel unsettled by the change. One parent describes her reactions to conferences with her children's teachers:

> *"I used to find conferences very uncomfortable. I almost felt as if I was back at school. I guess I thought I was being 'judged' on the basis of my son's performance."*

Keep in mind that you continue to have a profound influence on your children long after they begin attending school. Your love and support will play a key role in helping them cope with the pressure of making friends, getting along with teachers, and fitting in happily.

Ready or Not, Here We Come:
"Behavior Age" Versus "Birthday Age"

Dr. Louise Bates Ames and Dr. Frances L. Ilg, of the Gesell Institute of Human Development, contend that half of all school-related problems and failures could be prevented if we looked at a child's emotional readiness. This mother found out the hard way that "behavior age" is important:

> *"Perri turned two in June, and I was so excited about signing her up for preschool the following fall. She was going to be the youngest in the group, but I knew she was very intelligent and convinced the school that she would be fine. I expected her to have trouble separating for the first few days, but it went on for weeks and weeks. She just*

wasn't able to handle it or enjoy school at all. I finally took her out of the program and decided to wait. When we went back a year later, I couldn't believe the difference. This time Perri was obviously ready, and she loved going to school."

Some parents think that starting school will help an immature child:

"Henry was two and a half and he still had problems playing with other children in the park. He would take their toys and get angry when they wanted them back. I thought that school would be a good place for him to learn these things, but the additional rules of the classroom seemed to make him even more frustrated."

While it is true that children hone their social skills at school, this is not where they first learn them. It is like a couple deciding to have a child to save an unhappy marriage: it simply doesn't work. Similarly, an immature child will have problems with some of the basic tasks that are a part of school life: separating from parents, handling transitions from one activity to the next, sharing materials, working independently, and at other times conforming to the needs of a group.

For the child who is beginning to do these things at home, the positive reactions of a teacher enhance self-esteem. But for the child who cannot, school begins as a series of reprimands and negative interactions: with the teachers, with the other children, and eventually, with parents, who feel disappointed or even dismayed by their child's behavior. The only real "failure," however, may be a failure to wait until it makes sense to begin school.

Surely, the pressure felt by a family when both parents work has also helped push children into programs they aren't ready for:

"I work full-time, and I couldn't wait for Lauren to start kindergarten because it would be so much easier in terms of child care."

A young child's earliest school habits and attitudes are important clues. If Lauren, above, has had no problems separating and has always been happy in class, she may well be ready for a full day.

But what if Lauren is very small for her age, or she often gets sent home with stomachaches? If this is the case, a full day may be too much too soon.

"Mommy, Please Don't Leave Me!": Saying Good-bye at School

This mother poignantly recalls how her son's first school days affected her as a parent:

"I never expected to react so emotionally the first time I took Austin to school. I was excited, of course, but I really choked up watching him in the room with the other children. Here was my baby starting preschool! All of a sudden I realized how quickly these years go by."

But just as we cannot predict our own feelings, we have no way of knowing how our children will respond. This parent was pleasantly surprised:

"Mark is our first child, and I worried for weeks about whether he would cry when I left the classroom. The first day arrived, and he walked into the room without even looking back. I guess he was just ready for it."

But for every "Mark," there is a child who cannot easily let go, and a mother who worries that her son or daughter will never say good-bye without tears:

"Lisa is five now and she loves school, but I was always the last mother in the room. I remember worrying about it a lot. I wondered why my kid was the only one who started to cry, and whether I had done something terribly wrong. Her school was wonderful and kept reassuring me that her reaction was not unusual."

Attitudes toward separation are as individual and impossible to predict as when a child's first tooth will fall out. Each child is different, and so is each relationship between parent and child. Your older daughter may say good-bye on the first day of school, but her younger sister may insist on being held.

Starting school may be easier for a child with an older brother or sister. It's exciting to join the big kids and to have a schoolroom of one's own. But for many children the things we say to make them eager and excited may make them nervous instead. Parents naturally want to be supportive of a child's first school experiences, but even our positive comments no doubt put pressure on a young child:

"You're getting so big now. Soon you'll be starting SCHOOL."

"Oh, look! There's Jennifer. She goes to the same SCHOOL that you'll be going to."

"No, don't wear that dress! We're saving it for the first day of SCHOOL."

Children get the message that this "school" thing—whatever it is—is important, and they begin to worry: *What if it's a scary place? What if they're mean? What if I don't like it?* A more natural, concrete way to introduce the idea of school might be to read a story about children who go to school, or simply to pass by the building and casually point it out one day. At least it becomes a concrete place in the child's mind— like the store or the bank—instead of something unknown and unimaginable, like those monsters in the closet.

Ambivalence About "Letting Go"

If your child does have trouble separating, it's normal to be concerned, especially if this is your first child. It may help to bear in mind that ambivalent feelings arise from all that is right in the parent-child relationship: the closeness, comfort, and trust that you have provided all along.

Anna Freud was one of the first to look carefully at how young children feel when separated from their mothers. Freud wrote that separation is a transition for a young child. And like any skill, it requires time and practice. It should be neither a contest of wills nor a contest of speed. Like all transitions it simply takes time, as this mother found:

"I was very worried at first that I would only make things harder for my daughter by being overly sympathetic. But her teacher wanted

me to stay inside the room or just outside the door until Emma had really gotten to know the teachers well. Looking back, I can see how important it was to give her the extra security early on. At the time it seemed as if it took an eternity, but really it was just a matter of weeks before she felt completely comfortable."

You can help most by staying calm. If you act tense or comment on it to every other mother you know, you will only add to your child's anxiety, turning a normal reaction into an extreme one. When your child looks at your face, he wants to know whether you're anxious or angry—or whether you have faith that he can do it. If you relax, so will he. Your bright three-year-old may be slow to separate because his mind is reeling with all of the things that might happen to him when Mommy isn't there. As he comes to know and trust the teachers, though, he will feel more comfortable saying good-bye.

A child may also be reluctant to let go of you if there are younger siblings at home. School may be fun, but many big brothers and sisters feel they still get the short end of the stick. After a torturous first few weeks, one two-year-old finally confessed that she didn't want Mommy to go home and play with the baby.

These problems are normal, but they should never be dismissed or ridiculed. Avoid statements such as "You're being silly, sweetheart," or "Be a big girl now and give Mommy a kiss good-bye." They are only going to make your child feel worse. "Comments like these tell a child that you aren't listening," says Marcia Wishnick, a pediatrician with the Medical Center of New York University. "And if you aren't listening to me, how are you going to help me?" Nothing buttresses a child's fear more than to belittle it.

Neither should separation anxiety become the subject of every conversation, with your child or with anyone else. What starts as a legitimate fear can become a way of manipulating a parent's behavior, or getting your attention.

How can you know whether a problem with separation is normal or not? Your child's behavior after you've left the room says a lot. The expression on my oldest child's face always tugged at me when I said good-bye. But once I was gone, the teachers said, she participated fully. For her, then, it was a matter of easing the transition from being with me to being in school.

Helping Your Child to Say Good-bye

There are things you can do to make saying good-bye easier:

❧ *Accept your child's temperament.* By nature some children warm up slowly to a new place or experience. They may be more sensitive to transitions than other children. Give a cautious child extra support if she asks for it, whether it means accompanying her on playdates or staying with her at parties when the other mothers are dropping off their children.

❧ *Get to school early.* This is easier said than done. In our family just getting anywhere on time is a challenge; arriving early is a minor miracle. But it may help your child to be one of the first in the room as opposed to being the last to join in the activities. (Imagine how you feel entering the front of a hall after the speaker has begun a lecture, and you'll understand how your child feels about getting to school late.)

❧ *Enlist the teacher's help.* Take your child over to one of the teachers just before you say good-bye. Being with another adult is reassuring for an anxious child. A teacher who knows your child well can guide him or her to a favorite activity or playmate.

❧ *Offer to stay a few minutes—but set a limit.* Agree to stay a little while, until your child feels secure, but don't wait for your child to say it is okay for you to leave. It may not happen. Besides, the longer you stay, the harder it may be for your child to see you go. Many nursery schools begin with a circle time, so this may be a perfect time to say good-bye.

❧ *Talk openly about your child's feelings.* It is important for you and your child to talk openly, but *be careful about what you say to others.* Your child may overhear you on the phone, lamenting that morning's drop-off: *"Jessica made a scene again at school today. She's impossible. It's really embarrassing to have the only kid who acts this way."* This can be devastating to an already anxious child. It certainly won't make saying good-bye the next day any easier.

You can build a child's confidence by being sympathetic. Try discussing it later in the day (*not* on the way to school), when you have a quiet moment together: *"You seem to feel sad when Mommy has to leave the room."* If you really listen, you may find that there is a specific reason for your child's fears:

> *"My daughter had just finished toilet training but still liked to have company in the bathroom. She didn't know that the teachers would help her, and it turned out that's why she was so worried about my leaving."*

Another child may need to be reassured that you or your baby-sitter will be on time to pick her up, or that the school knows where to reach you if there is ever a problem. A child with allergies, for example, should be aware that the teachers know what to do in case of a severe reaction.

"I Don't Want to Go to School Today!": Understanding School Reluctance

School reluctance may be as benign as a child wanting to stay home because Grandma is visiting, or it can take the form of heart-wrenching battles five days a week:

> *"I try not to make a big deal about going to school, but my daughter just turned three and she gives me an incredibly hard time about getting ready to leave in the morning. I start out very calm and patient, but I usually end up screaming at her because we're so late by the time we leave the house."*

> *"Every Sunday night it's the same thing. Charles begins to complain about a stomachache. He's fine all weekend, but by Monday*

morning he feels sick as a dog. Our pediatrician says that I should just make him go to school, but that's easier said than done. Besides, the poor kid is really in pain."

"I finally noticed that Jocelyn was developing a mysterious illness every Tuesday. Three weeks in a row she either stayed home sick or got sent home by the school nurse. I finally learned that she had gym on Tuesday afternoons and hated it."

Some experts take a hard stand. Unless a child is ill, fever and all, he or she should attend school. If there is anxiety about going, then being away from school will only add to it.

Others are more moderate. If a child is worried about going to school, they reason, then the anxiety is valid. Just as it helps to take a child's fear of the dark seriously, a parent should be sensitive to school-related angst, and judge each situation individually. Different children have different reasons for wanting to miss school. The first thing to do as a parent is to figure out why *your* child would rather stay at home.

Is Something Bothering You?

Regardless of a child's age, there is usually a specific reason for school reluctance. With a preschooler it may coincide with the start of toilet training or the arrival of a new baby. If this is the case, then you can reassure older children that they aren't "missing anything" at home. An older child may not feel comfortable with a new teacher. A sympathetic ear, along with reassuring words, can help: *"Your new teacher doesn't smile a lot, and that's important to you, isn't it?"* Or for a child who pines for last year's teacher: *"I see how much you miss Mrs. Jacobs, but she was very strict at first, too, remember? It took weeks before you felt really comfortable in her classroom."*

Anytime your child resists going to school, assume that there is a good reason. Ask what you would ask a friend or a spouse who misses work and calls in sick: "Is something bothering you?"

Early Issues of Control

With a very young child parents must decide whether the goal is to miss school or simply to flex some muscle. As we saw in Chapter 6, mornings are rarely free of stress with young children. But you may add to the problem by acting as if school is optional.

"Are you ready to get dressed for school now?" *"Would you like to see your teacher today?"* These are questions, not comments, and they give your child the idea that he has a choice. It sends a different message to state, "Marcia is waiting to see you today. Let's get ready to go." And assuming that school is enjoyable for your child (after all, preschool should be fun), your toddler should look forward to going.

Try to act as you would if there were no milk in the house and you had to go to the store. In other words, approach getting ready in the morning as something that has to be done. Act as if you *expect* to get dressed and out the door.

When we overreact to a reluctant child, he can become even more determined to stay home. And for the next twenty-four hours we dread reliving the scene the following day. If protests arise, it can be more effective simply to repeat what the child has said. This is a conversation my husband had with our younger daughter one morning, shortly after she turned five:

> *"Daddy, I'm not going to school today."*
> *"You're not going to school today?"*
> *"No, I'm not. I'm staying home."*
> *"Oh, I see."*
> *"I'm not going to school, and I'm not taking the bus home."*
> *"Really? I thought you liked taking the bus home."*
> *"Yesterday the boys were mean to me. They kept teasing me, and I felt embarrassed."*
> *"That must have felt terrible."*
> *"It did."*
> *"You know, they have rules about teasing on the bus. Maybe those boys didn't know there was a rule. What if we talked to the teacher in charge of the bus and asked her to have a talk with the boys?"*
> *"Okay."*

Humor also helps, especially if you're pretty sure that your child is testing you:

> *"You're not going to school today? Well, I am. And I'm going to play with that big red truck in the corner."*
> *"You can't, Mommy! You're too big. That's for me to play with."*
> *"It is? Well, then, you'd better finish getting dressed so you can play with it today. Otherwise I'm going to play with it!"*

The Transition to Kindergarten

The start of kindergarten can be taxing for young children and their families. Where nursery school is intimate and protective, kindergarten classes are usually bigger, giving way to a more rough-and-tumble atmosphere. "Playground prowess" is important to children this age. More than we realize, egos become enmeshed in how many parallel bars can be conquered or one's agility on the rings. (Some grown women confess that they still look back enviously at the girl who effortlessly did a split in grade school.)

One mother recalls how upsetting it was to watch her daughter struggle with the "social" pressures of being in kindergarten:

> *"When Lindsay used to come off the school bus, I could see that she had been crying. It finally came out that she had trouble finding other girls to play with outside, during recess. It was very painful for me as a parent. Lindsay and I talked about it, but it was something she eventually learned to handle by herself."*

Some children show typical signs of regression when adjusting to a new class or school. A five-year-old may have trouble sleeping at night or resume sucking her thumb. Others may cling more during the day. Sometimes younger siblings bear the brunt of a bad day at school, as this mother found:

> *"My son usually came home from school in a good mood. But one day, he came off the bus like a different person. He was cruel to*

his younger brother, and he started yelling at both of us. I couldn't
take it anymore. In desperation I finally said, 'What happened at
school today?' He started sobbing. It turned out that he had forgotten
to bring his library book from home, so he hid while the rest of the
class went to return their books. He felt terribly guilty about it
afterward."

Imagine for a moment the range of emotions her son had endured: fear of letting down his teacher by forgetting his book, anxiety over perhaps being "punished," fear of being found out while hiding, and ultimately guilt over doing something that he knew he shouldn't have done. What a relief it was for him to talk about it!

For the mother the incident was also a clue to her son's high expectations of himself. And for all of us it is a reminder that children take to heart their new responsibilities and that they worry about measuring up and making mistakes.

Nervous Habits

School-age children soon learn that they are being evaluated by teachers and friends, and these pressures weigh on them. Many develop nervous habits that help them to cope, and parents can't help wondering whether these are normal or not. An older child may start twirling her hair or biting on the end of a pencil. One of our children began cracking her knuckles just before the start of kindergarten, and she still does this when she is nervous.

"It's very good for children to be able to comfort themselves," says psychologist Francesca Schwartz. Still, she says, parents need to consider whether a given habit is *compulsive* or not, and whether the child can control it. Ask your child's teacher if the habit is interfering with schoolwork or whether it is distracting to other children. Your daughter's humming may not bother you, but if other children are put off by it, you may want to intervene. You can begin with a small reward each time your daughter forgoes a nervous habit. Start with a short period of time, say, fifteen minutes, and gradually build up to a longer one.

In general, parents should also look for patterns to these nervous habits. "I noticed you were biting your nails a lot this morning. Were you worried about something?" Talking about anxiety is an effective way of relieving it. (A word of caution, however: Even if you are convinced that your child is nervous about the weekly spelling quiz, be careful not to interpret the anxiety for your child. It is a better idea to let children tell you what event, if any, is making them nervous.) Some experts believe that a habit such as nail biting should be curbed early. Most adult nail biters wish they had stopped as children. Your dentist or pediatrician may have a specific plan to recommend.

Understanding Hypochondria: Real Pressure, Real Pain

The term *hypochondria* is frequently used but rarely understood. This can be seen in the way we react to a child's complaints, as if the pain or discomfort is imagined.

But the expression is derived from the word *hypochondrium,* a region of the abdomen just below the ribs. A person who feels upset may unconsciously tense the stomach muscles, and this can cause nausea or stomach pain. It is important for us to understand this as parents. Often we sense that a sudden stomachache is an excuse, and it is tempting to dismiss it. When we realize that a child's pain or discomfort is as real as the anxiety the child feels, we may handle the situation with more patience and sensitivity. Parents should always try to find out what a child is really worried about.

When Do Children Learn to Read? When They're Ready

The issue of early education is rife with paradox. Research has consistently shown, for example, that children who learn to read later have fewer reading problems. Yet reading is being pushed earlier and earlier.

No one has challenged this trend more eloquently than David Elkind, a professor at Tufts University and the author of *Miseducation* and *The Hurried Child.* According to Elkind, today's preschool curriculum is yesterday's kindergarten, and today's kindergarten is yesterday's first grade.

Some children are ready to read at the age of five, but many others are not. And it is the latter who are at risk today when parents and teachers push academics for which children simply aren't ready.

Some children take their first step at eleven months; others begin walking halfway through the second year. Twelve months later, however, you cannot tell the early walkers from the late ones, and the same can be said of reading. By the end of the third grade, no matter when each child learned to sound out words (and assuming roughly equivalent abilities), most children will be reading at the same level.

There is a disturbing catch-22 occurring in early education today: To please the parents, the schools push early academics that do not benefit their students. The result is to raise the expectations of parents in a way that puts young children at a greater risk of failing.

In *The Hurried Child* Elkind describes a group of first-graders who began a rigorous reading program at age four or five. Elkind confesses that he is impressed by their fluency and ease. However, he continues, when the children read aloud to him individually, he is struck by the quietness of their voices. He writes:

> They were not reading aloud but whispering, so that I had to strain to hear. Although they had learned a skill, it had been at great cost, and I interpreted their low voices as a sign of embarrassment and fear. They experienced no pleasure in reading aloud or in my praise or approval of what they were doing. It almost seemed as if reading had been foisted upon them, at great cost in time and effort, without their having any real understanding of the value of what they were learning. They showed the apathy and withdrawal that are frequent among children who are pushed too hard academically.

Is it nonsense, then, when parents point to a four-year-old and claim that she "taught herself to read"? No. Some children, especially those with above-average visual memory, are ready to learn, and they begin recognizing words early. Your son may start pointing to words and asking you to read them, and then he will recognize the same word on a street sign or in a storybook. But there is no point in rushing a child who isn't ready. You will only make him anxious, and this could get in the way of a relaxed attitude toward learning to read later.

Perfectionism

Some parents wish their children cared more about school work. Others think their children care too much:

"Liza is only seven, but I'm beginning to see that she's very concerned about whether her work is all right. I know that kids that age don't like to make mistakes, but she really wants to be sure that everything is perfect, and that concerns me."

In her role as a school psychologist, Francesca Schwartz is often asked about perfectionism. Parents speak of children who are overly critical of themselves and too concerned about performance. Dr. Schwartz's first suggestion is that parents take an honest look at themselves. "With matters like these," she says, "the apple doesn't fall far from the tree." Temperament plays a role, of course, but our attitudes and expectations tend to influence and modify the child's.

Some childhood experts claim that firstborns typically set high standards for themselves. Even if siblings arrive later, firstborn children model themselves after their parents. They expect to be able to do things as competently as grown-ups, and get frustrated when they cannot.

But we convey high standards in other, subtle ways as well. One parent told me that if her daughter hadn't been accepted to a certain private school, she and her husband planned to move out of the city. I can understand a parent being concerned about a child's schooling and wanting to find a good fit. But a statement like this is extreme, and it is this kind of thinking on a parent's part early on (even if it is never explicitly stated to the child) that must create in the child a need to excel for fear of disappointing the parents.

It is tempting to blame a school for putting on pressure too soon. But children look to us to interpret these expectations. They take cues from the way we behave and from our expectations of ourselves. If you set high standards for yourself and tend to be unforgiving of your own mistakes, your child may do the same.

One mother tried to discuss this tendency openly with her son:

"I can see that Scott is a lot like me. He's a real perfectionist. I've talked to him about how hard I am on myself, and I try to

encourage him not to fall into that trap because I know how unhappy it's made me feel at times."

It may help to point out your own mistakes and to show your child that you can accept your imperfections without feeling defeated.

Whose Homework Is It, Anyway?

You may be told by the teachers that homework is "your child's responsibility," or you may be asked to play an active role. Either way, it brings you, your child, and the school into a new web of responsibility.

Try not to become too involved, though. The real purpose of homework is for a child to learn to work alone, and this will not happen if you take over. You can help most by establishing a time and place for your child to work uninterrupted. But as Haim Ginott suggests, homework should be between your child and his teacher. If you worry that your child isn't taking it seriously, then speak to the teacher about what's expected before you start criticizing your child. (If a teacher fails to collect homework, the children in her class will not feel accountable for doing it.) But try not to allow homework to become another battleground between you and your child.

One educator told me that parents focus too much on *product* as opposed to *process* when it comes to homework. Checking to see how many answers are correct, for example, is to focus on the product. Here are comments that show you care about the process:

❧ "I see you worked out all the answers in the margins. That must have taken a lot of time."

❧ "It looks like that fourth problem was much harder than the others, but you stuck with it. That's great."

❧ "You remembered to put your name on both pieces of paper. Mrs. Johnson will appreciate that."

There are very few perfect solutions in life. Children should know that how they approach an assignment is as important as getting the "right" answer. We can apply the *process of learning* to solving many kinds of problems; an "answer" is specific to only one.

Avoiding the "Earlier Is Better" Trap

One of the catchwords of parents today is *exposure*. Here are some comments that may sound familiar:

"I never learned to play an instrument when I was a child, and I've always regretted it. I want to expose my son to music early so that he won't miss out on it, too."

"I've read that children who are exposed to a second language have a real advantage. I remember how I struggled just to pass French in junior high school."

"My daughter is three, and she loves when I read to her. I thought I would start teaching her to read before she starts kindergarten. I know that a lot of children start to read early now, and I don't want her to feel insecure about being the only one who can't."

None of these parents is doing anything inherently wrong. But each comment belies a subtle misunderstanding of what motivates a child to learn and how often the price of "exposure" is a child's true enjoyment of learning.

The Extracurricular "Edge"

David Elkind, quoted earlier, traces this "earlier is better" mentality to the 1960s. At that time studies showed that underprivileged children who were enrolled in early-education programs did just as well in school as their affluent counterparts. The idea that early experience and "competence" were linked became known as the competent-child theory, and it led to the Head Start program.

A decade later, women began entering the workforce in record numbers, and family life changed. Elkind's theory may be controversial (it is not what a lot of mothers want to hear), but he believes that the "competent child" theory was subtly reinterpreted to fit the new needs of parents, especially mothers who were coping for the first time with the demands of family and career.

Elkind suggests that the term *Head Start* was an unfortunate one. In a short period of time the notion behind the program (that early exposure would help the disadvantaged child to do better) was used as proof that all children would benefit from early exposure to formal learning. Piaget's insistence that children can learn certain things only at certain stages was pushed aside in favor of a new notion: that since children could be taught so much at an early age, it was practically a disservice not to do so.

As parents we should be honest with ourselves about what is in the child's best interest. There is nothing wrong with planning activities that are appropriate and enjoyable for our children. But we should also give young children time that is unstructured and unhurried. It is "idle time" and contemplation that give rise to a child's creativity, and we need to value these experiences, too.

From Play to Work:
How Young Children Learn—and How
They Do Not

For young children, learning takes place on many levels. Here is one father's reactions to his daughter's new private school:

> *"My wife and I went to observe my daughter's kindergarten class recently, and all they did was play. We're spending so much to send her to this school—I guess I thought there would be more to show for it. I can't help wondering what she's really learning."*

If you have had a similar experience, then consider yourself lucky. A so-called "nonacademic" kindergarten is rare these days.

The tradition of kindergarten (whose literal translation is "children's garden") was one of unstructured play and exploration. In Chapter 7, about aggression, play was seen as a catharsis for a child's complex feelings. In the context of school, educator David Elkind explains, play is "the child's major defense against the feeling of helplessness." Through play a child conquers his foes (real and imaginary) and transforms the world into a place where he feels safe. This process is the development of *competence*. And without it, despite other signs of intelligence, a child cannot begin to tackle formal learning.

Parents today want to give their children an early "edge," Elkind observes. Our own parents, by contrast, saw themselves as providing an *opportunity* for learning. A nursery school mother asked the following question at a panel discussion I attended:

> *"I'm concerned about my daughter. She's three and a half and very bright, but I notice she doesn't want to finish a page in a workbook. Should I insist that she do it so that she learns to finish what she starts, or should I just back off? I know she could do it if she really tried, so I'm always tempted to make her finish."*

The real question, as one of the panelists quickly pointed out, is why a three-year-old is being given workbook pages at all! The more we look to these superficial signs of learning, the less we seem to value what children learn from simply being at home with an adult who is responsive and accepting.

There is a great deal of experience that must precede a child's learning to read or having the confidence to appear in a school play. The activities of playing at home and simple outings to the store or to a friend's house are more than adequate. "Intellectual curiosity is a psychological achievement," says Dr. Francesca Schwartz. "It means a child feels safe enough to wonder—and to *wander*—outside his natural environment."

To Quit or Not to Quit: Setting a Bad Precedent?

Most of us have found ourselves in this situation:

"Hannah is four and she started taking ballet lessons last month. At first she was thrilled, but by the third or fourth lesson, she didn't really want to go. This week she started to cry when I took out her leotard. I'm afraid that if I let her stop, she'll always be a quitter."

By being attentive to a child's interests, we can probably keep these experiences to a minimum. Many mothers envision ballet lessons the moment they give birth to a little girl. But again, the best reason for signing up for a class is that your child shows an interest in it. Children know themselves better than we think. Your active, robust five-year-old may be better suited for gymnastics than for ballet.

The more these classes mean to you, the harder it is for a child to find a way out. Maybe she overhears you telling Grandma about it: *"You should see Suzie in her pink leotard! I took her to her ballet class, and she looks adorable—just like a real ballerina!"* If Suzie isn't enjoying the class, though, neither does she enjoy the feeling that she is somehow disappointing her mother, too.

Don't be too quick to label your child a quitter. Focus instead on finding out why she no longer likes the class, and whether there is something that you or the teacher can do to help. Sometimes children begin to lose interest if they feel they are not the best in the class. Is there too much pressure on performance instead of enjoyment? Far more unhealthy than the precedent of quitting is setting up any learning experience as something that is done to please a parent. It is upsetting to a child to feel that our love or approval is somehow conditional on how well or how quickly a child masters an activity or a sport.

Ask Yourself:

What does your child need *now*?

Looking at your child's current needs is a good starting point if you are concerned about any school-related problem. With a two-year-old it may tell you whether it makes sense to begin preschool or to wait until the following September.

If you are looking at a private kindergarten, don't be overly impressed by the number of Ivy League colleges that the school's seniors will be attending. Focus on what will be expected of your child for the next few years and ask yourself if it seems like a good fit *today*. If children as young as seven or eight are being tutored, then you have a right to ask why. What is being demanded of students that the school is not adequately providing? I have heard parents bemoan the necessity of a school interview. But really, this is a chance for you to see a school firsthand and to think about whether your child would feel comfortable there.

Are you falling into the "earlier is better" trap?

In our eagerness to promote learning and nurture talent, we may try to do too much, too soon.

It is a mistake to think in terms of "giving an edge," instead of simply giving a child opportunities for learning. Concerned parents want to give children what they need to succeed in a tough, competitive world. The irony, though, is that while the world has certainly changed, "what it takes" for a child to succeed has not. Children still need to develop trust, autonomy, and feelings of self-worth. But this is possible only when parents have goals that fit with each child's age, experience, and personality. Trust your child to learn at his own pace, and let him take the lead in exploring new interests. The more we set out to create what David Elkind calls superkids, the more we undermine the qualities that children need most to enjoy school and feel good about learning.

Consider waiting a year if your child is borderline in terms of birthdate. A school curriculum is usually geared toward the *oldest* child in the class. As a result, the youngest children may be at a disadvantage. Since mastery of skills is linked with feelings of competence and self-esteem, it is especially important to think about your child's readiness for learning. No matter what a school tells you, children who have to repeat a year often feel stigmatized.

Do you choose activities that make sense for your child?

The challenge for parents is no longer finding activities to fill a young child's day; it is saying no to the hundreds of options available. If you are considering after-school activities, find classes that are right for your particular child. One mother found out why "fit" is so important:

> *"Ethan gets pretty wild, so I thought it might be good for him to take up a quiet activity, such as piano. My plan backfired, though. After having to sit still for thirty minutes with his music teacher, he was even more physical at home. We dropped the lessons, and I signed him up for a gym class instead, which is what he really wanted in the first place. The funny thing is, after being able to run around and play ball for an hour, he was happy to come home and play quietly!"*

An activity should complement a child's basic temperament. If you have a quiet child who enjoys arts and crafts, for example, she may learn to make friends in a small puppet-making class. But to sign her up for a drama class may be overwhelming.

Gymboree classes can be fun for mothers and children, and an active baby may enjoy climbing and running indoors without worrying about tables and lamps. But a child can also thrive without these classes. Happy social experiences contribute more to healthy growth than programs that promise "skills." Children also benefit from time alone, so resist the urge to program every minute of the day.

Are you respectful of your child's learning style and pace?

I once overheard two mothers standing side by side watching their two-year-olds inside a preschool classroom. "Look at Billy," said the first. "He's been playing with that truck now for twenty minutes. He hasn't even budged or looked at the other kids in the class." Meanwhile, the other mother was busy observing her own child: "Sophie's all over the place—look at her! She doesn't sit still for two minutes before she's off to a different part of the room. It must be nice to have a kid who can keep still."

Children have different learning styles. If it is the beginning of school, each child may be expressing anxiety differently. Adults do the same thing. Some of us become quiet and withdrawn when we're nervous, and others grow fidgety and talkative. Try to be accepting of each child's approach to the world.

Are you comparing your children's school performance?

You should expect your children to have different strengths and weaknesses at school. One mother told me that this is the biggest challenge to her as a parent:

> *"I have a son and a daughter with very different abilities. My son is very cerebral, and my daughter has always had a typical 'tomboy' profile. She's great at sports, and he excels at poetry and creative writing. Needless to say, these go against the usual stereotypes, so it can be difficult for them at times. My husband and I work very hard to show that no matter what anyone else may say or think, we love them both for who they are—not for who they aren't."*

If one of your children has trouble with math, he may resent a brother or a sister who is good with numbers. But you can focus on the wonderful stories that he writes and make him feel good about being so creative. It can be even more difficult when a younger child has a gift that leaves an older sibling feeling outperformed or "eclipsed." But there is no way to eliminate these rivalries. The best you can do is to reassure each child that his talents are valued and appreciated. You don't need to deny that these differences exist, but you can help a child to understand that they are part of what makes everyone special.

Do you have faith in your own instincts?

A mother told me why she decided to transfer her son to a new private school:

> *"Ted was in the first grade, and the school was pressuring us to have him tutored because the other children in his class were reading at a fourth-grade level. My husband and I thought that was ridiculous.*

A first-grader reading at the first-grade level seemed just fine with us. We decided it was the school that had a problem."

Unfortunately many parents find it difficult to stand up to school personnel with attitudes like this. But these people make mistakes, too. It is also important to accept that, from year to year, your child will find some teachers either easier or more difficult to get along with (see "Significant Others," on page 98).

In a parent-teacher conference, don't be afraid to challenge a teacher's assumptions about your child. You know your child's history, and you may be able to shed light on behavior that is puzzling in the context of a classroom.

Are you helping your child find ways to cope with the ups and downs of school?

When children begin a longer school day, they naturally spend less time with us, and more time coping with teachers and peers. The sad tales that your child brings home can be heartrending. *"I wasn't invited to Pauline's party." "Mrs Bryant didn't believe me when I said I didn't feel well." "Luke called me an idiot."*

As parents, we tend to feel these slights as deeply as our children. Be aware, though, that while you never want to be dismissive of a child's feelings, you also don't want to react in such a way that your child thinks that an insult or label may have merit. We get so caught up in our children's triumphs and defeats that we often lose perspective. But children watch our reactions to these incidents as a gauge of whether they are worth taking seriously.

Haim Ginott puts it this way: You want your doctor to be sympathetic to your ills, but if he faints at the sight of your blood, he isn't going to be much help. We need to react to a hurt child in a way that bolsters his positive image of himself, instead of grimly capitulating along with him. As one therapist says, parents need to convey to a wounded child, *"You* will be okay because *I* am okay."

Perhaps the most constructive thing we can do is to give our children the language they need to assert themselves at difficult times. To your child who is angry and ashamed because someone called him a dunce, you can simply ask, "Did you like that?" And when your child replies that he did not, you can add, "Well, I hope you said so." Teaching a child to do this is enormously empowering.

To be able to turn to another person and say "I don't like when you do that" is a constructive way to vent feelings. One of our children's teachers recommended these words to us, and they have been simple, effective, and surprisingly satisfying to the child who uses them. They also work well at home, encouraging siblings to assert themselves and settle things on their own.

RED FLAGS

Bullying Behavior

One teacher told me that in cases of aggression there are two victims: the bully *and* his target.

Intervene early if your child shows a pattern of aggressive behavior at school. A child who teases and attacks other children does so because he hasn't learned to trust the outside world. On an unconscious level, he feels vulnerable himself. And since he fully expects others to attack him, he chooses to strike out first. Children who are slow to develop language skills may also be more aggressive than their peers. Sadly the behavior becomes reinforced. "I don't like to play with Gabriel," your four-year-old tells you. "He always hits the other children." Now Gabriel feels rejected, and his frustration will only reinforce his aggressive tendencies.

"The most dangerous thing in human development is a lack of empathy," says Dr. Schwartz. Children who bully other children without remorse need help.

Anxious, Unhappy Behavior

Children come home with tragic tales of unfair teachers and cruel schoolmates. But if they go off to school happily in the morning, you probably do not need to worry. On the other hand, if your child seems genuinely anxious and unhappy and is without friends, you should speak to the teacher or the school head. An occasional stomachache is normal. But a pattern of overanxious behavior may signal too much pressure, a poor fit between your child and her teacher, or problems at home that need to be addressed. Anytime your child's behavior seems out of character, it is best to talk to someone about it.

School Phobia

School phobia is a form of *separation anxiety disorder* (see page 149). While some anxiety over separation is normal, separation anxiety disorder is a pathological condition, ranging from mild to severe. A child who suffers from this condition is chronically anxious about school and requires professional help.

Underachievement

Poor fit, mentioned above, is one reason why some children have trouble in school. Physical problems are another common reason. If your child doesn't seem to be learning, or is acting out at school, go for a full physical exam. One family consulted an analyst when their older son, who had always done well in class, began having learning problems. After weeks of therapy, the child commented one day: "Third grade was easy. But in fourth grade the letters are all blurry." You would be surprised how often children do poorly because of problems either seeing or hearing in school.

Nervous Tics

A tensional outlet such as a nervous tic is different from hair twirling or nail biting. Tics are of course less acceptable socially, but more important, experts see them as an unhealthy manifestation of anxiety. You want to think about what may be causing such a reaction in a school-age child, and talk to a professional to find out how you can help.

One parent recalls that her son, eager to learn, was disappointed when he came home from his first day of school and still couldn't read. Several years later, he still wasn't reading and had developed terrible tics. The parents finally learned that their son had dyslexia. They quickly compensated for his learning disability, but the child bore psychological scars and a sense of inadequacy for a long time afterward. If learning causes extreme frustration for your son or daughter, go for outside help to figure out the problem, and don't wait to do so.

Stuttering and Stammering

Stuttering is common, especially in preschool-aged boys, and parents should avoid overreacting, or it can become a stammer. If the problem exists for more than two months, however, then a professional evaluation is called for. Again, these behaviors are difficult for children socially.

Stark Contrasts in Behavior

Parents find that some children act like "angels" at school and "devils" at home, or the other way around. Some variations in behavior are to be expected. But if your child assumes an entirely different demeanor, it is worth asking why: Are the demands so rigorous in one environment that acting out becomes necessary in the other? Begin by speaking with your child's teacher to sort out such discrepancies in behavior.

Parting Words

In our rush to produce young men and women of letters, we would be wise to let children be children. This chapter covers a wide range of school-related behavior, but its emphasis on learning experiences that are age appropriate and unhurried is best summarized by John

Dewey. In *The School and Society,* a series of lectures published in 1943, Dewey wrote:

> Life is the great thing after all; the life of the child at its time and in its measure, no less than the life of the adult. Strange would it be, indeed, if intelligent and serious attention to what the child *now* needs and is capable of in the way of a rich, valuable and expanded life should somehow conflict with the needs and possibilities of later, adult life.

CHAPTER ELEVEN

Suddenly Mary Poppins turned and faced him, one hand on the handle of the perambulator.

"You," she began, "got out of bed on the wrong side this morning."

"I didn't," said Michael. "There is no wrong side to my bed."

"Every bed has a right and a wrong side," said Mary Poppins, primly.

"Not mine—it's next the wall."

"That makes no difference. It's still a side," scoffed Mary Poppins.

"Well, is the wrong side the left side or is the wrong side the right side? Because I got out on the right side, so how can it be wrong?"

"Both sides were the wrong side, this morning, Mr. Smarty!"

"But it has only one side, and if I got out on the right side—" he argued.

"One more word from you—" began Mary Poppins, and she said it in such a peculiarly threatening voice that even Michael felt a little nervous. "One more word and I'll—"

She did not say what she would do, but he quickened his pace.

from *Mary Poppins* by P. L. Travers

A Rhyme and a Reason: Difficult Behavior at Home

~~~~~~

One of my younger daughter's pet activities is to remove all of the cushions from the sofa and build intricate tunnels and bridges out of them on the floor. I walked into the living room one day after she had been playing there and found the pillows strewn about. Ordinarily, I would have muttered to myself while replacing them. That day, however, I decided it was enough. My daughter was almost five now, and I thought she should know better.

"Marina!" I exclaimed when I found her busy in her room. "You can't just play with the sofa cushions, throw them all over the living-room floor, and leave them there!"

She looked at me, horrified, and then stated with equal indignance, "Well, I didn't know that!"

The incident reminded me that, often, when we assume children know what is expected of them, they do not. There was nothing wrong with my wanting a five-year-old to clean up the mess she had made. But I had changed the rules of the game without any warning, and that's what she objected to. (Suppose you prepared a report for your boss the same way every month for four years and he suddenly decided that it needed a new format. Would you want to be told this *before* you submitted your next report or criticized *after* the fact for doing a poor job?)

This chapter looks at children's habits and reactions at home:

❧ Coercive behavior

❧ Fights over what to wear

❧ Sibling rivalry

❧ The messy room

❧ Personal responsibility

❧ The TV habit

❧ Whining

All of these conflicts begin behind closed doors. What happens at home is important, however, because what children see and learn there becomes the model for their behavior in the outside world.

A child who grows up in an atmosphere of tolerance learns forgiveness. He comes to view himself as someone to be loved in spite of his shortcomings. In a home where parents try to understand childhood urges and impulses, children come to believe in their own essential goodness. More often than not, they choose to act in a way that fulfills this positive view of them.

A child who grows up being criticized and shamed never learns to trust the world. This is why it is important to understand these patterns of conflict and, in many instances, to modify them. As one educator told me, parents have "a vast arsenal" available to them for managing difficult behavior and for keeping it to a minimum.

Coercive Family Behavior

There will always be conflict between parents and children, but it should not be incessant. If it is, we need to step back and ask why. A pattern of coercive behavior is unpleasant and exhausting in any relationship. In the early years it takes an unfortunate toll on a child's ego. A hostile parent, researchers have found, is likely to behave in a way that also teaches and engenders aversive behavior. Everyone in the family suffers as a result.

It is in the nature of all human relationships to attribute motives to another person's behavior. In a marriage that is fundamentally happy, or strong, the husband and wife tend to give each other the benefit of the doubt. By contrast, some couples do constant battle with each other. They not only expect the worst but this is what they see in a spouse and, ultimately, this is what they get.

The same cycle can occur in families with young children. And this is why researchers claim that a positive outlook on child behavior is the single best way to avoid these patterns at home. Angry and frustrated, parents may begin to anticipate conflict, and this only increases the odds that resistance will recur. What is probably most harmful about everyday stress, then, is its effect on *future* interactions between a parent and child.

A parent who misinterprets difficult behavior may come to expect it of a child. And the child, who uses the parent to define himself as worthy or unworthy, does not want to "disappoint" the parent, so the same behavior is repeated. It is ironic that we hear so much talk of self-esteem. Meanwhile, these daily battles at home chip away at a child's image of himself.

"Why Are You Doing This to Me?!"

Conflict at home has a way of escalating. Anytime you hear yourself saying or wondering, *Why are you doing this to me?* you probably need to step back and reassess a particular habit or behavior.

Despite what we may think, the messy room isn't designed to make us angry, although it certainly has that effect. Nor is it a sign of moral sloppiness. On the other hand, we have a right to expect children to pitch in as they grow older and to take responsibility for their actions. Teaching this is one of our most important jobs as parents.

"It always helps to know that there are reasons for these behaviors," writes Stanley Turecki, author of *The Difficult Child.* And finding these reasons is the first step toward dealing with conflict effectively. Often, it is a matter of making demands that are reasonable, given a child's age and temperament, and finding the right language for expressing them.

Whether you are agonizing about what your children wear to school or how often they fight, the key is to look for patterns. Try to figure out why certain behavior makes sense to the child and why you react negatively to it as a parent. If we begin by expecting the worst—by labeling young children or by forcing them into negative roles—we never give them a chance to show just how competent and cooperative they can be, too.

Negative-Reinforcement Traps

Parents who are physically abusive tend to interpret a child's behavior negatively. Such a parent will hit a two-year-old and claim afterward that the child was "bad" because he wouldn't sit still. However, most children that age are not capable of sitting still. Researchers have noted that to an outside observer abused children often appear more "obedient" than nonabused children. The parents of nonabused children have a different set of expectations and as a result they are less critical. There is a good fit between what they expect of a child and what the child is capable of doing at a specific age.

This isn't a book about child abuse. But even in homes that are basically warm and loving, the relationship between what we expect of a child and how we interpret that child's behavior are important. Some families find that conflict is fairly "localized." There may be one major issue: homework, the TV, sibling fights. In other homes, though, conflicts tend to snowball. The child who fails to do homework is also criticized for being a sloven or lazy and for always forgetting to take care of his pet. Then, when he knocks over a vase, he is called clumsy. When this happens, the censured child may have no choice but to become difficult, bringing even more disapproval on himself.

Added Pressures When Both Parents Work

When both parents work full-time, two things may happen at home. In some families, since the adults hardly have a chance to observe other children, expectations run too high. These parents may judge normal behavior too harshly, expecting a small child to behave as a miniature adult.

In other families, however, working parents may be loath to spoil what little time they spend with their children. Many working mothers feel guilty about not being at home. And when they are there, they wish it could be perfect:

"I have to remind myself not to take it personally if I come home and Nathan is in a bad mood. It's just that I miss him so much while I'm at work and I want to make the most of our evenings together."

This pressure to make every minute happy puts working parents in a bind when it comes to setting limits and modifying behavior, as this mother explains:

"There are a lot of times when I know I'm just giving in to make things easier at night, but the alternative is to spoil the hour or two that we have together as a family, and who wants to do that¿! I feel very guilty about not being there all day. I think it's much easier to set limits when you're not counting on that one hour together at the end of the day."

So Much Guilt, So Little Time

Guilt can be damaging. Parents who feel guilty have a hard time saying no to unacceptable behavior. Children quickly sense what is happening, though, and they may begin manipulating a parent who is afraid to lose the love of a child, even temporarily.

But children do not enjoy this kind of power. In fact, it can be frightening to them. Children may protest loudly when you set limits on their behavior, but they sense early on that these boundaries keep the world safe. When we fail to set these limits, the child suffers socially, too. A child who grows up manipulating his parents will not have an easy time making friends or getting along with teachers.

Getting Dressed:
Why Clothes Become the Culprit

By the second year what a child wears is terribly important to him. For some children comfort is critical, as one mother of a three-year-old discovered to her chagrin:

> *"Daniel has one pair of pants that he insists on wearing every day to nursery school. It's gotten to the point where it's a little embarrassing to me. I bought another pair in a different color (I wanted the teachers to know that he does have something else to wear), but he insists that the blue ones 'feel better.'"*

Some children, by temperament, are more sensitive to the way clothing feels. To them, wearing a new pair of stiff jeans can be as uncomfortable as putting on shoes that give you blisters. For another child, wearing the same worn-in shirt day after day becomes a source of comfort at the beginning of school. His friend, meanwhile, may not care about what he wears, but insists on taking a toy from home, deriving the same sense of security in a different way.

It is not unusual for first-time parents to have difficulty with issues of autonomy when they first arise, and to be better prepared for them with later children:

> *"My older daughter and I constantly fought about clothing. Kathryn only wanted to wear dresses to school, and in the winter it drove me crazy because it was so cold. We fought about it every morning. With my second daughter I learned to say, 'Fine. You can wear whatever dress you want, but put on a pair of leggings underneath because it's cold today.'"*

Obviously, some parents will have more problems than others allowing their children to dress as they wish. A mother who longs to see her daughter in pink party dresses may feel alienated (or even rejected) by a daughter who insists on boyish clothing. Sadly, there are families where conflicts such as these touch on every aspect of a parent-child relationship.

Autonomy and Control . . . Again

Most of us can recall the satisfaction of learning to ride a two-wheeler. For a toddler, zipping the zipper or buttoning the buttons "all by myself" is just as exhilarating. Your child needs to sense that your pleasure in these accomplishments outweighs your occasional impatience because simple tasks now take longer.

More than we realize, a child who insists on dressing himself is asking us to let go. And our response to these habits will either support the move toward independence or discourage it. A mother may begin calling her daughter "willful," growing impatient with each "impossible" demand to do things by herself. So the child begins to think that the more she relies on her mother—the more dependent she is—the more her mother approves of her. One year later the same parent complains because her child *still* needs help getting dressed!

Obviously there is more to be gained in the long term (by parent and child) if we appreciate the meaning of these new demands and accommodate them whenever possible.

Parents hurry children along in the morning because it is time for nursery school, or Gymboree. But a child's self-esteem soars when he is allowed to help dress himself. If you can, allow an extra fifteen minutes in the morning. The chance to prove himself competent probably means more to your child than the class or activity you are rushing to.

If you aim to give a child autonomy in this area half of the time, or three-quarters of the time, you will probably find less resistance on those days when you must hurry the child along. "I know you want to button all the buttons like you usually do, but we're really running late now. Let Mommy help you today, and you'll do it by yourself next time."

The Search for a Middle Ground

Once again, the key is to find a middle ground to avoid conflict. Even with a child as young as two and a half or three, you can decide together on a special place for school clothing and let your child pick any shirt or any pants from that shelf or drawer. You have a right to object if clothing is dirty, but stains that bother you may not trouble your toddler. Some mothers are disappointed if a child refuses to wear a new outfit to a party or on the first day of school. Again, though, children may feel uncomfortable in something brand new. Try to present a few acceptable options, and let your child choose.

When Little Girls Want Frills

Many women who work are baffled when their daughters insist on wearing dresses. A friend who works full-time reports that by age three her daughter knew exactly what she wanted to wear to nursery school every day: "Purple dress, party shoes, tights."

These are some other comments I have heard from women who worry that their daughters will grow up to be antifeminist:

> *"Sometimes if we're about to leave the house and I'm wearing slacks, my daughter will drag me back into my bedroom and tell me to put on a skirt. When I ask her why, she insists, 'Girls wear dresses.' "*

> *"The other day my four-and-a-half-year-old told me that she didn't think she looked pretty without makeup on. I was appalled! I've always worked and avoided stereotypes like that about women and appearance."*

For children, clothing is also a way of sorting out their sexual identities. Although women work hard today to provide positive models for their daughters, the signals we send are mixed at best. For every mother who works conscientiously at presenting a "nonsexist" image, little girls are bombarded daily by images of women that are just the opposite. A life-sized image of a scantily clad Madonna makes a tremendous impression on a young girl, and so does Barbie, with her lacy, low-cut dresses, spike heels, and *hair*.

We tell our children that appearances don't matter, but children are perceptive. They see us putting on eye makeup and wondering aloud which dress to wear, or they hear us complaining because the hairdresser took off an extra half an inch of hair. It should not surprise us if little girls associate ruffles and hair ribbons with being "feminine." (My daughter struggled one year as Halloween approached. She wanted to be a witch but hated the idea of not wearing a "pretty" costume. She made her peace that year by trick-or-treating as a "ballerina witch" instead.)

Try to keep these concerns in perspective. By the time your daughter is six, she will probably have no interest in wearing the same smocked party dresses that she now begs to wear to preschool.

What Sibling Fights Are Really All About

Parents have an influence on what happens between siblings, and this begins when they bring home the new baby. I have heard parents say plaintively, "I know Kevin really loves the new baby, but he keeps pinching him." The truth, however, is that Kevin deeply resents the little intruder! (For more on the new baby, see page 63.)

Don't deny or dismiss the firstborn's feelings. The more attuned you are to your older child's ambivalence, the easier it will be for that child to accept the new baby. Some parents report that an older child with serious behavior problems never quite "recovered" from the arrival of a new baby, so troubling were his feelings of being displaced. Allowing a child to express resentment early on can help to prevent such lasting anxiety.

Psychologists use the word *narcissistic* to describe the child in the first three years. In other words, every event is seen egocentrically. Two- or three-year-olds see the birth of a sibling in terms of how it affects them directly and their relationship with you. Anna Freud suggests that an older child may feel "abandoned" by the mother, who leaves for the hospital to give birth. He feels rejected as well, since so much of her energy and attention is now turned over to the helpless infant.

A child of four or five has grown used to his role as the baby of the family, which changes with the arrival of a new sibling. Be prepared to reassure the older child, and don't be surprised if he or she acts more needy, or babyish, just before or after you give birth. It may help to bestow new privileges on this child, such as a later bedtime, to make him feel good about being bigger.

As happy as you feel about the new baby, accept an older child's sense of loss. No matter how much help you have from family or friends, a new baby intrudes on the child's time with you. You may be tired from the birth or busy feeding the baby. If you accept the other children's feelings, you will probably try to be as reassuring as possible. A few weeks later, after the "novelty" has worn off, you won't be happy if your older son squeezes the baby's head and makes him wail (nor should you permit your son to do this). But you also won't be shocked by such reactions.

In general the sooner parents accept these hurt, angry feelings, the sooner a child passes through them. Why? Because when parents accept the mixed feelings, the child at least feels understood. But when parents fail to hide their dismay, the child feels even more confused. Now, because of emotions and impulses that he cannot control, he has jeopardized his mother's and father's love and approval.

A "Trickle-Down" Theory

It didn't take long for us to see that the more time and attention we lavished on our older daughter, the more "benevolently" she behaved toward her new sister. And since all of this occurred at the height of the Reagan years, we called this our "trickle-down" theory of sibling relations. Simply put, we kept the two-year-old's feelings of displacement to a minimum. And the more attention we gave our older daughter, the more acceptance "trickled down" to her new sister.

This isn't easy, especially if you are clinging to the memory of spending undivided time with your first child. If possible, arrange to have a relative or sitter come and stay with the baby while you spend some time alone with the older child. There will be plenty of other opportunities to do things as a family. Your older child just lost a monopoly on parental attention and needs a chance to adjust.

Whatever the new baby "loses" by not being with you is more than compensated for later if siblings are more accepting.

When Older Children Fight for Their Parents' Benefit

Sibling rivalry is usually a contest for the parents' attention and approval. Children may be playing together happily until they catch sight of a parent, and then an argument erupts immediately. (This is why many of us skulk around corners at home to avoid detection.)

Parents may not realize how much they influence these patterns among siblings. Eager to see their children get along, parents try to help settle a fight between siblings, but this usually puts more of a wedge between them. The message is that these arguments will in fact end with a parent taking one side or another, and this reinforces the rivalry instead of arresting it. One child feels that he or she has been treated unfairly, and it is only a matter of time before a new fight begins.

Every family has what one analyst calls an "emotional currency," and children quickly figure out what it is. If parents reward sibling fights by becoming involved and setting up winners and losers each time, then these contests for their favor will continue. But if children see that there is nothing to be gained by running to their parents, there is no incentive for them to do so.

When Parents Are Partial, Problems Will Follow

Judith Dunn, a foremost researcher on siblings, finds that when a mother gives her children different degrees of affection, or is more responsive toward one child than another, there is a better chance of more conflict *between* siblings within the family.

In general, Dunn has written, mothers tend to be more solicitous of the younger sibling, and this breeds resentment. But when mothers are less partial—when they are as forgiving of a first child's flaws or respond with the same enthusiasm to the comments and ideas of all her children—a lot of rivalry is eliminated. This supports the notion that attunement to each child in the family is an important goal and that it can make family life happier all around.

Attachment to the parent is a powerful force in early childhood, and siblings are bound to compete for your love and approval. But trying to pour two perfectly equal glasses of milk each time, in an effort to appear impartial, simply isn't the answer. To take their complaints too seriously ("She got a bigger scoop of ice cream than I did!") is to perpetuate the rivalry well beyond the first six years. Focus instead on the more subtle signals you send and whether you interact with your children in a way that conveys greater warmth or love for one than the other.

Confessing that she still feels insecure as an adult, a mother of two recalled her own experiences growing up in a family where her older brother's interests always seemed to take priority over her own:

> *"I remember we would travel to the city for the day and go to the Metropolitan Museum. I would have loved to see the costume exhibit, but my brother never wanted to. Instead we would look at the armour or whatever part of the museum he found more interesting."*

Speaking to parents, one pediatrician urged parents to watch home videos carefully. Does one child always seem to demand (and receive) more attention, while another always goes quietly off on her own? Try to see that each child is given a turn to decide on a family outing, or to bring along a special friend. It is an effective way of letting your children know that everyone's opinion is important.

"You Never Spend Any Time with Me!"

When a child accuses you point-blank of liking a brother or sister more, it hurts. The temptation—difficult to resist—is to deny the statement and prove or insist that you do not. But this is futile. If you seem too defensive, a child may feel worse, as if he has somehow come to the truth of the matter.

It can be far more satisfying to the child to acknowledge how terrible he feels ("Is that what you're thinking? That must make you feel awful.") and to do something constructive about it ("Would you like to spend some special time together, just the two of us?"). Your child is really looking for reassurance. Perhaps during the last few weeks, without realizing it, you have been busy helping one child in the family get ready for a school play, and now the others are beginning to resent it.

Setting Guidelines for What's Acceptable

Sibling fights are to be expected, but parents clearly need to set guidelines for these arguments. Dr. Harold Koplewicz urges parents to tell their children that they are to negotiate their differences. In his home if parental involvement is necessary, all the participants suffer as a result (some TV time is taken away, or fewer stories are read together at bedtime). This method takes parents out of the role of police and jury. It also encourages siblings to work together as a team, since everyone loses out the minute Mom and Dad become involved. The real goal is to have siblings aligned together, so that parents encourage the relationship but do not intervene by siding with one child or another.

Cruelty toward a sibling should never be tolerated. Children can learn to argue fairly, without injuring one another either physically or emotionally. The same rules of decency that we extend to those outside the home should govern behavior within it.

"This Is Between the Two of You"

One mother explains how she has taught her children to resolve arguments on their own:

> "My husband and I have friends who always step in, and I think they're doing their kids a disservice. It's obvious that the arguments are a way of getting a parent's attention. It may be tempting to get involved at times, but we try very hard to be neutral. They get our attention a lot faster by settling a fight than by starting one."

Another mother also learned that, left to resolve their differences, her children would fight and then make up quickly:

> "It amazed us to see how quickly our children would reconcile their own fights if no one interfered. It was like watching puppies who roll around on the ground together and then snap or growl at each other, and then start to play again."

If we can stay on the sidelines, brothers and sisters learn a remarkable lesson about resilience in human relationships—that we can feel terribly angry at people and then feel loving toward them again with no loss of intimacy. This is the gift of a sibling.

When siblings develop real resentments of each other, then it is up to parents to see why these angry patterns have emerged. One mother discovered why her younger daughter often instigated trouble:

> *"I didn't see it at first, but Erica was obviously jealous of my relationship with her older sister. At first I would deny that I spent more time with Bethany. Then I realized that 'perception is reality.' I started planning time alone with Erica, too, and it helped. They still fight, but there's much less bitterness on Erica's part."*

Many parents have an easier time understanding one child than another, and they feel guilty about it. One mother told me:

> *"I was very independent growing up, and I can identify much more with the willfulness of my older children than with the 'neediness' of my youngest daughter. But one day I remembered how vulnerable I felt in first grade because one of the boys used to pull my hair and nobody would do anything about it! Just thinking about those feelings enabled me to identify more with Joanna, instead of being impatient with her or critical of her insecurity."*

Try to find some common ground with the child whose temperament or outlook is different from your own. Otherwise, that child has no choice but to resent a brother or sister with whom you relate more easily. This is one way to keep sibling fights from flaring. You don't have to feel guilty about the heart-to-heart talks you enjoy so much with your younger child and that your first born has no interest in. But do find some other path to intimacy.

Working Parents: Trying to Meet Each Child's Needs

Being able to spend time alone with each child is one way to minimize jealousy. One mother who works full-time described what it is like to walk into her house at seven P.M.:

"When I come home from the office, it can be very stressful. My older daughter needs help with her homework. My middle one may have had a fight with her best friend, and the baby, who's two, wants to show me her painting from school. I wish I could split myself in three sometimes."

There are no easy answers, and honesty may be the best approach: "I want to listen to all of you, but it's very hard when everyone talks at once." It is difficult to determine who needs you most at the moment, and being exhausted after working all day makes it even harder. You may have to rely on good old common sense: "Listen, everyone: Since today was Leah's first piano lesson, let's give her a chance to tell us about it, and then each of you will have a chance to talk."

Siblings for Life: Taking a Longer View

For all the conflict and emotional reckoning that they bring, siblings also have the potential of giving each other lifelong solace and support. The petty arguments of the early years may leave parents exasperated. At other times it moves us beyond words to watch brothers and sisters soothe and console one another. We need to teach children early on that a parent's love can be shared without in any way being diminished. If we can convey to our children how much they stand to gain by reconciling the inevitable rivalries, we give them a real incentive to work these things out.

Judith Dunn makes the point that a relationship with a sibling is usually the longest that a person has. With this in mind, parents may be more inclined to help form family ties that are as emotionally enriched as they are enduring.

RED FLAG

Even close siblings will fight heatedly at times. I've noticed that our children argue most at times of transition. The end of the school year, for example, is often stressful, and they seem to be less tolerant of one another.

But if your children constantly behave cruelly toward one another, and if there are no peaceful moments to compensate for callous behavior, then the fighting may be outside the normal range. A child will not learn true empathy if his brother's and sister's feelings somehow don't count.

If your husband loves sports and grew up playing ball with his father, he may have an easier time relating to a son who is athletic. But he should find different activities to share with less active offspring to avoid fueling jealous feelings.

Children often use younger brothers or sisters as scapegoats. A child who has had a bad day at school may be unusually sharp toward a younger sibling. Don't be alarmed if this happens. (You're probably less patient with your spouse, too, at the end of a bad day.) But a pattern of putting down brothers and sisters is often a sign of other problems, such as low self-esteem, and should not be ignored.

"It's Time to Put the Toys Away": Living with a Messy Room

When the writer Calvin Trillin is asked for baby advice by anxious, expectant parents, he tells them, "Try to get one that doesn't spit up." He might add, "Try to get one that puts his toys away."

The sight of a room strewn with toys sends many mothers into a frenzy of anger. We cannot help thinking that children who behave this way are spoiled and ungrateful. Here is how one father expressed his frustration:

> *"I can't stand to look at Phoebe's room anymore. She's a complete slob. I didn't mind it as much when she was younger, but now she's five and I expect her to start taking care of her things. I've even threatened to stop buying her anything new until she learns to take care of what she has."*

Making a mess is childish behavior, but it isn't a criminal offense. When we criticize a habit like this, we're probably more concerned about the adult a child will become. We forget that cleaning up, like a lot of behavior, must be learned and reinforced.

In her parent-education workshops, Nancy Samalin asks parents to think ahead ten years and list the qualities that they would like to see in their children. Typically, the list includes words such as *honest, self-confident, independent, self-sufficient.* Samalin notes that the word *neat* rarely appears. (Nor does the word *happy,* she points out sadly.)

The point of this exercise is to help parents focus on what really matters. If character development is the issue, then parents would do better to stop criticizing this behavior so harshly and find positive ways to elicit cooperation. The fact that children must learn to become responsible should be no less dismaying than that they need to be taught to brush their teeth or to tie their shoes.

"Messing" in Childhood

There are instances of children defiantly dumping an entire bucket of toys at their mother's feet. But most of the time the child, because he is so fixed in the present, simply forgets about what's on the floor and enthusiastically moves on to the next activity. If you know that most young children are careless about putting toys away, then you will not judge your toddler too harshly. But more important, you will not perpetuate the behavior by overreacting to it.

As children grow, you can create opportunities for positive reinforcement, as this mother found:

> *"Now that my kids are a little older, I find I can create incentives for them to help cleaning up. If they're about to have their snack in the kitchen, the cookies don't come out until everyone has helped put the toys away. Or if they want to watch a video, they know that they can't just leave stuff all over the floor. I think they're slowly getting into the habit of cleaning up after themselves."*

In general try to make cooperation something reciprocal. If your son surprises you by cleaning the table or making his own breakfast, you can return the favor later in the day: "Since you were nice enough to clear the dishes, I'll be happy to put the puzzle away." If you can create a spirit of cooperation in this way, there will be less bickering in general.

It is easy to be vocal about what children do wrong. Try instead to emphasize what they do right. "I noticed you put the paints away today instead of leaving them out. I really appreciate it. Thanks." Children are eager for such praise, and it gives them a positive image to live up to.

With a school-age child try to talk openly about why it is important to keep things organized, as this woman did:

> *"I happen to have a very messy bedroom. My office reading is piled up on the desk, and so are old newspapers and magazines. I obviously wasn't practicing what I was preaching, so I talked about it with my daughter one day. I told her that I wasn't particularly proud of the way my room looked and that it was frustrating not to be able to find the things I needed. It didn't change her behavior overnight, but it gave her something to think about. It probably made her realize that she has a choice about how she takes care of her own things."*

What I like most about this approach is its honesty, and its understanding that children have to want to change behavior for themselves.

A Helpful Note: The Power of Descriptive Words

Haim Ginott urges parents to use descriptions instead of diatribes in many situations at home. No one enjoys being put on the defensive. But this is exactly what we do when we exclaim, "You're so irresponsible! You never take care of that animal!" A child is more likely to take action if you simply describe the problem: "The bird cage hasn't been cleaned in a while." Other examples: "I see a lot of toys on the floor." "Shoes belong in the closet."

The TV Habit

Children's TV habits are as varied as they are. Some become bored after fifteen minutes and play regardless of whether the TV is on. Others enter an altered state, becoming oblivious to the world around them. There are good reasons for being concerned about the amount of time young children spend in front of the TV, and parents shouldn't hesitate to set limits on what, and how much, children watch.

When children play quietly at home, without benefit of TV, they learn to entertain themselves. This kind of quiet time is in short supply for many children today, who, from an early age, go from one structured activity to the next. You can avoid developing a TV habit by simply keeping the set unplugged.

Even if the program is "educational," children benefit more from the games they invent for themselves. Children who develop an early love of books and reading typically do well in school and enjoy learning. Unfortunately, if the TV is constantly on, children may never develop this wonderful habit. (I find it sad when children come to our house to play and, despite a closet full of games, toys, and dress-up clothes, they ask to watch a video.) Another good reason for keeping the TV off is that many of the programs, even those that air during prime time now, are frightening and highly inappropriate for young children.

Parents should also think twice before watching the evening news with young children in the house. Local coverage amounts to gory, "eyewitness" accounts of murder, child abuse, and other violent crime. You shouldn't worry for a moment that this attitude is overly protective. Many experts agree that children feel vulnerable enough. It is our job, not theirs, to worry about violence and other social ills.

Recent research has delivered two new strikes against TV, both psychological and physical. In the first case, after watching TV for extended periods of time, children become agitated, and adults are found to be slightly depressed. As for physical health, a recent study found that the metabolism *slows* during TV viewing to a point lower than if you were sitting and reading. And since watching TV and eating often go hand in hand, it is easy to see why this is an unhealthy connection.

It is your right as a parent to say no to television. (For more about parents' rights, see page 232.) Certainly, it is unrealistic to expect children to limit their own viewing. It may help to establish certain times of the day or week. Some families find it works to keep the TV off altogether on school nights and to be more lenient on the weekend. Other parents prefer allowing children to watch an hour or so each day.

Whatever you decide, bear in mind that, as one school advises parents, less is more when it comes to TV.

Modifying Child Behavior: Rewarding, Ignoring, and "Time-out"

Understanding a child's behavior does not mean accepting or condoning it. One of the most important things a child must learn in the first few years is to control many impulses and urges. Whether the source of conflict is sibling fights, a sloppy room, or that "special" pair of stained leggings, there are effective ways of modifying bad habits at home.

Redirecting Behavior

With a young, preverbal child, the best we can do early on is to redirect difficult behavior. A good example is a scene I witnessed recently in a nursery school, when a three-year-old boy threw a toy across the room. The teacher simply said, "Connor, if you want to throw something, I'll take you outside and we can play ball. But we can't throw toys in the classroom. Someone could get hurt. Would you like to go outside and throw a ball with me, or do you want to stay inside and play with the toys?" Connor chose to remain in the room, and he stopped throwing toys.

We can use the same technique at home. When a child begins walking toward the living room with a box of paints and crayons, we don't have to accuse or attack ("What are you doing? You're impossible! You know you're not allowed to paint in there. Give me those paints. That's absolutely not allowed!"). We can assume innocence and offer a choice instead: "The paints aren't allowed in there. I can read a story to you in the living room, or we can set up the paints in the kitchen. Which would you like to do?"

A young child can be told, "You may not hit the baby. I see that you're angry, so we'll have to find something else to hit instead. Do

it the pillow on your bed? Would you like to go outside
l? Would that make you feel better?"

Ignoring and Rewarding

"Excessive attention, even if it's negative, is such a powerful 'reward' to a child that it actually reinforces the undesirable behavior,"
writes Dr. Stanley Turecki in *The Difficult Child*. This is why experts
advise parents to prioritize: Ignore the behavior that you can live with
and focus on rewarding a child for what he or she does right.

Since play is such important work, it may be worth it to allow the
child some free rein, even if the result is a room that makes you recoil.
Believe me, you can't *force* a two-year-old to clean up. (There will be
marks on your floor where he digs in his heels.) But you can try offering
a choice.

A three-year-old is beginning to understand that if the blocks are
scattered on the floor, there will be no room for the dollhouse and the
cars, too, so he sees that there is a good reason for putting away some
of the toys.

"Hmm . . . I have a problem. How am I going to get all these blocks
back in the box?" The idea of helping Mommy with a problem is
appealing to a young child. There are other ways of making the choice
theirs. "Do you want to put away the blocks or the puzzle?" It won't
always work, but if it does, you have something positive to build on.

When it does work, find a way to reward the gesture. That night
you can be sure that your child is in earshot when you tell his grandmother on the phone, "Brian is getting to be such a big boy. He helped
me clean up the blocks today, and I was so proud of him."

Most children whine from time to time, especially if they're hungry
or overtired. But again, if a child whines excessively, the parents have
to look objectively at whether they are rewarding the behavior:

*"I didn't realize that I was encouraging the whining until I saw
how differently Victoria behaved at school. The teachers had made it
clear that this was not acceptable in the classroom. They weren't
punitive or anything. They just made it clear that a 'big-girl' voice
was expected, and that's what they got."*

You can try to do the same at home. Some parents insist from the start that they can't understand a child unless he uses a different voice, and this gradually lets children know that there are no rewards for this behavior. The same approach can be used to discourage tantrums. But this will only work if you reward the child when he succeeds—not with a new toy necessarily but by acknowledging the effort: "I notice you used a grown-up voice just now. Good for you!" "I know you wanted to go to the toy store, but you didn't make a big fuss when I said no. Why don't you choose something special to do when we get home?"

Parents may not be aware that they are "rewarding" sibling rivalry, as this parent found:

> *"It has taken a lot of discipline, but I'm finally learning not to be dragged into my children's fights. I used to try to settle each one 'fairly,' because I really wanted them to feel close to one another. I couldn't understand why it wasn't working, until I saw that the fighting was just a way of getting my attention and seeing who I would side with. Now that I refuse to get involved, they fight much less."*

Another way of rewarding the behavior we like is to keep a chart, as in the section about oral habits. One mother found this was helpful with a six-year-old who still wanted her mother to dress her:

> *"I knew that Alice's refusal to get dressed by herself was partly a reaction to my starting work again, but I still felt it was important for her to do her share in the morning, so we started a chart. If she managed to get dressed four mornings a week on her own, I took her out for tea on Saturday. In the end the time together was what she was after anyway, so it was a very powerful incentive. Getting out in the morning has been much easier as a result."*

Time-out

The time-out procedure is used by many teachers, and it is just as effective at home, especially when children have trouble controlling their temper. A child with a short fuse can be told, "I see you're getting upset with your cousin. Why don't you cool off in my room for a few minutes until you feel better."

If your child hits you or kicks his sister, you can take him to his room and insist that he stay there. Even if you only close the door for thirty seconds or a minute, the message is clear: "If you behave in that way, we don't want your company. If you want to be with us, then you cannot do those things."

In general, when parents follow through on these discipline techniques, children are easier to live with. It is when parents make idle threats that children continue to fall back on the same annoying behaviors.

Your "Rights" as a Parent

This book defends a child's right to certain feelings, even if he cannot always be allowed to act upon them. As a parent, you have certain rights as well, and, contrary to what you might think, exercising them can make life with a young child easier:

The right to say no: Every parent has a different comfort level when it comes to such things as eating sweets or cleaning up. But if you feel strongly about imposing some limits in these areas or others, you needn't apologize for them.

At a recent forum on parenting, one panelist spoke of his work with highly creative children. The most exceptional young people he had studied, he said, rarely watched TV. Some of the parents didn't even own one, but those who did strictly limited its use. Thinking out loud, the same professor ventured that these parents' *willingness* to curb TV viewing had probably been just as important as the fact of its absence. The boys and girls who grew up in these homes displayed not only intelligence and innovative thinking but, like their parents, they had the courage of their convictions.

We never want to invoke rules that are unreasonable or punitive. But if you are thoughtful about the standards you set in your home—and if you take the time to explain these to your children—you teach them what it means to have values and, most important, to stand by them.

The right to think before answering: Parents sometimes forget that they do not always have to answer a child right away. The first time your daughter asks for a pet puppy, you don't have to respond immediately. "That's a big request, and I need some time to think about it." Even if you do end up refusing, a child at least feels that you have taken the request seriously. You can also wait until a quiet time to discuss your answer when you know your child will be more willing to consider your reasons.

The right to exit: As we've seen in Chapters 7 and 8, it is important to stand by an anxious, fearful child, and this includes one who is having a tantrum and could hurt himself. There are many situations, however, when you do have the right to leave the room. A child who has grown deaf to your angry tirades will quickly see that your disappointment or anger is real. Whether the problem is warring siblings, rudeness, or language that you refuse to tolerate from your child any longer, your absence—that is, the message that you do not even want to be in the same room with him—can effectively bring an end to offensive behavior. Being with you is so important to him that to be deprived of your company, even for a minute or two, sends a powerful message about what is acceptable to you and what is not.

Language Can Help, Too

As we've seen, you can modify behavior by choosing the right words and avoiding others. Nancy Samalin notes that when parents begin sentences with the word *You*, they immediately put a child on the defensive ("You never put your things away." "You're a complete slob!"). Children recoil from these accusations, and nothing constructive comes of them.

The next time your child asks for help finding a toy, say to him, "As soon as you get some of the toys off the floor, I'll be happy to help you look." Those words have a magical effect on children. I once heard a nursery school teacher tell a group of two-year-olds, "As soon as you finish your snack, boys and girls, we'll go outside to play." Fourteen small arms mechanically lifted up their cups, and the children finished their juice in an instant.

Ask Yourself:

Do you enlist your child's help?

Don't try to address problem behavior in the heat of the moment. Whenever you're upset about something, wait for a quiet time to say, "We have a problem." We did this when weekday mornings became too frantic. Our daughters came up with the idea of a checklist for their school things. They can refer to it at bedtime and gather what they need for the following day.

Given the chance, children are great problem solvers. Even with a child as young as four or five, you can sit down, talk about a problem, and ask for help in solving it. It is supremely satisfying to a young child's ego to be asked for his opinion. And you will be surprised at how practical their solutions can be.

Children learn from these experiences not only that their opinions matter, but that there is usually a way to change things for the better.

Have you established enough routines in your home?

Having routines at home can help to eliminate a lot of arguments. A child who studies an instrument can be asked to decide on a special time of day to practice: when she finishes her after-school snack, for example, or before taking a bath in the evening. You will fight less over homework if your child knows that it is to be done each night immediately after dinner. The atmosphere at home will be more agreeable in general if your children know what they are expected to do, and when.

Are you being overly critical or negative?

Try to have perspective—and a sense of humor—when your children do "childish" things. Drs. Ilg and Ames, of the Gesell Institute, note that as children grow up, their behavior proceeds "toward an optimum regardless of parental handling." I have found this to be true. It isn't long before the child who rises at five A.M. must be shaken several times after the alarm bell rings at seven. Your son, whose table manners are atrocious, begins dining at a friend's house, and suddenly these things become important to him, too. The challenge is in getting from here to there with our warmth and affection intact.

Do you spend time with other families?

It is easier to have perspective if you see a broad range of child behavior. But families today are probably more insular than in the past, and this no doubt affects a parent's perceptions of bad habits, both inside and outside the home. Today there is rarely a grandmother or an elderly aunt living neaby to reassure us that while growing up, we engaged in the same bewildering behavior as our children. It helps to know that the habit you find vexing in your own child—shouting, whining, or a revolting method of eating cookies—is clearly the norm for boys and girls that age. And as most mothers will admit, nothing is more comforting than to see other children do the same dreadful, perplexing things as your own.

Are you creating "roles" for each of your children?

Dr. Virginia Burlingame once attended a workshop in which the participants were asked to introduce themselves based on the "role" their parents assigned to them while growing up. "I'm the selfish, spoiled older sister," one person began.

Parents create these roles without meaning to, and it begins with being overly critical or judgmental of a child's behavior. It is difficult for children to escape these labels, and many are burdened by them well into adulthood. Today, Burlingame tells her adult patients that they do not have to live with these roles forever. "I tell them they can resign from them," she says, and it is an empowering thing for them to hear.

CHAPTER TWELVE

It was Dad. My stomach felt as if it was dropping to the floor, the way it always does when I hear his voice. "How're you doing, kid?" he asked.

"Fine," I said, thinking of the great success of my burglar alarm. "Great."

"I got your letter," he said.

"That's good," I said. His call took me so by surprise that I could feel my heart pounding, and I couldn't think of anything to say until I asked, "Have you found another dog to take Bandit's place?" I guess what I really meant was, Have you found another boy to take my place?

"No, but I ask about him on my CB," Dad told me. "He may turn up yet."

from *Dear Mr. Henshaw* by Beverly Cleary

A Child's-Eye View of Divorce and Remarriage: Single-Parent and Stepparent Issues

A happy, two-parent family continues to be seen as an ideal environment for raising children, and divorce is still seen as disruptive, putting strains on all of those involved. But there is also greater acceptance today that a single parent can, indeed, give children the security they need for healthy growth. This is good news, considering how many young children are now affected by divorce.

Researchers predict that half and possibly three-quarters of all children born in the last decade will spend at least one year living in a single-parent home. This includes a small but growing number of mothers who never marry, but the large increases in the number of single-parent families are mainly a result of divorce.

No two families will experience a separation in the same way. The personalities and the specifics are too diverse, and it would take an entire book to do justice to such a complicated subject. Nevertheless, when children are involved, certain issues and behaviors can be expected. This chapter, written primarily for single parents and stepparents, looks at divorce and remarriage from a child's point of view.

It is painful to witness a child's grief. And it is not unusual for parents to persuade themselves that young children will not be affected by a divorce. "At first, I tried to convince myself that it was somehow 'good' for the kids," one mother said of her separation. "It's as if I was trying to deny that I had done something to hurt them." But if a divorce is emotionally draining for you, it is also a burden for your children, who do not have the same defense mechanisms as an adult.

You are in a better position to help a child in distress if you begin by accepting that a divorce raises difficult issues for children. Although it takes time, families can adjust "intact" to their new status.

"Winners, Losers, and Survivors"

E. Mavis Hetherington, a psychology professor at the University of Virginia, has studied the effects of divorce on children for more than two decades. Initially, she assumed that divorce would automatically be damaging, or "pathogenic," for children. Twenty years later, her views have changed.

A separation, she contends, is disruptive for families. "Few children wish for their parents' divorce," she wrote in 1989. But she concedes now that the event, while stressful, need not be damaging in the longer term. She observes that children have typically fared better in a harmonious, well-functioning single-parent or stepparent home than in a conflict-ridden family with warring mother and father. Hetherington insists that depending on many factors that are under a parent's control, children may emerge "winners, losers, or survivors" of divorce and remarriage.

Victoria Ryan, a psychologist in full-time practice in Glen Cove, New York, and herself a stepparent of three grown children, agrees with this view. When parents ask her if their breakup is going to hurt their children, Dr. Ryan is honest: "I tell them, 'Yes, it's damaging for children. What most children want is the family they had.'" But, she quickly adds, "There are many things parents can do to make it less damaging to children."

This chapter looks at some of the ways in which parents can either help or hinder a young child's adjustment. Throughout this book we've seen that a great deal of behavior in the first six years can be explained by normal child development, by temperament, and by the interactions that take place every day between parent and child. The same model helps to explain how children feel and behave when a parent moves out.

Normal Development or a Reaction to Stress?

A divorce may compound the normal problems of raising children. All siblings will fight from time to time, and a child may occasionally become withdrawn or anxious about school. It isn't always possible for divorced parents to distinguish between conduct that might occur anyway in the normal course of growth and reactions that are linked to the end of a marriage.

Bedtime is a good example. During the day, one divorced father explained, his five-year-old daughter seemed fine. Her conduct at night, however, was a clue to the turmoil she felt but couldn't express:

"Kathryn was always a great sleeper. But after my wife and I separated, she would cry inconsolably at night and insist that someone stay with her until she fell asleep. During the day she didn't seem upset about the divorce, and there were never any problems at school. But obviously, she felt troubled, and it all caught up with her at night."

For children and adults alike, stress makes it more difficult to relax at bedtime. The more pressure we feel, the more elusive sleep becomes. Even in intact families preschool children may protest when a parent says good night and leaves the room. But in a family where the father has just moved out, a small child's fear of abandonment may understandably turn urgent. On a subconscious level children can't help worrying: *Daddy left me, and Mommy might do the same thing.* Psychologist Robert Wolf treats many school-age children. "Following a divorce," he says, "fears start to mushroom." If you are worried, look at the severity of your child's behavior.

Where Temperament Comes In

Within the same family, reactions to a separation will vary. Feelings of sadness and loss are common. But each child is different, and there is no way to predict how children will express these emotions, or whether in fact they will find an outlet at all. The best guide to your child's behavior following a divorce is probably his or her personality prior to it.

Reactions to a divorce are often consistent with a child's basic temperament. In fact, earlier patterns of behavior may intensify. A child who never separated easily may pale now at saying good-bye. A little boy with a quick temper may begin hitting children again at school or acting out. As a parent, you can be understanding of these tendencies, but you still want to help children find avenues for anxiety that are in their best interest. Even in a situation such as a divorce, problem behavior—whether it is a habit of withdrawing or of acting out—is highly malleable.

Hetherington notes that some children are temperamentally "difficult" from birth. If transitions are a challenge for these boys and girls, then the changes that come with a divorce can be traumatic. The ability to verbalize feelings or to control anger are qualities that help "easy" children to cope; so do strong peer relationships. But a difficult child, who is more vulnerable to feeling isolated or inferior to begin with, may have none of these coping mechanisms to fall back on. His aversive behavior only brings about more rejection, and this reinforces his need to attack others.

One father noted that differences in personality, apparent from birth, could be seen in the way his children reacted to his moving out:

> "Janice was always more thoughtful and introspective, and she could talk easily about what was on her mind. But Casey was very different. Even as a toddler she cried a lot and acted out more when she was upset. We knew she was troubled, but it was harder to get her to talk about her feelings. We found that therapy was an important outlet for her."

A child's behavior can also be deceptive. Therapists offer many examples of parents claiming that a particular child (often described as "sturdy") seems to be coping beautifully, with no outward signs of strain. One custodial father insisted that his four-year-old son had fully accepted his mother's leaving—until they attended a Broadway show one weekend. During the play, it seems, the son was enchanted by the female lead. When the cast took their bows, he bolted toward the stage, yelling to the actress, "Will you be my Mommy? Will you be my Mommy?!" The father, shocked, finally accepted his son's feelings of loss.

Ten years after she became a stepmother, one woman recalls:

> *"My stepson kept a lot inside after his parents divorced, but my husband's daughter had a completely different reaction. She made life difficult for everyone, so it was clear she needed to talk to someone and get out some of her resentment. But looking back, I think Allan's son needed an outlet just as much as his daughter. In fact, I think the therapy helped her to let go of certain issues that her brother is still carrying around to this day."*

Even a child who appears to be coping needs to talk about these changes. Sensitive children, aware that a custodial mother is under a lot of pressure, may not want to burden her with their own anxiety. If you are unable to provide a sympathetic ear as a parent, then be sure that your child has a friend or relative to turn to.

Between Parent and Child

Needless to say, if you are going through a divorce, you may find yourself less patient with a child, less sensitive to his needs for the time being. Some researchers call this *diminished parenting*. Briefly, it means that a custodial parent may not be as sympathetic or effective, especially during the early, stressful stages of a separation.

A mother of two children, ages five and eight, was aware that after becoming a single parent, and struggling for the first time to support her family, she had grown more critical of her children's foibles:

> *"I'm not as patient with my children now as I used to be, and that has been a very difficult adjustment for me. But what can I do? The reality is that I've been under a lot of pressure since my husband moved out."*

A custodial mother has to handle all of the normal tasks of child care at a time when she may feel angry, disappointed, or depressed about a marriage that didn't work out. The strain can be enormous, especially if it is compounded by financial pressure. Some parents react by becoming more permissive. They "excuse" behavior that would normally be unacceptable, whether it is because they are too exhausted to deal with discipline issues or because they think a child is under too much pressure already. But from a child's perspective this may be interpreted as a lack of caring. Acting out can become a way of regaining a parent's attention.

In other families, by contrast, a custodial mother may become critical and demanding, like the authoritarian model described in Chapter 2. This pattern can also create problems, with parents less attuned to a child's individual needs. Children will feel more vulnerable if a custodial parent becomes either too permissive or too controlling after a divorce.

But it is also important to acknowledge the struggles and remorse of a parent who moves out. One noncustodial father, when asked what had been most painful for him, replied that it was the loss of intimacy he had previously enjoyed with his young daughters:

> *"I miss not being able to go into their rooms at night and make sure that they're safe . . . the routine of coming home and getting involved, giving them their bath, drying their hair. It's taken a long time to get to the point where I don't feel rushed during a weekend with them."*

In some families parents make a point of continuing to discuss issues that affect the children—decisions about school, for example, or plans for music lessons, or summer camp. But in others, parents plainly lose touch. The loss of physical proximity can give way to emotional distance, and a noncustodial parent may feel shut off from his children. When this happens, children can misread a father's behavior as aloof and assume that he is less interested in their lives than before. It takes time for new living arrangements to normalize, and you should expect relationships to enter a state of flux.

It helps to be flexible. A family may try joint custody but find that one parent's travel schedule during the week makes it too unpredictable for everyone. In this case, weekend visits may reduce friction, providing a stable routine that young children prefer.

Understanding Why Divorce Is Disruptive

Today, instead of laying the blame for problem behavior on the divorce per se, researchers look at the specific changes that come with a divorce. Decisions about custody, for example, profoundly affect a child's everyday life. If a divorce is followed by an ugly custody battle, then conflict between parents may escalate. Obviously, children suffer from these ongoing disputes.

From your child's perspective, these are some of the harsh realities of a family's breaking up:

Emotional Confusion

When children aren't given a chance to talk about a divorce, they come up with their own theories of what went wrong and why. And children often conclude that they are to blame.

How does this happen? Dr. Wolf explains that in homes where there is frequent fighting or verbal abuse between parents, a child is more likely to think he caused his parents to go separate ways. "The child remembers spilling the milk, for example," he explains. "And then Mommy got upset and Daddy started yelling at Mommy. But from the little boy's perspective, it was the spilled glass of milk that started all the fighting, and therefore the divorce is *his* fault."

Even in a home without fighting, it can be difficult to explain a divorce to young children or to gauge their reactions. "My husband and I never fought in front of the children," one mother said. "I think they must have been very surprised to hear that he was leaving, and I still have a hard time finding the words to explain it to them."

Divided Loyalties

"Children are very loyal creatures," says Dr. Victoria Ryan, who counsels adolescents and their families. She contends that it is confusing for children when parents put down or criticize each other. A child who looks forward to a weekend with his father may begin to feel guilty for enjoying their time together, since it is obviously upsetting to the mother.

Changes in Financial Security

It is an added burden to a child when a family's financial status plummets, which is often the case when a father moves out or remarries. Now, after moving to a less expensive neighborhood, a child may also be starting a new school, so that nothing quite remains the same. A mother who was previously at home may begin working full-time, which means changes in child care. All of these pressures take a toll on a custodial parent, who is already more emotionally and physically drained than ever. And sadly, all of this occurs at a time when children, also strained by a divorce, need a patient, loving hand.

Continued Conflict Between Parents

"Divorce is about troubled relationships," says Dr. Francesca Schwartz. Its effect on a young child is largely determined, she explains, by how the conflict between the parents is resolved. From a child's perspective what matters most is your capacity for "control, resolution, and reparation." Children who continue to see their parents hurt and insult each other long after the papers have been signed will continue to suffer the ill effects of divorce. In families where divorced parents learn to get along, children learn that a relationship can end without injury. If parents can set aside their conflicts and put the family's interests above their own, a child has a better chance of emerging, to use Hetherington's word, a "winner."

RED FLAGS

Changes in Behavior, Mood, or Outlook

In growing up, children normally go through changes in behavior. But according to Dr. Wolf, this can be a symptom of anxiety or withdrawal for a child whose parents have separated. He gives the example of an excellent softball player who suddenly lost interest in the sport, claiming that he couldn't hit the ball well anymore. Clearly, though, it was a clue to depression arising from many unresolved conflicts, and some counseling helped. "It's hard for us to admit to ourselves that children experience the same intense feelings and reactions that we do," says Dr. Wolf.

Sudden Fears and Withdrawal

Again, fear is a common element of childhood. Look at the *intensity* and *duration* of any problem behavior, including a child's phobic reactions. A common pet may become terrifying to your child, or she may suddenly refuse to walk down a certain street. When a child won't go to a best friend's house, says Dr. Wolf, parents may make excuses for the behavior, claiming that it's "just a phase." But these can all be symptoms of anxiety, a sign that your child needs reassurance.

The danger of allowing extreme reactions to continue untreated is that they may become permanent patterns of behavior. Of special concern is a child who begins to lose interest in playing with other children, or who becomes aloof. The ability to form and maintain close attachments is something that we learn in childhood, but this can occur only if children feel that they can trust others not to hurt or disappoint them.

Naturally, divorce can interfere with this process, since many children feel rejected when a parent moves out. After a divorce children may have to establish their ability to trust and to form close attachments again with others. It is not unusual for children to carry a fear of loss, and a consequent lack of commitment, into adulthood, with the unhappy result that they never learn to form happy, lasting relationships of their own.

Ask Yourself:

Have you explained the divorce to your child in an age-appropriate way?

It can be dangerous to assume that the less said, the better. Obviously, what you say will depend in part on your child's age. A school psychologist or private therapist can suggest ways of informing a six-year-old as opposed to a two-year-old. But every child is entitled to some explanation. Otherwise, children will "fill in the gaps" with their own theories. When this happens, young children may conclude that they are to blame.

If you have more than one child, try speaking to each one's immediate concerns. Your preadolescent son may need to hear that Daddy will still coach the soccer team. But your youngest child needs more basic information. A preschooler's first concern is: *Who is going to take care of me?* Nico Carpenter, a social worker who counsels divorced families on Long Island, urges mothers to tell a preschool child, for example: "We will always be your parents. I will always be your mommy, and Daddy will always be your daddy. We will always take care of you. We will always love you." This can be more reassuring to a child than confusing statements such as, "Daddy and I still love each other, but not in the same way."

At the same time that it's important to clarify and reiterate your new living arrangements (where your children will sleep, when they will see Daddy, and so on), you also want to be honest in acknowledging what a big change this will mean for everyone and that getting used to these changes will, of course, take time.

Do you talk about the divorce, and do you encourage your child to do the same?

Most parents would never set out to do something harmful to their children. Discussing a divorce is difficult, though, and many mothers and fathers try to convince themselves that "the kids will be fine." Children are adaptable and malleable, yes, but they do not always know how to articulate what is troubling to them.

An absence of symptoms should be treated with suspicion. One of the most exasperating misperceptions is that a child who doesn't show any emotion is not affected by a divorce. But this is to deny a child's feelings, when they have simply been hidden. "There are assumptions that kids can deal with all sorts of things," says one therapist. "But children are children, and they need help."

Are you supportive of your child's relationship with the noncustodial parent?

The more a noncustodial parent stays involved, the better it is at any age. Again, this may not be possible if a spouse moves to another city or has no interest in staying close with the children. This can also be complicated because it means coordinating at least three schedules. When parents succeed, however, they send a child two important signals: first, that they can resolve their own disagreements and, second, that they are willing to put the child's interests first. Many studies today show that children do best when they continue to have a relationship with both parents.

Even in two-parent families mothers and fathers have different ways of handling children. One parent may be the disciplinarian, while the other tends to be more lenient. One custodial mother found these differences were even harder to accept when her children started spending weekends with their father:

> *"My ex-husband doesn't know anything about cooking, and the kids would eat hot dogs and pizza when they were with him. I'm very health-conscious, and at first it bothered me a lot. Now I've learned to let it go. In the end it's more important that they spend the time together, so I've learned to be more relaxed about it."*

It may take a lot of self-restraint, but try to avoid criticizing your former spouse. It puts children in the position of feeling disloyal to you if they love someone who causes you grief. You can be honest about things that you and your former spouse disagree about (children nearly always intuit your real feelings anyway), but try to speak about each other as neutrally as possible.

Are you putting your child in the position of having to "choose" between parents?

Again, young children should never be made pawns in parental strife. Yet parents do this inadvertently in many ways. While some parents make the mistake of saying too little about their marital problems, others say too much. When a mother talks to a school-age child about the father's affair with another woman, it is not only inappropriate but harmful. It puts terrible pressure on a child to feel that his love for one parent is an act of disloyalty to another. Again, if you aren't sure about how to explain a divorce to your children, speak with someone who can help you to do this in a sensitive way.

Even after custody arrangements have been worked out, parents should never ask young children with whom they would rather spend time. To you it may be just one afternoon or one weekend. But from their perspective the children are being asked to state a preference, and this only adds to the burden of coping with divorce.

Is your child learning to form close, trusting relationships with other adults and children?

Learning to trust is one of the most important tasks of childhood. At its worst, divorce may threaten a child's ability to form close attachments. Many children exhibit signs of mourning for a parent who moves out. Try not to belittle these feelings ("How can you miss him? You see him every weekend. In fact, he spends more time with you now than before the divorce."). If these feelings are not addressed, a child may withdraw from others as a way of avoiding another painful loss. An uncle may not be the same as a father, but children benefit richly from close relationships with members of their extended family.

Do you constantly feel guilty?

Many parents feel terrible about subjecting their children to the experience of divorce, but it is important to overcome these feelings. "When they're working off guilt, parents make the worst decisions," says Nico Carpenter. As an example, she notes that each parent will probably have different rules at home. Your husband may let the children eat in the living room in front of the TV, whereas you may insist that the food stay in the kitchen. But you don't have to apologize for being less lenient. "Children can adjust," she insists. "They learn early on, for example, that the rules at Grandma's house are different than the rules at home." She suggests a gentle reminder when your children return from being with a noncustodial parent: "I know Daddy lets you watch TV at his house, but remember that the rules here are different: No TV until you've finished all your homework."

Do you expect and allow each child to respond differently?

Be wary of studies that oversimplify how children react ("Boys act out, and girls withdraw"). Focus on each child in your family and do your best to help them individually. For preschool children free play is an important outlet for emotions and anxieties that cannot be easily expressed. Most children want a mommy and a daddy and, through fantasy play, they can compensate for the parent they miss.

Similarly, expect the duration of each child's adjustment to vary. Some boys and girls need three months to adjust; others need a year or two. What's more, depending on a child's stage of development, the issues may change and reappear over time. A boy entering adolescence, for example, may suddenly ask to spend more time with a noncustodial father.

Are you attentive to changes in your child's personality?

This can mean any departure from normal behavior, from eating habits and outgoingness to brushing teeth and bathing. If you aren't sure whether the change signals a real problem, talk to someone about it anyway. It isn't always necessary to involve a child in treatment. Your pediatrician or the school psychologist may have suggestions for how to handle a specific situation with your child. Parents risk more by not dealing with issues that may be troubling to children.

Stepfamilies

The first year after a divorce is typically the hardest, but most children adjust to life with just one parent. About three-quarters of divorced mothers remarry, however, and this means another transition for a child who has experienced a divorce. Along with the rise in step-families has been a new language used to describe them. "Blended" or "reconstituted" families are more and more common today, and researchers are just beginning to study them.

Frank F. Furstenberg, a professor at the University of Pennsylvania, finds that many remarriages also end in divorce. (In fact, there is a greater chance of divorce in remarriages involving children than we see in first marriages.) Furstenberg estimates that when custodial parents remarry, about one third of the children go through a redivorce. (Approximately one child in ten, he contends, "will see their parents divorce, their custodial parents remarry and then divorce again before reaching the age of sixteen.")

In other words, remarriage does not automatically "stabilize" a child's life. Children whose parents separate and divorce may see their family situation transformed many times over.

Overcoming the Obstacles to Stepfamilies

As with divorce, there is no "typical" stepfamily scenario. When a noncustodial parent remarries, the stepparent can easily become the target of a child's resentment. "Think of it this way," says one therapist. "If your parents get divorced and your father remarries, it's easier to get mad at your stepparent because she doesn't count as much. It's a lot safer."

On the bright side, there are families for whom the arrival of a sympathetic stepmother is welcomed. She may help a noncustodial father to renew ties with his children, especially a father who found it difficult to "mother" his children during weekend visits.

Despite the complications—and there are many, especially when two families with children try to become one—certain problems can be avoided if the biological parents and stepparents are sensitive to the child's point of view. The following are some suggestions that may ease the arrival of a stepparent.

See It as Another Transition for Your Child

Young children are easily shaken at times of transition, so don't be surprised if your normally self-sufficient four-year-old seems more needy than usual. Your child has already coped with a divorce and grown accustomed to life with one parent. Now, after perhaps being the exclusive focus of your attention, your son or daughter has to share you with someone new. Jealousy and resentment of your new spouse are common reactions, but you can prevent problems by continuing to spend some time alone with your children. They need to feel that your new marriage isn't a threat to the intimacy that was once reserved for them.

Let the Biological Parent Handle Discipline

It helps to have the natural parent handle discipline issues, especially in the beginning. Research has shown that children resent an overzealous stepparent. When two divorced or widowed parents marry, each with children from a previous marriage, anger and disappointment run high. Each family unit has a different idea about how to spend vacations, for example, or what to do in the evening, says Dr. Ryan. A child cannot help but think, *These other people are doing it so differently!*

In essence, to make both families work as one, a new family unit has to be formed. You must be able to talk openly. Work together to develop a new code whereby both families have a chance to air their preferences and everyone is asked to compromise a little.

Expect Children to React Differently

Again, reactions will vary within the same family. A very young child may welcome a live-in father, especially one who is kind and loving and not overly demanding. But an older son who has assumed the role of "the man in the family" may be full of resentment if a custodial mother remarries. Be sensitive to each child's reactions to a new stepparent and try to get these out into the open. As with childhood fears, once these feelings are accepted as valid, it is much easier for children to let go of them.

Be Sensitive to Issues of Allegiance

Children frequently act rude or abusive toward a stepparent. This usually occurs because children are angry at the natural parent and need to be reassured. Rudeness toward a stepparent should be handled with understanding, but it should never be condoned. Focus on finding a better form of release, such as imaginative play, for a young child's anger.

Children with stepparents worry about where a parent's real allegiance lies. One social worker tells of a seven-year-old girl whose noncustodial father remarried, becoming stepfather to a girl just a year or two older than his daughter. One day the natural daughter surprised everyone by asking a neighbor with whom she had become close if she could call him "Dad." It was as if she were saying to her father, "Okay, you got yourself a new daughter. Now I'm going to get myself a new father."

In this case, the social worker noted, the father saw what was happening, and he made a point of spending more time alone with his daughter.

Even when children have embraced a stepmother, issues of allegiance may arise from time to time. It is understandable, for example, that when a remarried father is expecting a new baby, children from the first marriage will feel "displaced." To lash out at the father would be to put that relationship at risk. It is safer for children to behave poorly toward a pregnant stepmother.

Despite her training, Dr. Ryan recalls that becoming a stepparent was harder than she had anticipated. "My stepchildren's reactions to me had nothing to do with me," she explains, "but with loyalty to their own family or parents."

Avoid Rushing the Relationship

Finally, stepparents are often eager to be loved and accepted by their stepchildren. But experience proves that children need time to get to know this new member of the family. Insisting that a child call your new spouse Mom or Dad is a mistake. Many children resent the idea of "replacing" their real mother or father.

Children may also be mistrustful of the new parent in their lives. One stepmother took a realistic stance toward her husband's children:

"For me, it was never an issue of getting Bob's kids to 'love' me. I knew there was resentment. They already had a mother, and I knew they didn't need or want another one. In the beginning I gave them a lot of time alone with their dad because I knew they needed him to themselves. It's taken a long time, but today we're good friends, and I know they like and respect me a lot."

When stepparents try to impose feelings of intimacy, children feel rushed and even more resentful. It is not unlike what happens in an intact family when a second child comes along, and parents are eager for the older child to welcome the new baby. Children feel guilty about the gulf between what they're expected to feel and what they do feel, and this only generates more anxiety.

But stepparents may also feel guilty about not "loving" a spouse's children. Experts suggest that couples be realistic about these bonds. It takes time to form attachments, and there are no guarantees that stepparents and children will form genuinely loving relationships. The lesson of most stepparents who succeed is that patience pays off.

CHAPTER THIRTEEN

The tellyfone rings in our house and my father picks it up and says in his very important tellyfone voice "Simpkins speaking," Then his face goes white and his voice goes all funny and he says *"What! Who!"* and then he says "Yes sir I understand but surely it is *me* you is wishing to speke to sir not my little son?" My father"s face is going from white to dark purpel and he is gulping like he has a lobster stuck in his throte and then at last he is saying "Yes sir very well sir I will get him sir" and he turns to me and he says in a rather respeckful voice "is you knowing the president of the United States?" and I says "No but I expect he is hearing about me." Then I is having a long talk on the fone and saying things like "Let me take care of it, Mr. President. You'll bungle it up if you do it your way." And my father's eyes is goggling right out of his head and that is when I is hearing my father's real voice saying get up you lazy slob or you will be late for skool.

from *The BFG* by Roald Dahl

A Few More Words About Language: What We Say and What Children Hear

This chapter looks at language and the happy effects of using words as they should be used with a child: to create intimacy, to convey understanding, to show that mistakes can be forgiven (and, indeed, forgotten), and to acknowledge that we know childhood is anything but easy.

Dr. Haim Ginott, the late child psychologist and author, believed that between parent and child, habits of speech influence habits of behavior. In his books he noted that for children to respect themselves—which they must do before they can respect others and act humanely—they must be spoken to with respect. Instead, we sometimes speak to our own children in a way that we would never use to address a stranger or someone else's child. The effect is not only to attack and diminish a child but to reinforce the behavior that made us critical in the first place.

When parents choose their words carefully instead of callously, the results are often heartening. Here are some examples:

"That Must Hurt Like the Devil"

My father is a man of few words, and enormous compassion. One of my most vivid memories of childhood was his reaction whenever my brothers or I got hurt, and it was almost always the same: "That must hurt like the devil." Those words took the sting out of many stubbed toes and skinned knees, and I believe they have done the same for my own children, so often have I used them.

Bettelheim wrote that nothing is more satisfying to a child than to be taken seriously, and I see now that this is why my father's words were like an elixir.

A more typical reaction to a child's distress is to say, "It's nothing." "Never mind." "It's a tiny scrape. I can't even see it!" When children wail inconsolably, I am convinced that they are working hard to persuade us that their pain is real. If you think that too sympathetic a response will only prolong a child's tears, you needn't worry. Typically (assuming no broken bones, of course), the response to a heartfelt "That must hurt like the devil" is a stoic "Thanks, Mommy. I'm okay."

The Sleepover That Wasn't

A mother told me that her eight-year-old son, Peter, had been invited to a sleepover party one night but was reluctant to attend. It was given by a boy he knew at school, but they weren't in the same class, and Peter said he didn't know any of the other boys who would be there. After her son agonized over whether or not to go, his mother offered to pick him up later in the evening if he wasn't having a good time. Here's what happened:

> "At about nine-thirty Peter called and asked me to take him home. I probably could have talked him into staying—he didn't sound miserable or anything—but I wanted him to know that I meant what I said about the choice being his."

When children fret about sleepovers, we have a tendency to turn it into something much bigger. I admired this mother's ability to focus on what was important—namely, the trust between parent and child.

She rescued him from an uncomfortable evening, but she also taught him to respect his own feelings.

When You Have to Miss the School Play

If a business trip keeps you from attending a school play and your daughter has said nothing about it, don't assume that she is not affected by it. Try turning this around, and you will see why. Your child is probably looking at you and thinking the same thing: "Mommy hasn't said anything about missing my play, so it must not be very important to her."

Nor should you assume that talking about it will only make your child feel sadder. The disappointment you feel about not being able to share something meaningful is being felt just as deeply by your child, and honest words from you can help: "I feel just awful about not being there tomorrow. What can we do together when I get back? I know it won't be the same, but it's important for me to be with you and to hear all about it." Words like these can buoy a child who feels let down.

Make arrangements to film the play, or to have someone else attend in your place and take pictures. Children appreciate such gestures, especially when they come from the heart. One father had to miss his daughter's farewell party on the last day of school. The day before, however, he arranged to visit her class and join her for lunch. She was thrilled and didn't feel dismayed about his absence the following day.

Torn Between Two Friends

Even when the evidence appears to be stacked against your child, try to give her the benefit of the doubt.

Nicole's mother was told that Nicole, six, and another little girl had excluded a classmate and hurt her feelings. It was the mother of the aggrieved party who told this to Nicole's mother. In a case like this, it is easy to feel outraged and disappointed by a child's behavior. But Nicole's mother waited until after dinner that evening, when things were quiet, and said, "Do you ever get to play with Molly at school?"

Nicole's face fell. She looked up at her mother and said, "I feel as if I'm being split in half. I want to play with Molly, but Rachel says she won't be my best friend anymore if I do."

Her daughter clearly felt anguished. What followed was a heart-to-heart talk about how difficult it is when friends become possessive. They were able to arrange time for Nicole and Molly to play together and to reassure Rachel as well. How easy it would have been for Nicole's mother to assume the worst. Instead, she had faith in her daughter, chose her words carefully, and listened.

Nervous About the First Day of Camp

I was walking my daughter to her first day of camp one morning and couldn't help noticing, a few feet ahead of us, a little boy who was crying. He was obviously frightened and kept pulling at his father's arm. But his father, who looked a little embarrassed, kept walking ahead, saying, "C'mon, we'll be late."

Can't he be a little more sympathetic? I thought. *Can't he just tell his son that it's okay, everyone is a little nervous the first day of camp? Or tell him that his counselor is probably going to be great?*

Then I asked myself how "relaxed" I would have been if my own child had been making a scene in front of everyone! It occurred to me that we often save our kindest, most sympathetic words for someone else's children. With our own, we lose perspective. Fretting too much about the future (*How will he ever go away to college?!*), we neglect to offer the comfort they need today.

A Big Brother Who Became the Baby Expert

Through her gestures and her language one mother ensured that the new baby provided a lift for her older child's confidence:

"If Brandon and I were reading a book together and the baby started to cry, I never rushed over to her. I would say to him, 'What are we going to do?' It was always Brandon's idea to go over and see what was the matter. After a few months, he was the one who got the biggest smiles from Stephanie, so we called him the baby expert. You could see that he loved that. Instead of the baby making him less important in the house, she made him more important."

(The same woman admitted that she sometimes worried because, a year later, the baby would run to greet Brandon before she ran to her mother, and she wondered if maybe there was something wrong with that. I suggested that the baby must be very secure in both relationships. Most parents of siblings, I added, would welcome such a problem!)

"It's Hard to Make New Friends . . ."

A mother of a four-year-old told me,

"I never asked Lizann whether the first few days of school were difficult or lonely, because I didn't want to 'make her' feel afraid, and she never indicated that she was having any problems. Then at dinner one night I was talking about my grandmother, who had just moved into a nursing home. I was concerned about her because she still hadn't made any new friends. Suddenly, Lizann looked up and said, 'I feel sad at school because I don't know anybody.' "

Once Lizann said this, her parents reassured her that it takes time to make friends and feel comfortable in a new school. They also asked her which children she wanted to get to know better and decided to invite them over to play. Instead of making Lizann more anxious, as her parents had feared, the discussion seemed to bolster her. She seemed not only relieved but eager to go back to school in the morning. Her parents learned that children, like adults, can work through difficult issues by discussing them.

"I Could Never Do That!"

Perhaps the most extraordinary thing about words is how often they backfire, having the opposite effect of what we intended. Even words of praise may fall short. My daughter brought home an art project one day, and we started to admire her work. She was delighted—until I made the mistake of saying, "I could never do that when I was younger." Her expression changed immediately, and she began reassuring me that I could.

Children are protective of our feelings, too. If a child senses that his accomplishments make you feel inadequate, he may well avoid that activity. (It is more effective, I learned, to praise a child's work by *describing* what you see. See the sidebar that follows.)

Words may fail us when we try to help a child with homework, too. "That's an easy one," we say, trying to offer encouragement. But as Haim Ginott points out, this has the opposite effect. Now the child thinks he must *really* be dumb if he can't even answer an "easy" problem.

Reacting to a Child's Artwork

"It's beautiful!"

This is the first thing many parents say when their child shows them a drawing. According to many educators, though, there are more effective ways of commenting on children's art, and parents should avoid comments like these, which "validate" each piece of work.

"The best thing is to talk about exactly what you see on the paper," advises Barry Goldberg, a nursery school teacher and sculptor. If one corner of the page is filled with orange shapes, then he suggests commenting on that color ("I see that you used lots of orange today"). Focus on what the child did ("I see you put a triangle and a circle together in the corner"), instead of what he or she didn't do ("Why didn't you draw anything on the rest of the page?"). Describing the work takes time, and you can't do this without really looking at it. Hanging art work in a prominent place at home is also a way of showing that you appreciate a young child's creativity.

As with homework, discussed in Chapter 10, *process* is just as important as *product* when it comes to a child's artwork. Instead of rushing to compliment his handmade picture frame, ask your son how he made it. Did he paint it first and then add the glue on the sparkles, or the other way around? You will probably be amazed at what a detailed explanation a three-year-old can provide, and by how much he appreciates your interest.

Goldberg offers another reason why a three-year-old's paintings can leave parents as tongue-tied as a Jackson Pollack. "We're taught [from an early age] that understanding is the ability to translate into language," he explains, "but that isn't what art is about."

For parents, trying to name or identify what's in a picture is especially risky. If you exclaim that a drawing looks "just like a tree" but the young artist never intended to make one, then he will feel easily defeated, as if the work is a failure.

"The child is choosing a certain way to 'behave' on the paper," says Goldberg. The more your words show that you see and appreciate these choices, the happier your child will feel.

"My Best Friend Isn't in My Class!"

One mother said that her daughter typically came home from the first day of school full of enthusiasm. But after her first day of second grade, she looked and felt crushed. "Mary's not in my class this year," she told her mother. "I kept waiting for her to come into the room, but she's in a different class. This is the first year we haven't been together." The mother continued:

> *"There wasn't a lot I could say, so I just listened and nodded sympathetically. I remembered feeling upset like that when I was about the same age, but I also made some wonderful new friends that year. When I told my daughter that, she seemed to appreciate it. 'Y'know,' she told me, 'Amy is in the class, and she seems pretty nice.' We went through the list of names and came up with a few other girls she wanted to invite over."*

We all know how tempting it is to say, "They didn't put you and Mary together? That's terrible! I can't believe they split up you and your best friend." These words might convey sympathy, too, but they would hardly have been as constructive in helping a child learn to deal with disappointments.

When Children Show Off for Their Friends

We feel a lot less sympathetic toward our children when they talk back or put us down in front of their friends. Most of us have suffered this embarrassment. If possible, though, resist the urge to yell and embarrass your child. Use damage control while friends are over. Call your child into your room and say, "Look, I don't want to embarrass you in front of your friends, but the way you're acting is not acceptable. Cut it out. We'll talk about this later."

At dinner or at bedtime, talk about what happened. Children have to learn that our feelings matter, too. You can also say, "I know you were excited, and it's fun to show off sometimes, but how would you feel if I called you names like that in front of my friends?" Children learn empathy by being taught and reminded to think about how others feel.

CHAPTER FOURTEEN

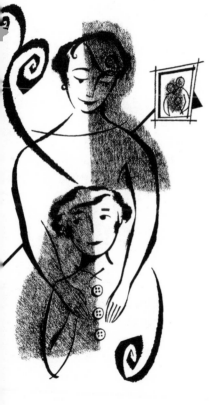

Of course the reason that all the children in our town like Mrs. Piggle-Wiggle is because Mrs. Piggle-Wiggle likes them. Mrs. Piggle-Wiggle likes children, she enjoys talking to them and best of all they do not irritate her.

When Molly O'Toole was looking at the colored pictures in Mrs. Piggle-Wiggle's big dictionary and just happened to be eating a candy cane at the same time and drooled candy cane juice on the colored pictures of gems and then forgot and shut the book so the pages all stuck together, Mrs. Piggle-Wiggle didn't say, "Such a careless little girl can never look at the colored pictures of gems in my big dictionary again." Nor did she say, "You must never look at books when you are eating." She said, "Let's see, I think we can steam those pages apart, and then we can wipe the stickiness off with a little soap and water, like this—now see, it's just as good as new. There's nothing as cozy as a piece of candy and a book."

from *Mrs. Piggle-Wiggle* by
Betty MacDonald

14~

Turnabout:
Ten "Good Habits"
for Ending
"Bad Habits"

1. Little by Little, Letting Go:

Understanding Autonomy and the Need to Be Separate

The child's need to "be his own person" gives rise to many of the issues discussed in this book. At the same time that we struggle to feed or to dress or to bathe them, children are struggling with something much bigger: self-worth.

Often, it is easier to do things for our children. If *we* pour the milk, there probably won't be a puddle to mop up afterward. If *we* insist on holding the spoon, the food has a better chance of finding its way into a child's mouth. But as children grow, we must surrender these tasks. Consider the significance of something as small as a hairbrush.

Fascinating research has been done on primates and how they nurture their young. The author of one article, an anthropologist, noted that chimpanzee mothers, for example, brush the infant's fur a great deal. "At times it is clear," he observed, "as the infant is growing older, that the grooming by the mother serves to keep the infant close to her at a time when he is on the verge of leaving."

The same "tug" occurs in human mothers, too, and this is why we sometimes perform a small task such as hairbrushing longer than we should. Children are as destined biologically to break away as we are, emotionally, to hold on and protect. But thinking independently comes of acting independently. It begins with a two-year-old doggedly pulling on flannel pajamas during a July heat wave and with parents accepting that the impulse is a good one. When we let go of these small tasks—without anger or sorrow but with pleasure and pride—we give each act of independence our blessing.

Accepting autonomy is the first step toward acceptance of the child. And this, I think, is the key to making our children feel positively about themselves. How can any child grow up to feel good about achieving if each act of independence threatens the approval of those he loves most?

2. Finding What Is Special in Each Child

Another theme of this book has been temperament, and the "fit" between parent and child. Being a good-enough parent means being attuned to each child in the family, which is easier to say than to do.

One of your children runs to you with open arms and kisses you roughly on the cheek each time you return. It is easy to return this kind of bold affection. But some children, despite what we read about the importance of early touch and "bonding," don't feel comfortable being cuddled. They may not express affection as easily. Don't assume, however, that the child who stands patiently at the door is any less happy to see you.

Shortly after the birth of our son, his two big sisters (then ages two and a half and five) came to see me at the hospital. I hadn't realized how much my younger daughter had missed me until weeks later, when I looked at the photographs we took that day and remembered that she had crawled into the hospital bed and nestled there beside me during the entire visit. My older daughter had gushed, "Mommy, it's so good to see you! When are you coming home?!" Her younger sister said little, but her quiet gesture spoke volumes.

Children differ in their interests and outlooks, and we need to nurture these with enthusiasm. But they share the same intense need for our love and approval. They simply have different ways of showing this.

3. Understanding Child Development: A Slippery Slope

Unlike physical growth, which proceeds in one direction, a child's emotional growth is marked by starts and stops. The psychology of early childhood is probably best summarized as one step backward for every two steps forward.

Transition and separation are two pervasive themes in the life of a young child. They occur in the first three years, and they recur forever afterward. These two principles alone help to explain the milestones that are most stressful in a young child's life and why these often lead to "bad habits" and troubling behavior. The sooner we understand how children internalize the events of their lives, the better we can handle reactions to any change: the beginning of school, the arrival of a new baby, the start of homework, and many other challenges of the first six years.

No one defends the child's erratic behavior (what she calls the "disharmonies" of development) more vigorously than Anna Freud. She argued that no child should be expected to function always at the same mature level. "On the contrary," she wrote, "occasional returns to more infantile behavior have to be taken as a normal sign."

As a parent, you can't help worrying about a child who starts waking up from nightmares or who resumes baby talk during the day. But these tendencies, however wearing, are to be treated as normal. A child cannot conquer the world all at once. In her writing, Anna Freud constantly makes the point that there is much more cause for alarm when these setbacks do *not* occur than when they do.

4. Giving a Child the Benefit of the Doubt

When a child challenges us with difficult behavior, we can feel overcome with anger. Often, though, habits that are upsetting to you are also troubling to your child. A little boy who hits, for example, quickly sees that his nursery school teacher disapproves of it and so do the other children.

In the introduction to one of her books, Nancy Samalin writes that she railed about her child's learning problems for a long time, until someone pointed out to her how unhappy her son must feel about school. It was only when she began to see the situation through his eyes that she could help him manage and overcome his anxiety.

It is much easier to give a child the benefit of the doubt if we put aside our feelings of disappointment and anger. If your child yells at you in front of someone else, you may feel outraged and embarrassed. Even so, try to see the incident from your child's perspective and discover what compelled him to act this way ("You must have been pretty angry to speak to me that way"). If you can do this, you can put an unpleasant incident behind you and in the process gain insight into your child.

5. Aiming Not to Be Perfect, but to Be "Good Enough"

As concerned parents, we want to do "the right thing" at all times: to read the right books, to say the right thing, to be the best parent possible. But this is not an attitude that serves children well in the long term. Just as children are entitled to their flaws, so are we.

The more we set out to be perfect, the more pressure we put on children to do likewise, and this is why they ultimately suffer when we expect too much of ourselves. Parents often "confess" to Francesca Schwartz, a psychologist, that they have a bad temper. What matters, she says, isn't that parents get angry (we all do) but how they handle these feelings. There is a world of difference between punching a hole in the wall and expressing anger without injury or insult. What children learn from us is how accepting we are of our own limitations and imperfections—and, indirectly, of their own—and what to do with errors in judgment or behavior once they are made.

Children, who begin life with an eagerness to please, need to know that *not* pleasing is also all right now and then. They learn tolerance for others' faults through our tolerance of their own. A child who grows up in a home with exacting standards cannot help but set impossible goals for himself. His parents take him to the skating rink for the first time, but he won't even step out onto the ice. When the standard is perfection, the risk of failure multiplies. Who can blame the child for not even wanting to try?

6. Having Confidence, Resisting Guilt

Many childhood experts contend that parents today feel guilty and that this affects the way they raise young children. The guilt felt by working mothers shouldn't surprise us. Consider the subplot of *Beethoven,* a recent Walt Disney movie that was seen by millions of children, including my own.

In the film, about a rambunctious sheepdog, the husband urges his wife to return to work, but she is reluctant. She wants to be home with her three children, the youngest of whom is about five, but finally agrees. On her first day at the office, however, one of the children nearly drowns in a neighbor's pool, thanks to an inept baby-sitter. The mother then announces that she will not work again because she loves her children, and that's the end of it.

I couldn't help wondering how children interpreted that message, especially the millions of boys and girls whose mothers do go to an office or a factory five days a week.

It is important to come to terms with your own decision to work or not to work. Research has never shown that children of mothers who work are either better or worse off than the children of mothers who do not. It has been found, however, that how a mother feels about whether or not she works matters a great deal. A mother who wants to work but does not tends to be less happy—and less effective as a parent—and so does a mother who does work but doesn't want to.

Feelings of guilt may prevent you from saying no to your children and setting limits when they are needed. And this can contribute to a child's problem behavior. Keep in mind that children easily learn to manipulate a guilty grown-up's behavior, but that it is harmful for them to do so.

Don't look to your children or to anyone else to validate the choices you make. You know your family's needs (financial and otherwise), and to the extent that you feel confident about how you meet them, you will make better decisions as a parent. At some point, whether you work or not, your child will wake up in the middle of the night or be afraid of dogs or refuse to get into the swimming pool. You can help your child most by being sensitive and sympathetic, not by assuming that it is all your fault.

(If you are still convinced that June Cleaver and Donna Reed were model moms, consider this: In his new book about the fifties, David Halberstam, who wrote *The Best and the Brightest,* reexamines "Ozzie and Harriet" and concludes, finally, that the real Nelson family was hopelessly dysfunctional!)

Part-time Work, Full-time Parent

"It's only work if you want to be somewhere else."
Sir J. M. Barrie

Many women find that their attitude toward the office changes with childbirth. For those of us who prided ourselves on sixty-hour weeks, the feeling that work is work—that, as Barrie put it, we would rather be somewhere else—comes as a shock bordering on sacrilege, as this woman found:

"For the first time in my life I had trouble concentrating on my work. I had made up my mind to go back full-time, but I really wanted to be with my baby. I never expected to feel so torn."

The media still leans toward one stereotype or the other: the corporate "supermom" or the ethereal, full-time "stay-at-home." For many of us, however, the reality of family life lies somewhere on a vast spectrum between these two extremes. Given the option economically, many mothers are finding work schedules and careers that allow some flexibility while their children are still young. It can be gratifying to schedule work around school vacations and birthdays, for example, and comforting to stay home with a sick child. But if a flexible work schedule has its rewards, it also brings on special pressures, as many mothers find:

> *"Before I had children I felt driven to do the best job possible at work. Now I feel the same 'drive' with respect to my children. I really want to be the best mother possible, and working part-time helps, but I still constantly wish I could be in two places at once."*

> *"I feel as if it's hard for my kids because I work part-time. Sometimes I can pick them up at school, sometimes I can't. It's so unpredictable, and I wonder if that's harder for them than if I worked full-time."*

As for any working parent (full-time or otherwise), both worlds will invariably come into conflict: your child wakes up feverish on the same day as a pivotal meeting or a career-making presentation to a new client. But even without such crises, working at all (whether it is fourteen hours a week or forty) will put a well-meaning parent in the position of juggling almost daily, as this mother found:

> *"I'm constantly torn between working a few more hours or picking my daughter up at school. She sees how ambivalent I am in the morning, and then she works herself up until I feel I have no choice but to leave work early. Then I'm not as patient with her because I'm thinking about how much I didn't get done at the office."*

Keeping to a fairly regular schedule can help. It is easier for you and your child if you can get into the habit of saying, "It's Tuesday. Don't forget that Dolores will be picking you up today because I'll be at my office." For a small child, the certainty of knowing to expect someone else after school may be better than wondering all morning whether it will be your face or the baby-sitter's at the door.

Most important, give up on the idea of being able to do it all, as this mother learned:

> *"It's taken me more than a year of part-time work to get it right. I used to exhaust myself trying to do everything, every day. Now I've learned that I can't, and I try to be more realistic. Sometimes my kids are disappointed if I can't be there in the afternoon, but I think I make up for it by being happier and more relaxed on the days when we're together."*

Some part-time working mothers find it's best to put in two or three full days a week. Others prefer spending five mornings at work and the rest of the day with the children. What works when your child is two may change by the time he turns five and starts kindergarten, so be flexible. Take the time to find a schedule that works for you, and then expect to modify it as your children go through changes in their emotional lives and start attending school for longer periods of time.

For many women, having work outside the home is a welcome and satisfying antidote to the demands of caring for a young family. And a happy consequence may be having more reasonable expectations of our children. That we can derive satisfaction outside of our children may be the best way of learning to enjoy and appreciate them for what they are.

Trying to be in two places at once can be draining, both physically and emotionally. If you succeed one week in achieving a perfect equilibrium, enjoy it—but write it off as a happy accident. Your goal is elusive, but it is worthwhile nevertheless. A balanced approach to life—one that leaves room for personal satisfaction and yet enables a family to be child centered—is an awfully nice legacy to give our children.

7. Rethinking What "Quality Time" Really Means

Recent surveys of older children have found that what they want most is more time with their families. Parents, meanwhile, get caught up in making extravagant plans that aren't necessary. Give thought to how you define "quality time." The objective is to be together. Tickets to a show or a ball game are a wonderful treat. But most young children would be just as happy, if not happier, to spend an hour alone with you in the park or read a favorite book together. These are the occasions that build intimacy and a true sense of shared experience. Don't let your child get into the habit of thinking that an afternoon is special only if it includes a trip to an amusement park or to the toy store.

We are all under pressure to support our families financially, and doing this often means spending time away from them. But compensate with time together that is meaningful to the particular child and that shows you appreciate his special needs and interests. Teaching a fearful child to ride a bike can be enriching for both of you, as long as it is done without pressure.

Above all, keep in mind that when you spend time with your children, you show them that you enjoy their company, that they are people you like to be with. And children who grow up feeling this way have a good reason for liking themselves.

8. Giving Childhood Back to Children

In his book *The Disappearance of Childhood,* author Neil Postman likens children today to "miniature adults" in the manner of thirteenth- and fourteenth-century paintings. The truth is that our children are barely distinguishable from grown-ups, from the way they dress to the places they go.

It doesn't have to be this way, but it takes enormous time and effort to keep childhood "innocent." We spend a lot of time convincing ourselves of what children are ready to do or to learn at an early age. David Elkind objects to infant swimming classes that promise to keep a baby "safe" if he falls into the water. He believes that it is the parent's job to keep a young infant safe, not the child's.

You may find his example too extreme, but the principle is sound. Many teachers are appalled by the movies and videos—even the TV news—that children today are permitted to watch. "Young children don't have the means to understand what they see on television," one educator explains, "and this only adds to their anxiety about whether the world is a safe place or not."

Our job in the first few years is to convince children that the world is, indeed, safe for them. It isn't "overprotective" to limit what children see on TV. On the contrary, it can be enormously liberating to a young child *not* to have to worry about certain problems. A child who feels secure is in a much better position to develop confidence, good judgment, and faith in his instincts. And this is what ultimately helps children to avoid dangerous situations in the world at large. Within the family, a child deserves to know that his needs are at the center, that the decisions made about his life are, to the extent possible, made in his best interest.

9. Coming to Terms with Your Own Childhood: Taking Stock of Yourself

When we become parents, we bring into the nursery many unresolved issues from our own upbringing. As we've seen, this affects issues such as feeding and disciplining a child, but it also influences how we nurture and support a child's growth. Whenever you find a child's behavior to be especially disquieting, or you find yourself reacting emotionally, look to your own childhood for clues.

Many therapists use the term *family of origin* when describing the patterns that persist from one generation to the next and how our own history influences that of our children. We have no real role models other than our own mothers and fathers. This is why parents who are basically happy with the way they were parented have an easier time raising their own families. Parents often set out to "correct" the mistakes their parents made. When we do this, however, we tend to "overcorrect" and make other mistakes instead.

In general, the more reconciled you are about your upbringing, the easier it will be for you to accept a child's behavior and idiosyncrasies. Instead of trying to bury a troubled relationship with your parents, this may be a good time for coming to terms with it.

10. Appreciating the Resilience of Parents and Children

There is no doubt that the first few years play an important role in a child's development. But it is never too late to improve your relationship, even if this requires outside help.

The important thing is for you to be able to see what is good in your child. If a specific habit has you losing sleep at night, or if you are worried about how the behavior will manifest itself down the line, then you are wise to do something about it. Otherwise, it may come between you and your child, and these effects may be more difficult to unravel than the original symptom or habit.

Sometimes, talking to a sympathetic friend can be helpful. We have a tendency to isolate ourselves in our concerns about our children. It can be reassuring, for example, to discover that your neighbor's child, who seems so well rounded and happy, exhibited the same fears or anxieties when he was your child's age. Parent groups, in which mothers and fathers can air the issues that concern them, are also helpful for gaining perspective. Find an approach that makes you feel comfortable.

A good pediatrician can answer questions about normal development. For a more serious problem he or she might refer you to a specialist. (Many schools also have a resident psychologist who is available to families.) Keep in mind that you can consult a psychiatrist or psychologist without involving your child in treatment. In fact, you should be wary of a professional who rushes to diagnose your child over the phone. After meeting with *you* first, a professional can suggest whether the child needs to be seen at all, or whether there are things you can do as a parent to modify a pattern of behavior. Some children benefit from one or two sessions with a therapist who can help ease specific problems and anxieties.

Finally, make use of the many wonderful books available today about early childhood. Many of these are listed in the Bibliography.

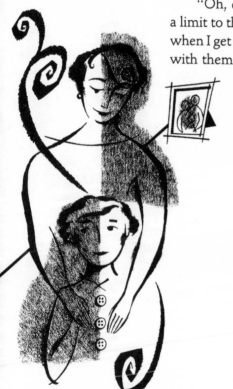

"Oh, don't you see, Marilla? There *must* be a limit to the mistakes one person can make, and when I get to the end of them, then I'll be through with them. That's a very comforting thought."

from *Anne of Green Gables*
by Lucy Maud Montgomery

Parting Words: The Spirit in Which We Act

The danger of any book about raising children is that it can either raise parents' expectations too high or else make us more critical of ourselves than before. Certainly, we can learn to anticipate some reactions, become more sensitive and sympathetic listeners, and try to separate our own fears and insecurities from those of our children. But for all our devotion and effort, there is no way that we will act wisely 100 percent of the time, no matter how many books we read or experts we consult.

We can occasionally congratulate ourselves on doing the right thing at the right time when faced with a child's challenging ways. But more often we will probably look back and wish we had acted otherwise. For every baffling reaction that we manage to figure out, there are many others that will remain at best a mystery. What may be most reassuring in the end is to know that there is plenty of latitude for the mistakes we make along the way.

There is so much good and useful information about the psychology of childhood, and we are wise to seek it out. But there is probably only one factor that prevails with any certainty, as undefinable as it is unscientific. It is what Jane Kessler has called *the spirit in which we act*. When words fail us or, quite the opposite, when they rush from our mouths faster than we would like, we can console ourselves that if no single moment is going to define our relationship with a child, neither can a single lapse of good judgment or patience destroy it.

At a recent forum on parenting, the pediatrician and author Penelope Leach made a confession. In her books she has always advised parents not to allow children to take a bottle to bed. And yet, she admitted, one of her own children did so until he was almost five years old! In an auditorium filled with anxious parents, the relief was palpable.

At one time, the child psychologist Bruno Bettelheim protested that Maurice Sendak's *Where the Wild Things Are* would be too disturbing for small children. But Bettelheim went on to write *The Uses of Enchantment,* a rousing endorsement of fairy tales in their most brutal, unadulterated form. Over time Bettelheim had come to appreciate that children need such fantasy as a way of working through their fears and anxieties.

If the experts who study children can be allowed their foibles and changes of heart—and *still be the experts*—then surely the rest of us should be allowed them as well. We try so hard to be consistent, and yet one lesson we can learn from the experts is that in parenthood, as in childhood, there is room to grow and evolve. The same learning curve that applies to any other skill or profession can surely be applied to the job of raising children.

Dr. Spock's book on child care became a bible for many of our parents, and over time he has earned a reputation for being "permissive." But this is a misnomer. If Dr. Spock was lenient, it was only in giving parents "permission" to trust their instincts and make mistakes.

The spirit in which we act counts for so much in this business of being parents. Nothing can be easy or simple when we care so deeply and the stakes appear so high. But time has a way of softening, smoothing, even erasing the mistakes that we once thought to be indelible. With a little perspective, we may just succeed in turning a daunting task into a rewarding and enjoyable one. And as Anne of Green Gables concludes, that's a very comforting thought.

Bibliography and Suggested Reading

Books

Ames, Louise Bates; Frances L. Ilg; and Sidney M. Baker. *Child Behavior.* New York: Harper Perennial, 1992.

Bettelheim, Bruno. *A Good Enough Parent.* New York: Alfred A. Knopf, Inc., 1987.

Bowlby, John. *Attachment and Loss.* New York: Basic Books, 1980.

Brazelton, T. Berry. *To Listen to a Child.* New York: Addison-Wesley Publishing Co., 1984.

Bruch, Hilde. *The Golden Cage/The Enigma of Anorexia Nervosa.* Cambridge, Massachusetts: Harvard University Press, 1978.

Chess, Stella and Thomas Alexander, *Temperament and Development.* New York: Brunner-Mazel, 1977.

Colao, Flora, and Tamar Hosansky. *Your Children Should Know.* Indianapolis: Bobbs-Merrill, 1983.

Cott, Jonathan. *Pipers at the Gates of Dawn: The Wisdom of Children's Literature.* New York: Random House, 1983.

Dewey, John, *The School and Society,* University of Chicago Press, 1943.

Elkind, David. *The Hurried Child.* Addison-Wesley Publishing Co., 1981.

———. *Miseducation: Preschoolers at Risk.* New York: Knopf, 1987.

Faber, Adele, and Elaine Mazlish. *How to Talk So Kids Will Listen & Listen So Kids Will Talk.* New York: Rawson-Wade, 1980.

———. *Liberated Parents—Liberated Children.* New York: Grosset & Dunlap, 1974, 1990.

Fraiberg, Selma H. *The Magic Years.* New York: Charles Scribner's Sons, 1959.

Freud, Anna. *Normality and Pathology in Childhood: Assessments of Development.* Madison, Connecticut: International Universities Press, Inc., 1965.

Ginott, Haim. *Between Parent and Child.* New York: Macmillan, 1963.

Hetherington, E. Mavis, and Josephine D. Avasteh, eds. *Impact of Divorce, Single Parenting, and Step-parenting on Children.* New Jersey: Lawrence Erlbaum Associates, Inc., 1988.

Kagan, Jerome. *The Nature of the Child.* New York: Basic Books, 1984.

Kaplan, Louise. *Oneness and Separateness: From Infant to Individual.* New York: Simon & Schuster, Inc., 1978.

Kessler, Jane. *Psychopathology of Childhood.* Englewood Cliffs, New Jersey: Prentice-Hall, Inc., 1966.

Leach, Penelope. *Your Baby & Child.* New York: Alfred A. Knopf, 1984.

Lytton, Hugh. *Parent-Child Interaction.* New York: Plenum Press, 1980.

Postman, Neil. *The Disappearance of Childhood.* New York: Delacorte Press, 1982.

Samalin, Nancy. *Love and Anger: The Parental Dilemma.* New York: Penguin Books, 1991.

———. *Loving Your Child Is Not Enough.* New York: Penguin Books, 1987.

Sheldon, Dr. William H. *Varieties of Temperament.* New York: Harper and Row, 1942.

Spitz, Rene. *No and Yes: On the Genesis of Human Communication.* Madison, Connecticut: International Universities Press, 1957.

Spock, Benjamin, M.D., and Michael B. Rothenberg, M.D., *Dr. Spock's Baby and Child Care.* New York: Pocket Books, 1985.

Stone, L. Joseph, and Joseph Church. *Childhood & Adolescence: A Psychology of the Growing Person.* New York: Random House, 1973.

Turecki, Stanley. *The Difficult Child.* New York: Bantam Books, 1985, 1989.

Winnicott, D. W. *Home Is Where We Start From.* London: Penguin Books. New York: W. W. Norton & Company, Inc., 1986.

———. *The Child, the Family and the Outside World.* Reading, Massachusetts: Addison-Wesley Publishing, 1964.

Academic Articles and Journals

Azar, S. T.; D. R. Robinson; E. Hekimian; and C. T. Twentyman (1984). "Unrealistic Expectations and Problem-solving Ability in Maltreating and Comparison Mothers." *Journal of Consulting and Clinical Psychology,* Vol. 52, No.4, 687–691.

Baumrind, D. (1971). "Current Patterns of Parental Authority." *Developmental Psychology Monograph,* Vol. 4, No. 4, Part 2.

Belsky, J. (1981). "Early Human Experience: A Family Perspective." *Developmental Psychology,* Vol. 17, No. 1, 3–23.

Belsky, J. and Fish, M. (1991). Temperament and Attachment Revisited: Origin and Meaning of Separation Intolerance at Age 3. *American Journal of Orthopsychiatry,* 418–427.

Birch, L.; S. L. Johnson; G. Andresen; J. Peters; and M. C. Schulte (1991). "The Variability of Young Children's Energy Intake." *The New England Journal of Medicine,* Vol. 324, No. 4, 232–235.

Bullock, J. R. (1989). "Parental Knowledge and Role Satisfaction and Children's Sociometric Status." *Child Study Journal,* Vol. 18, No. 4, 265–275.

Connor, K. (1989). "Aggression: Is It in the Eye of the Beholder?" *Play & Culture,* Vol. 2, No. 3, 213–217.

Crnic, K. A., and M. T. Greenberg (1990). "Minor Parenting Stresses with Young Children." *Child Development,* 61, 1628–1637.

Crockenberg, S., and C. Litman (1990). "Autonomy as Competence in 2-Year-Olds: Maternal Correlates of Child Defiance, Compliance, and Self-Assertion." *Developmental Psychology,* Vol. 26, No. 6, 961–971.

Dadds, M. R. (1987). "Families and the Origins of Child Behavior Problems." *Family Process,* Vol. 26, 341–357.

Dodge, K. A. (1990). "Nature Versus Nurture in Childhood Conduct Disorder: It Is Time to Ask a Different Question." *Developmental Psychology,* Vol. 26, No. 5, 698–701.

Felson, R., and M. A. Zielinski (1989). "Children's Self-Esteem and Parental Support." *Journal of Marriage and the Family,* 51, 727–735.

Hetherington, E. M. (1989). "Coping with Family Transitions: Winners, Losers, and Survivors." *Child Development,* 60, 1–14.

Hetherington, E. M.; M. Stanley-Hagan; and E. R. Anderson (1989). "Marital Transition, A Child's Perspective." *American Psychologist,* Vol. 44, No. 2, 303–312.

Holden, G. W. (1983). Avoiding Conflict: Mothers as Tacticians in the Supermarket. *Child Development,* Vol. 54, 233–240.

Johnston, C., and E. J. Mash (1989). "A Measure of Parenting Satisfaction and Efficacy." *Journal of Clinical Child Psychology.* Vol. 18, No. 2, 167–175.

Johnston, C., and E. J. Mash (1983a). "Parental Perceptions of Child Behavior Problems, Parenting Self-Esteem, and Mothers' Reported Stress in Younger and Older Hyperactive and Normal Children."

Kaler, S. R., and C. B. Kopp (1990). "Compliance and Comprehension in Very Young Toddlers." *Child Development,* 61, 1997–2003.

Kochanska, G. (1992). "Children's Interpersonal Influence with Mothers and Peers." *Developmental Psychology*, Vol. 2, No. 3, 491–499.

Kuczynski, L., and G. Kochanska (1990). "Development of Children's Noncompliance Strategies from Toddlerhood to Age 5." *Developmental Psychology*, Vol. 26, No. 3, 398–408.

Kuczynski, L.; G. Kochanska; M. Radke-Yarrow; and O. Girnius-Brown (1987). "A Developmental Interpretation of Young Children's Noncompliance." *Developmental Psychology*, Vol. 23, No. 6, 799–806.

Lewis, M. (1992). "Commentary." *Human Development*, Vol. 35, 44–51.

Londerville, S., and M. Main (1981). "Security of Attachment, Compliance, and Maternal Training Methods in the Second Year of Life." *Developmental Psychology*, Vol. 17, No. 3, 289–299.

Maccoby, E. E., and M. Parpal (1985). "Maternal Responsiveness and Subsequent Child Compliance." *Child Development*, Vol. 56, 1326–1334.

Maccoby, E. E. (1983). "Presidential Address: Socialization and Developmental Change." *Child Development*, Vol. 55, 317–328.

Mills, R. S. L., and K. H. Rubin (1990). "Parental Beliefs About Problematic Social Behaviors in Early Childhood." *Child Development*, 61, 138–151.

Patterson, G.; B. D. DeBaryshe; and E. Ramsey (1989). "A Developmental Perspective on Antisocial Behavior." *American Psychologist*, Vol. 44, No. 1, 329–335.

Patterson, G. (1986). "Performance Models for Antisocial Boys." *American Psychologist*, Vol. 41, No. 4, 432–444.

Pettit, G. S., and J. E. Bates (1989). "Family Interaction Patterns and Children's Behavior Problems from Infancy to 4 Years." *Developmental Psychology*, Vol. 25, No. 3, 413–420.

Plomin, R. (1989). "Environment and Genes, Determinants of Behavior." *American Psychologist*, Vol. 44, No. 2, 105–111.

Sanders, M. R., and A. P. Christensen (1985). "A Comparison of the Effects of Child Management and Planned Activities Training in Five Parenting Environments." *Journal of Abnormal Child Psychology*, Vol. 13, No. 1, 101–117.

Sanders, M. R.; M. R. Dodds; and W. Bor (1989). "Contextual Analyses of Child Oppositional and Maternal Aversive Behaviors in Families of Conduct-Disordered and Nonproblem Children." *Journal of Clinical Child Psychology,* Vol. 18, No. 1, 72–83.

Stevens, J. H., Jr. (1984). "Child Development Knowledge and Parenting Skills." *Family Relations,* 33, 237–244.

Stocker, C.; J. Dunn; and R. Plomin (1989). "Sibling Relationships: Links with Child Temperament, Maternal Behavior, and Family Structure." *Child Development,* Vol. 60, 715–727.

Story, M., and J. Brown (1987). "Sounding Board: Do Young Children Instinctively Know What to Eat?" *The New England Journal of Medicine,* Vol. 316, No. 2, 103–105.

Wahler, R. G. (1990). "Who Is Driving the Interactions? A Commentary on 'Child and Parent Effects in Boys' Conduct Disorder.' " *Developmental Psychology,* Vol. 26, No. 5, 702–704.

Webster-Stratton, C. (1990). "Stress: A Potential Description of Parent Perceptions and Family Interactions." *Journal of Clinical Child Psychology,* Vol. 19, No. 4, 302–312.

Webster-Stratton, C. (1988). "Mothers' and Fathers' Perceptions of Child Deviance: Roles of Parent and Child Behaviors and Parent Adjustment." *Journal of Consulting and Clinical Psychology,* Vol. 56, No. 6, 909–916.

Williams, C., and R. Forehand (1984). "An Examination of Predictor Variables for Child Compliance and Noncompliance." *Journal of Abnormal Child Psychology,* Vol. 12, No. 3, 491–504.

Index